The Mediterranean World in Late Antiquity AD 395–600

The Mediterranean World in Late Antiquity AD 395–600 deals with the exciting period commonly known as 'late antiquity' – the fifth and sixth centuries. The Roman empire in the west was splitting into separate Germanic kingdoms, while the Near East, still under Roman rule from Constantinople, maintained a dense population and flourishing urban culture until the Persian and Arab invasions of the early seventh century.

Averil Cameron places her emphasis on the material and literary evidence for cultural change and offers a new and original challenge to traditional assumptions of 'decline and fall' and 'the end of antiquity'. The book draws on the recent spate of scholarship on this period to discuss in detail such controversial issues as the effectiveness of the late Roman army, the late antique city and the nature of economic exchange and cultural life. With its extensive annotation, it provides a lively, and often critical introduction to earlier approaches to the period, from Edward Gibbon's *Decline and Fall of the Roman Empire* to the present day.

No existing book in English provides so detailed or up-to-date an introduction to the history of both halves of the empire in this crucial period, or discusses existing views in such a challenging way. Averil Cameron is a leading specialist on late antiquity, having written about the period and taught it for many years. This book has much to say to historians of all periods. It will be particularly welcomed by teachers and students of both ancient and medieval history.

Averil Cameron is Professor of Late Antique and Byzantine Studies at King's College London.

ROUTLEDGE HISTORY OF THE ANCIENT WORLD

General Editor: Fergus Millar

THE GREEK WORLD 479–323 BC
Simon Hornblower

THE MEDITERRANEAN WORLD IN LATE ANTIQUITY
AD 395—600
Averil Cameron

The Mediterranean World in
Late Antiquity AD 395–600

Averil Cameron

London and New York

First published 1993
by Routledge
11 New Fetter Lane, London EC4P 4EE

Simultaneously published in the USA and Canada
by Routledge
29 West 35th Street, New York, NY 10001

© 1993 Averil Cameron

Typeset in 10 on 12 point Garamond by
Florencetype Ltd
Printed and bound in Great Britain by
T. J. Press (Padstow) Ltd,
Padstow, Cornwall

British Library Cataloguing in Publication Data
A catalogue record for this book is available from the British
Library

Library of Congress Cataloging in Publication Data
Cameron, Averil.
The Mediterranean world in late antiquity AD 395–600 /
by Averil Cameron.
p.   cm. – (Routledge history of the ancient world)
Includes bibliographical references and index.
1. Mediterranean Region–Civilization.
2. Romans–Mediterranean Region. I. Title.
II. Series.
DE71.C25 1993
909'.09822–dc20   92-34600

ISBN 0–415–01420–4
0–415–01421–2 (pbk)

Contents

Figures and plates

FIGURES

PLATES

Preface

The shape and parameters of this book are explained by the fact that it was conceived as part of a series designed to replace the earlier Methuen History of the Ancient World, though of course the latter had no volume with the present scope, and the concept of 'late antiquity' still lay firmly in the future. As it happens, while the present volume (the last chronologically in the series) antedates the writing of that projected on the fourth century, it follows on from my own book in another series, the Fontana History of the Ancient World. Though entitled simply *The Later Roman Empire*, the latter effectively ends where the present book begins, with Augustine as the bridge. The effect therefore is that despite minor differences of format and scale between the two, the reader will find in them an introduction to the whole period of late antiquity from, roughly, the reign of Diocletian (AD 284–305) to the late sixth century AD, where A. H. M. Jones also ended his great work, *The Later Roman Empire* (Oxford, 1964).

As most people will be well aware, this period has been the focus of a great upsurge of interest in the generation that has passed since the publication of Jones's massive work; in the past twenty years it has found its way for the first time on to ancient history syllabuses in many universities, with corresponding effects on courses in medieval history and (where they exist) Byzantine studies. The addition of two extra volumes to the new edition of the *Cambridge Ancient History* (now in progress) is also symptomatic of this changed perspective; together, they will cover the period from the death of Constantine (AD 337) to the late sixth century. Peter Brown's small book, *The World of Late Antiquity* (London, 1971), still provides an exhilarating introduction from the perspective of cultural history. The influence of that book has been enormous, yet despite this tremendous growth of interest in the period, and despite a mass of more specialized publications, many of them excellent, it is still difficult to find a book or books in English which provide a general introduction for students to the many and varied aspects of the period about which they need to know.

The present book adopts an approach that is part chronological and part thematic. No real attempt can be made in such a compass to provide a full narrative of events, and I have tried to do this only in those parts where it seemed particularly necessary or where the evidence was particularly difficult of access. Luckily, a useful brief narrative is provided in Roger Collins's recent *Early Medieval Europe 300–1000* (London, 1991). The present book has a different and wider scope. I devote particular attention to issues currently debated, such as urban change and patterns of settlement, where much of the evidence is archaeological, partly in order to point up the great change that has taken place in our approach to and understanding of the period since Jones, fundamental though his work remains in many other spheres. Cultural and social history occupy a large amount of space for similar reasons. Ideally, too, a book of this kind would be much more fully illustrated than has been possible here; however, there are fortunately many accessible guides to hand, which I have indicated as often as possible in the notes. The book's main emphasis is on the empire rather than the periphery or the emergent kingdoms of the west, and so it points towards the east, where the institutions of Roman government survived at least until the seventh century when a more 'Byzantine', that is 'medieval', state gradually emerged. There are many excellent introductory works on the medieval west, and other areas given less coverage here (Spain, Italy, the northern provinces, the Balkans) have been treated in specialist works mentioned in the notes. But there are few, if any, recent books which do justice to or even include in any detail the equally important history of the eastern provinces in the fifth and sixth centuries. We still need a detailed history even of the crucial reign of Justinian (AD 527–65). Finally, some parts of the book necessarily have a certain provisional or exploratory character, precisely because the necessary research is proceeding at very uneven rates, and many questions are still without answers. That is of course also one of the greatest attractions of the field.

I wish to thank several friends and colleagues for spotting errors and providing advice, among them Lawrence I. Conrad, Han

Drijvers and Bryan Ward-Perkins, and especially Wolfgang Liebeschuetz. Ian Tompkins and Lucas Siorvanes generously read the whole typescript, and Fergus Millar, the series editor, was not merely encouraging but also patient. The book is meant as a starting-point, not a terminus. If readers are annoyed by it or frustrated at not finding what they want, I hope they will also be stimulated into pursuing it somewhere else and finding the right answers for themselves.

Averil Cameron
London, July 1992

Date-list

AD 395	Death of Theodosius I
	Honorius, 395–423 (west)
	Arcadius, 395–408 (east)
AD 406	Vandals, Alans and Sueves cross Rhine
AD 408	Alaric and Visigoths enter Italy
AD 407–11	Constantine III (Britain)
AD 410	Withdrawal of Roman army from Britain
	Sack of Rome by Visigoths
AD 408–50	Theodosius II (east)
AD 425–55	Valentinian III
AD 429	Vandals cross to Africa, take Carthage AD 439
c. AD 430	Monastery of Lérins founded
AD 431	Council of Ephesus
AD 440 onwards	Huns raid Balkans
AD 450–7	Marcian (east)
AD 451	Huns invade Gaul
	Council of Chalcedon
AD 453	Death of Attila
AD 455–7	Avitus (west)
	Vandal sack of Rome, AD 455
AD 457–74	Leo I (east)
AD 468	Expedition of Leo against Vandals fails
AD 474–91	Zeno (east)
	Patrick in Ireland
AD 476	Deposition of Romulus Augustulus
c. AD 481–c. 511	Clovis in Gaul
AD 491–518	Anastasius (east)
AD 493–526	Theodoric (Ostrogothic Italy)
AD 507	Battle of Vouillé

AD 524	Execution of Boethius
AD 518–27	Justin I
AD 527–65	Justinian
AD 527–33	Justinian's codification of Roman law
AD 531–79	Chosroes I
AD 533–4	Reconquest of Africa
AD 535	Belisarius sent to Italy
AD 540	Sack of Antioch by Persians
	Rule of Benedict
AD 551	Justinian intervenes in Spain
AD 554	'Pragmatic Sanction' (settlement of Italy)
AD 563–5	Foundation of Iona
AD 565–78	Justin II
AD 568	Lombards invade Italy
c. AD 570	Birth of Muhammad
AD 578–82	Tiberius II
c. AD 580	Death of Cassiodorus
AD 580s	Slav invasions of Greece
AD 582–602	Maurice
AD 589	Third Council of Toledo, following conversion of Reccared (586–601) to Catholicism
AD 591	Restoration of Chosroes II by Maurice
AD 590–604	Pope Gregory the Great
AD 594	Death of Gregory of Tours
AD 597	Augustine arrives to convert Britain
AD 602–10	Phocas
AD 610–41	Heraclius
AD 614	Persian sack of Jerusalem
AD 622	Muhammad leaves Medina (Hijra)
AD 626	Avar and Persian siege of Constantinople
AD 630	Heraclius restores True Cross
AD 632	Death of Muhammad
AD 633–42	Oswald (Northumbria)
AD 636	Battle of R. Yarmuk
AD 638	*Ekthesis* of Heraclius
AD 638	Surrender of Jerusalem to Arabs
AD 640	Arab conquest of Egypt
AD 647	Exarch Gregory killed by Arabs near Sbeitla

Abbreviations

Alföldy, *Social History*	G. Alföldy, *The Social History of Rome*, Eng. trans., London, 1988.
Blockley	R. C. Blockley, *The Fragmentary Classicising Historians of the Later Roman Empire*, I–II, Liverpool, 1981, 1983.
Blockley, *Menander the Guardsman*	R. C. Blockley, *The History of Menander the Guardsman*, Liverpool, 1985.
Bury, *LRE*	J. B. Bury, *The Later Roman Empire from the Death of Theodosius I to the Death of Justinian*, 2nd edn, 2 vols, London, 1923.
Cameron, *Procopius*	Averil Cameron, *Procopius and the Sixth Century*, London, 1985.
Clark, *Life of Melania*	E. A. Clark, *The Life of Melania the Younger*, Lewiston, NY, 1984.
CTh	*Codex Theodosianus*, Eng. trans., Clyde Parr, *The Theodosian Code*, Princeton, NJ, 1952.
de Boor	Theophanes, *Chronographia*, *Chronicle* of Theophanes, ed. C. de Boor, 2 vols, Leipzig, 1883, 1885.
de Ste Croix, *Class Struggle*	G. E. M. de Ste Croix, *The Class Struggle in the Ancient Greek World*, London, 1981.

George, *Venantius Fortunatus*   Judith W. George, *Venantius Fortunatus. A Latin Poet in Merovingian Gaul*, Oxford, 1992.

Giardina (ed.)   A. Giardina (ed.), *Società romana e impero tardoantico*, Rome, 1986.

Hodges and Whitehouse   R. Hodges and D. Whitehouse, *Mohammed, Charlemagne and the Origins of Europe*, London, 1983.

trans. Jeffreys   Elizabeth Jeffreys, Michael Jeffreys and Roger Scott, *The Chronicle of John Malalas*, Melbourne, 1986.

Jones, *LRE*   A. H. M. Jones, *The Later Roman Empire 284–602. A Social, Economic and Administrative Survey*, 2 vols, Oxford, 1964.

Maas, *John Lydus*   M. Maas, *John Lydus and the Roman Past*, London, 1992.

MacMullen, *Corruption*   R. MacMullen, *Corruption and the Decline of Rome*, New Haven, Conn., 1988.

Mango, *Art*   C. Mango, *Art of the Byzantine Empire 312–1453*, Englewood Cliffs, NJ, 1972.

Martindale, *PLRE*   J. Martindale (ed.), *Prosopography of the Later Roman Empire*, II–III, Cambridge, 1980–92.

trans. Ridley   Zosimus, *New History*, trans. R. Ridley, Sydney, 1982.

Rostovtzeff, *SEHRE*   M. I. Rostovtzeff, *Social and Economic History of the Roman Empire*, 2nd edn, rev. P. M. Fraser, Oxford, 1957.

trans. Russell, *Lives of the Desert Fathers*   N. Russell (trans.), *The Lives of the Desert Fathers*, with an introduction by Benedicta Ward, London, 1980.

Saffrey   H.-I. Saffrey, 'From Iamblichus to Proclus and Damascius', in A. H.

Armstrong (ed.), *Classical Mediterranean Spirituality*, London, 1986.

Stevenson, *Creeds*   J. Stevenson, *Creeds, Councils and Controversies*, London, 1983.

Turtledove, *Chronicle*   H. Turtledove, trans., *The Chronicle of Theophanes*, Philadelphia, 1982.

trans. Whitby and Whitby   *Chronicon Paschale*, trans. Michael Whitby and Mary Whitby, Liverpool, 1989.

Introduction

THE DIVISION BETWEEN EAST AND WEST

In the year AD 395 the Emperor Theodosius I died, leaving two sons. Arcadius received the east and Honorius the west. From then on the Roman empire was effectively divided for administrative purposes into two halves, which, as pressure from barbarians on the frontiers increased through the fifth century, began to respond in significantly different ways. AD 395 was therefore a real turning point in the eventual split between east and west.

Until then, and since the time of Diocletian (AD 284–305), the late Roman empire had been a unity embracing all the provinces bordering on the Mediterranean and much more besides (Figure 1). In the west it stretched as far as Britain and included the whole of Gaul and Spain, in the north the frontier extended from Germany and the Low Countries along the Danube to the Black Sea; Dacia, across the Danube, annexed by Trajan in the early second century, was given up at the end of the third after a series of Gothic invasions, but otherwise the empire of Diocletian was impressively similar in extent to that of its greatest days in the Antonine period. To the east, it stretched to eastern Turkey and the borders of the Sasanian empire in Persia, while its southern possessions extended from Egypt westwards to Morocco and the Straits of Gibraltar; Roman North Africa (modern Algeria and Tunisia) was one of the most prosperous parts of the empire during the fourth century.

In Diocletian's day, though Rome was still the seat of the senate, it was no longer the administrative capital of this large empire; emperors moved from one 'capital' to another – Trier in Germany, Sirmium or Serdica in the Danube area or Nicomedia in Bithynia – taking their administration with them. By the end of the fourth century, however, the main seats of government were at Milan in

1

the west and Constantinople in the east (see Chapter 1). The empire was also divided linguistically, in that while the 'official' language of the army and the law remained Latin until the sixth century and later, the principal language of the educated classes in the east was Greek. But Latin and Greek coexisted with a number of local languages, such as Aramaic in Syria, Mesopotamia and Palestine, and with Coptic in Egypt (demotic Egyptian written in an alphabet using mainly Greek characters) or with the languages of the new groups which had settled within the empire during the third and especially the fourth century, one of which was Gothic. Even in the early empire, laws had circulated in the east in Greek, and there had always been translation of imperial letters and official documents, so that on the whole the imperial administration had managed to operate successfully despite such linguistic variety. But from the third century onwards local cultures began to develop more vigorously in several areas, and the eventual divide between east and west also became a linguistic one; as has often been noted, Augustine's Greek was not perfect, and his own works, in Latin, were not read by Christians in the east.

The period covered by this book thus saw a progressive division between east and west, in the course of which the east fared better. Even though it had to face a formidable enemy in the Sasanians, its economic and social structure enabled it to repel the threat from the Germanic tribes from the north far more successfully than the western empire could do, with the result that the institutional and administrative structure of the fourth-century empire remained more or less intact in the east until at least the later sixth century, only undergoing substantial change with the Persian and Arab invasions which took place in the early seventh.

In the west, by contrast, the government was already weak by the late fourth century, and the power of the great landowning families was correspondingly strong. Furthermore, the western provinces had been badly hit earlier by the invasions and civil wars of the third century. The disastrous defeat of the Roman army at Adrianople in AD 378 marked a critical stage in the weakening of the west, and barbarian pressures grew steadily until in AD 476 the last Roman emperor ruling from Italy was deposed and power passed to a barbarian leader. The eastern Emperor Justinian's much-vaunted 'reconquest' (Chapter 5), launched from Constantinople in the 530s, aimed at reversing the situation; but while a Byzantine presence was maintained in Italy in the exarchate, the west was divided

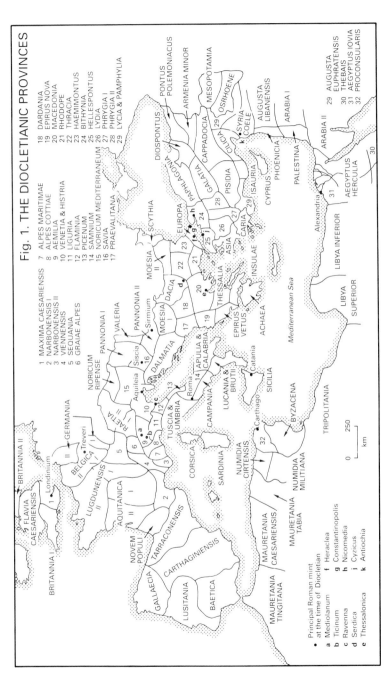

Fig. 1. THE DIOCLETIANIC PROVINCES

1 MAXIMA CAESARIENSIS
2 NARBONENSIS I
3 NARBONENSIS II
4 VIENNENSIS
5 SEQUANIA
6 GRAIAE ALPES
7 ALPES MARITIMAE
8 ALPES COTTIAE
9 AEMILIA
10 VENETIA & HISTRIA
11 LIGURIA
12 FLAMINIA
13 PICENUM
14 SAMNIUM
15 NORICUM MEDITERRANEUM
16 SAVIA
17 PRAEVALITANA
18 DARDANIA
19 EPIRUS NOVA
20 MACEDONIA
21 RHODOPE
22 THRACIA
23 HAEMIMONTUS
24 BITHYNIA
25 HELLESPONTUS
26 LYDIA
27 PHRYGIA I
28 PHRYGIA II
29 LYCIA & PAMPHYLIA
29 AUGUSTA EUPHRATENSIS
30 THEBAIS
31 AEGYPTUS IOVIA
32 PROCONSULARIS

• Principal Roman mint at the time of Diocletian

a Mediolanum   f Heraclea
b Ticinum   g Constantinopolis
c Ravenna   h Nicomedia
d Serdica   j Cyzicus
e Thessalonica k Antiochia

Figure 1 The Diocletianic provinces of the late Roman empire.

by the late sixth century, the Merovingian Franks ruling in France and the Visigoths in Spain; in Italy, eventual Byzantine victory (AD 554) was quickly followed by a new invasion by the Lombards, producing even greater fragmentation, as a result of which the papacy, especially under Gregory the Great (AD 590–604), acquired considerable secular power. All the same, much that was recognizably Roman survived in the barbarian kingdoms, and the extent of real social and economic change remains a controversial matter. The Belgian historian Henri Pirenne argued in a classic book, *Mohammad and Charlemagne* (Eng. trans. 1939), that the real break between east and west, and between ancient and medieval history, came as a result not of the barbarian invasions but with the Arab conquests. This is the famous 'Pirenne thesis' about which historians have debated ever since; while nowadays the evidence on which they rely has changed (see Chapter 8), the essential questions remain. However, some historians are replacing this emphasis on division (chronological or geographical) by a much broader view. Thus K. Randsborg, *The First Millennium AD in Europe and the Mediterranean. An Archaeological Essay* (Cambridge, 1991), argues on the basis of archaeological evidence that despite the obvious political changes, the patterns of settlement and material culture in the countries round the Mediterranean did not themselves begin to change in a drastic way until the eleventh century. Another recent work, P. Hordern and N. Purcell, *The Mediterranean World. Man and Environment in Antiquity and the Middle Ages* (Oxford, 1993), discusses the shared environmental, biological and anthropological factors which characterized Mediterranean culture in this period. Finally, a question of obvious current concern to western medievalists in particular is that of the emergence of the conception of Europe, the subject of an ambitious series, 'The Making of Europe', edited by Jacques Le Goff. Not least, these newer approaches illustrate how much conceptions of history, including our own, are coloured in all ages by contemporary concerns.

PREVIOUS APPROACHES AND THE PRESENT STATE OF RESEARCH

The 'transition' from classical antiquity to the medieval world was the subject of Edward Gibbon's great work, *The Decline and Fall of the Roman Empire* (1787), and, indeed, very few themes in history have been the subject of so much hotly debated controversy or so much partisan feeling. For Marx and for the very many historians in the Marxist tradition, the end of Roman rule provided cardinal proof that states based on such extreme forms of inequality and exploitation as ancient slavery were doomed eventually to fall. On the other hand, many historians, including Gibbon himself and the Russian historian M. I. Rostovtzeff, who left Russia for the west in 1917, also saw the later empire as representing a sadly degenerate form of its earlier civilized and prosperous self, which they regarded as having reached its apogee under the Antonines in the second century. Rostovtzeff's views, if in somewhat watered-down form, are still extremely pervasive, and may indeed still be regarded as the 'standard view'. This book will suggest in contrast that such evaluative notions as 'decline' and 'degeneration' must be discarded once and for all.

The theory of decline has been a tempting one. As a rationalist, Gibbon attributed the moral and intellectual decline which he saw setting in in the later empire to the effects of Christianity, while Rostovtzeff read the late Roman state in terms of brutal totalitarianism. Each saw the 'golden' days of the early empire in the image of the society he knew – eighteenth-century Enlightenment or late nineteenth-century bourgeoisie. In our own day the fall of empires has again become news, and the recent theory of 'systems-collapse' (see Conclusion) provides in essence a modern version of the idea of decline and fall.

The period covered in this book has been dominated in English scholarship for a generation by A. H. M. Jones's massive *The Later Roman Empire 284–602. A Social, Economic and Administrative Survey* (Oxford, 1964), also issued in shortened form as *The Decline of the Ancient World* (London, 1966). Jones was much influenced by the emphasis given by Rostovtzeff to social and economic factors, and his great work consists in the main of thematic chapters on individual aspects of late Roman society rather than political narrative. Jones had travelled extensively over the Roman empire himself, and took part in archaeological work, but he wrote before the explosion of interest and activity in late Roman archaeology and consequently made little use of material evidence; nevertheless, his book still provides the basic guide to which most English-speaking students must turn. Jones also defined the period chronologically as reaching from the accession of Diocletian (AD 284) to the death of Maurice (AD 602), a controversial but justifiable interpretation which this book essentially follows.

Jones's approach was pragmatic and concrete; he was not very interested in the questions of religious history which many now regard as primary and exciting factors in the study of late antiquity. For him, studying the development and influence of the Christian church in this period meant following its institutional and economic growth rather than the inner feelings of Christians themselves. Most famously, he included Christian monks, nuns and clergy in the category of 'idle mouths' who now had to be supported by the dwindling class of agricultural producers, and who in Jones's view contributed to the difficulties to be faced by the late Roman government, and to its eventual decline.

When Jones published his work in the 1960s, the later empire featured only rarely on university syllabuses, and the majority of ancient historians still regarded it as beyond their scope. Historians like Moses Finley who were interested in economic history, and aware of Marxist and other kinds of social and economic historical interpretation, of course did not, nor did those who were in touch with the broader continental tradition. But Jones's work opened up the period to a younger generation, who were further stimulated by the very different approach of Peter Brown, vividly expressed in his brief survey *The World of Late Antiquity* (London, 1971), which appeared only a few years after Jones's *Later Roman Empire*. Brown is altogether more enthusiastic, not to say more emotive, in emphasis; indeed, 'late antiquity' is in danger of having become an exotic territory, populated by wild monks and excitable virgins and dominated by the clash of religions, mentalities and lifestyles. In this scenario, Sasanian Persia in the east and the Germanic peoples in the north and west bounded a vast area within which several new battle-lines were being drawn – for example, between family members who as individuals wrestled with the conflicting claims of the church and their own social background. Great new buildings, churches and monasteries, epitomized the rising centres of power and influence; the Egyptian and Syrian deserts became the home of several thousand monks of all sorts of backgrounds, and the eastern provinces a heady cultural mix, ripe for social change.

This very different perspective is, however, largely based on the evidence of religious and cultural development; whether it can be extended to economic and administrative history remains to be seen. All the same, it has had immense value as a stimulus to further work and to the establishment of 'late antiquity' as a field of study in its own right. Indeed, one of the most notable and important developments in this field in recent years has been the amount of interest shown in the period by archaeologists, not least after the pioneering work done since the 1970s on the dating and identification of late Roman pottery, which at last makes possible an accurate chronology for late Roman excavation. The UNESCO-sponsored international excavations at Carthage in the 1970s were also extremely important in this respect, in that they made available a large amount of data which could then be used for comparison at other sites. One should also mention the level of interest shown at present in urban history, which is specially relevant to this period in view of the fact that the latter part saw a basic transformation in urban life and indeed the effective end of many classical cities in the eastern Mediterranean (Chapter 7). But the synthesis of the new archaeological material is still incomplete and in many cases controversial. One issue much debated at present is that of the nature and extent of trade in the later empire (Chapter 4), amounting to a re-examination, from a completely different starting point, of the very questions posed by Pirenne.

THE PERIOD 'LATE ANTIQUITY'

The terminology used by scholars for historical periods, in this case terms like 'late antiquity', 'medieval' or 'Byzantine' (even 'proto-Byzantine'), is largely a matter of convenience. Many books on Byzantium logically choose the foundation of Constantinople by Constantine the Great (AD 330) as their starting point, since Constantinople remained the capital of the Byzantine empire until its fall in AD 1453. Most Roman historians however would probably be more comfortable with a history of the fourth and fifth centuries AD described in terms of 'the later Roman empire' or 'late antiquity'; the same scholars might be inclined to apply the term 'Byzantine' to the reign of Justinian (AD 527–65); and some Byzantinists in turn are uncertain about when Byzantium became Byzantium, placing the real break in the seventh century. From a quite different perspective, theologians sometimes tend to place a break at AD 451, the date of the Council of Chalcedon. The term 'medieval' might seem to present fewer problems – until we come to the controversial issue of the supposedly 'medieval' elements in late Roman society and vice versa.

But terminology does matter: whether we like it or not, it shapes our perceptions, especially of controversial issues. The title of this book, *The Mediterranean World in Late Antiquity*, suggests in its use of the term 'late antiquity' that some of the basics of classical civilization still survived, albeit in fragmented form in the barbarian west. Thus it bypasses AD 476, the traditional date of 'the fall of the Roman empire', and invites the reader to look more broadly, both geographically and chronologically. It may seem paradoxical, then, that it starts with AD 395, the year in which the empire was both symbolically and actually divided into two halves. But above all, this is a transitional period, one which saw great changes as well as many continuities; that is of course precisely what makes it so interesting.

THE SOURCES

The source material for this period is exceptionally rich and varied, including both the works of writers great by any standards, and plentiful documentation of the lives of quite ordinary people. Changing circumstances also dictated changes in contemporary writing: St Augustine, for example, was a provincial from a moderately well-off family, who, having made his early career through the practice of rhetoric, became a bishop in the North African town of Hippo and spent much of his life not only wrestling with the major problems of Christian theology but also trying to make sense of the historical changes taking place around him. Instead of a great secular history like that of Ammianus Marcellinus in the late fourth century, Augustine's Spanish contemporary Orosius produced an abbreviated catalogue of disasters from the Roman past which was to become standard reading in the medieval Latin west, while numerous calendars and chronicles tried to combine in one schema the events of secular history and the Christian history of the world since creation. In the sixth century one man, the Roman Cassiodorus, composed *Variae*, the official correspondence of the Ostrogothic kings, a history of the Goths, and later, after the defeat of the Goths by the Byzantines in AD 554, his *Institutes*, a guide to Christian learning written at his Italian monastery of Vivarium. A century earlier Sidonius Apollinaris, as bishop at Clermont-Ferrand in Gaul, had deplored barbarian rusticity and continued to compose verses in classical style. A host of Gallic ecclesiastics in the fifth century, especially those connected with the important monastic centre of Lérins, wrote extensive letters as well as theological works, and this was also the age of the monastic rules of John Cassian and

St Benedict. At the end of the sixth century, the voluminous writings of Pope Gregory the Great, together with the lively *History of the Franks* and hagiographical works by Gregory of Tours, another bishop of Roman senatorial extraction, and the poems of Venantius Fortunatus, combine with other works to provide a rich documentation for the west in that period.

These are only some of the many western works composed at this time. The Greek east was equally productive, if not more so. Secular history continued to be written in the classical manner, and although the works of several fifth- and sixth-century writers survive only in fragments, we have all the *History of the Wars* in which Procopius of Caesarea recorded Justinian's wars of 'reconquest'. Procopius is undoubtedly a major historian; in addition, his *Buildings*, a panegyrical account of the building activities of Justinian, provides an important checklist for archaeologists, while his scabrous *Secret History*, immortalized by Gibbon's description of it, has provided material for nearly a score of novels about the variety artiste who became Justinian's wife, the pious Empress Theodora. With its greater cultural continuity, the east was better able than the west to maintain a tradition of history-writing in the old style, and the last in the line was Theophylact Simocatta, writing under Heraclius about the Emperor Maurice (AD 582–602). Other writers, however, composed church history, including Socrates and Sozomen, both of whom continued Eusebius' *Church History* in Constantinople in the 440s, the Syrian Theodoret, bishop of Cyrrhus, and the Arian Philostorgius, whose work is only partially preserved. In the late sixth century the tradition was continued, again in Constantinople, by the Chalcedonian Evagrius Scholasticus, writing in Greek, and the monophysite John, bishop of Ephesus, writing in Syriac. The Christian world-chronicle characteristic of the Byzantine period also begins now, with the sixth-century chronicle of the Antiochene John Malalas, ending in the year AD 563, and there are very many saints' lives in Greek and Latin, and sometimes in other languages such as Syriac, Georgian, Armenian or Ethiopic; the frequency of translation to and from Greek and eastern languages, especially Syriac, is a very important but often neglected aspect of eastern culture in this period.

In addition to the abundant literary sources, there is much documentary material, from the proceedings of the major church councils (Ephesus, AD 431, Chalcedon, AD 451, Constantinople, AD 553) to the law codes of Theodosius II and Justinian. The official document known as the *Notitia Dignitatum*, drawn up some time after AD 395 and known from a western copy (see Jones, *LRE*, app. II), constitutes a major source for our knowledge of the late Roman army and provincial administration. There are also many dedicatory inscriptions from the Greek east in the fifth and sixth centuries, sometimes interestingly written in elaborately classicizing Greek verse, and while major public inscriptions are few in comparison with their number in the early empire, large numbers of simple Christian funerary epitaphs survive, often inscribed in mosaic on the floors of churches, which also frequently carry dedications by the builder or the local bishop. Important papyri also survive from the desert region of the Negev in modern Israel, notably from Nessana, and from Ravenna in Italy, as well as from Egypt itself. Finally, the archaeological record is now large, and increasing all the time, and while it is still necessary to consult individual excavation reports, there are fortunately several recent publications which provide surveys of archaeological evidence; these are noted at suitable points below, especially in Chapters 7 and 8.

MAIN THEMES IN THE PERIOD

A major problem in the period was that of unity and diversity. While in the west writers such as Sidonius have left us an impression of the interaction of barbarians and Romans in fifth-century Gaul, the Greek epigraphic record indicates the changes in social composition and government in eastern cities and the impact of Christianity on well-off families in such towns as Aphrodisias in Caria. We are faced both by cultural change and by the juxtaposition of contrasting ideas and lifestyles. The major themes to be considered, therefore, necessarily include the process of Christianization; this is particularly so as pagan practice had been declared illegal only by Theodosius I, an initiative which, though it provoked some violent scenes (Chapter 3), by no means succeeded in its object. The great church councils, and the usually abortive efforts made by successive emperors to find doctrinal compromises, are also indicative of the problems inherent in achieving some kind of church unity over so sprawling and diverse a geographical area, and in the face of so much rapid change. A second major theme is that of defence. Diversified, localized and fragmented, the Roman army, or rather armies, of the fifth and sixth centuries were far different in composition and equipment from those of earlier days, even if not demonstrably inferior, as is often argued. Whether the army could now effectively keep out the barbarians, and if not, why not, were questions as much debated by contemporaries as by modern historians; the nature of the late Roman army, and the whole context of defence and frontiers, need therefore to be discussed in some detail (Chapters 2, 5 and 8). Third, the late Roman economy – was it really 'in decline' (Chapter 4)? How much long-distance exchange continued, and if it did, in whose hands was it? Closely related to these issues is the difficult question of the place of slaves in the overall labour situation, and especially in relation to *coloni*, tied peasants, who have often, though probably wrongly, been seen as the prototypes of medieval serfs. Finally, though not last in significance, comes the attempt to understand the educational and ideological adjustments that accompanied these changes. In broad terms, classical culture was now more and more open to challenge from alternative mentalities, a situation which contemporaries often found extremely uncomfortable. The contradictions that ensued can be seen in the example of the Emperor Justinian, who aimed at 'restoration' and the reconquest of the west, while simultaneously attacking intellectuals as subversive pagan elements in the Christian state. While it is arguable that ideological change came earlier in the west, and particularly with the barbarian settlements of the fifth century, the east had to wait longer for a similar process to take place, until the Persian and Arab invasions of the seventh century; even then, many classical survivals remained. This book will how-ever end before those invasions, which demand detailed treatment elsewhere in their own right.

1

Constantinople and the eastern empire in the fifth century

THE CITY OF CONSTANTINOPLE

On the death of Theodosius I in AD 395, Constantinople had been an imperial seat for over sixty years, since the refoundation of the classical city of Byzantium as Constantinople ('the city of Constantine') by Constantine the Great. Although it is common to refer to it as the eastern capital, this is not strictly correct: Constantine founded it along the lines of existing tetrarchic capitals such as Nicomedia and Trier, and although he naturally resided there for most of the time from its dedication in AD 330 to his death in AD 337 he seemed to envisage a return after his death to an empire partitioned geographically between several Augusti (Eusebius, *Vita Constantini* IV.51).[1] This division did not work out in practice: fighting soon broke out after Constantine's death, and by AD 350, with the death of the second of his three surviving sons, the third, Constantius II, became sole emperor like his father. Nevertheless, there were often two or more Augusti ruling together during the later fourth century, and it was not a novelty in itself when on the death of Theodosius I the empire was 'divided' between his two sons Honorius and Arcadius. What was different now however was the fact that the two halves of the empire began to grow further and further apart.

Constantinople itself was not yet a fully Christian city. Though Eusebius, writing of Constantine's foundation, would have us believe that all traces of paganism were eliminated (*Vita Constantini* III.48), this would have been impossible to achieve in practice short of deporting the existing population, and indeed, the later pagan writer Zosimus tells us that Constantine even founded two new pagan temples there (*New History* II.31). It was probably Constantine's son Constantius II (AD 337–61) rather than Constantine himself who was mainly responsible for the first church of St Sophia (burnt down in the Nika riot of AD 532 and replaced by Justinian with the present building), and the church of the Holy Apostles adjoining Constantine's mausoleum.[2] Constantius was extremely pious himself, but the effects of the attempted restoration of paganism by his successor, Julian (AD 361–3), were felt at Constantinople as elsewhere, and there were still many pagans at court – indeed, Constantius' panegyrist, Themistius, was himself a pagan. At the end of the century, John Chrysostom, who became bishop of Constantinople in AD 397, directed many of his sermons against the dangers of paganism. We should therefore see the fourth century, after the death of Constantine, as a time of ferment and competition between pagans and Christians, when despite imperial support for Christianity the final outcome was still by no means certain. It was only in the fifth century that church building began to take off on a major scale, and it was as much the powerful personalities of late fourth-century bishops such as the forceful John Chrysostom in the east and Ambrose of Milan in the west that advanced the church at that period. The fact that Constantinople was now an important bishopric added to the political prominence of Christianity in the city, though the two patriarchates of Antioch and Alexandria were older, and this could prove a source of friction. But despite the advances that had been made, Christianity was by no means evenly spread in the cities of the east at the end of the fourth century, and much of the countryside remained pagan for far longer.[3]

By the reign of Justinian in the sixth century the population of Constantinople had reached its greatest extent, and has even been thought to have approached half a million. So large a number of inhabitants could only be supported by public intervention, and Constantine had instituted an elaborate system of food distribution based on that at Rome.[4] It was from the late fourth century onwards that much of the expansion took place – something of its scale can be imagined from the fact that the original number of recipients of the grain dole was set at only 80,000. The aqueduct constructed in AD 373 by the Emperor Valens provided the essential water supply, but the city also possessed an elaborate system of cisterns and reservoirs; new harbours were also necessary. The walls built in the reign of Theodosius II in the early fifth century, and still standing today, enclosed a much larger area than that of the original Constantinian city. Though Constantinople did not

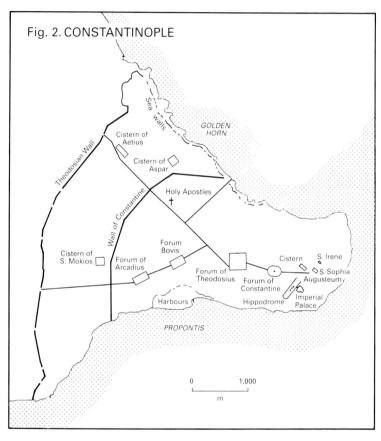

Figure 2 Constantinople.

14

equal Rome in population size, even at its height, it nevertheless provides a remarkable example of urban growth taking place during the very period of the 'fall of the Roman empire in the west'. Pagan critics of Constantine, like Zosimus, were highly critical of his foundation:

> the size of Constantinople was increased until it was by far the greatest city, with the result that many of the succeeding emperors chose to live there, and attracted an unnecessarily large population which came from all over the world – soldiers and officials, traders and other professions. Therefore, they have surrounded it with new walls much more extensive than those of Constantine and allowed the buildings to be so close to each other that the inhabitants, whether at home or in the streets, are crowded for room and it is dangerous to walk about because of the great number of men and beasts. And a lot of the sea round about has been turned into land by sinking piles and building houses on them, which by themselves are enough to fill a large city.
>
> (*New History* II.35, trans. Ridley)

Perhaps indeed the city failed to live up to modern standards of urban planning, but the description brings out both the extent of public investment and the consequent hectic growth. The heart of the city had been planned by Constantine himself – it included the imperial palace (greatly extended by later emperors), the adjoining Hippodrome and a great square leading to the church of St Sophia, a main processional street (the Mese) leading to Constantine's oval forum with its statue of himself on the top of a column of porphyry marble, and Constantine's own mausoleum, where he lay symbolically surrounded by sarcophagi for each of the twelve apostles. Despite the later proliferation of churches, it is notable that this is less a new Christian city than a complex of public buildings expressive of imperial rule.

Whatever Constantine's own intentions may have been, Constantinople did gradually assume the role of eastern capital. It had its own senate, and there were both eastern and western consuls; as the *Notitia Dignitatum* recognizes, by the end of the fourth century the same basic framework of administration existed in both east and west, and a division of the empire into two halves therefore posed no administrative difficulties.[5] But in practice, during this period the eastern government grew stronger while the western one weakened. Why the east should have prospered in this way is the subject of the rest of this chapter.

THE EAST IN AD 400

The turn of the century indeed found the east facing some severe problems, chief among which were the threats posed by the pressure of barbarians, mostly Germans, on the empire, and by the so-called 'Arian question'. The two were linked, for the Goths, who constituted the principal danger, had already been converted to a form of Arian Christianity in the fourth century by the missionary bishop Ulfila.[6] Arianism itself was named from the early fourth-century Alexandrian priest Arius, who preached that God the Son was secondary to God the Father and, though officially condemned by the Council of Nicaea (AD 325) and strongly opposed by the orthodox establishment represented, for example, by John Chrysostom, still had many adherents throughout the fourth century. At the turn of the century, certain Gothic leaders and their military retinues had acquired considerable influence over the government at Constantinople, and when Synesius, a landowner prominent in local administration, arrived there as an envoy from his native Cyrene in AD 397 he found city and court deeply divided about how to deal with this potentially dangerous situation.[7] This was not the only problem, however: like Honorius, Arcadius was young and easily influenced by unscrupulous ministers. In this way the eastern and western governments became rivals, and the western court poet Claudian, the panegyrist of the powerful Vandal general Stilicho, gives a luridly pro-western account of the situation, especially in his scabrous attacks on the eastern ministers Rufinus, master of offices, consul and prefect of the east, and the eunuch Eutropius, head of the young emperor's 'Bedchamber'.[8] Though he cannot rival Claudian's level of invective, Zosimus' account is similar in tone:

> the empire now devolved upon Arcadius and Honorius, who, although apparently the rulers, were so in name only: complete control was exercised by Rufinus in the east and Stilicho in the west . . . all senators were distressed at the present plight.
>
> (V.1.9)

Even allowing for distortion, matters looked unpromising.

Considerable danger was posed to the east in AD 400 by a certain Gainas, a Goth who had reached prominence in the Roman army only to stage a military coup and briefly occupy Constantinople. The weakness of the imperial government is shown by the fact that Gainas himself had only recently been given the job of suppressing the troops led by his Gothic kinsman Tribigild who were devastating Asia Minor, only to join them himself and march on the city. The choice for the eastern government was stark: either it could follow a pro-German policy and continue to attempt to conciliate such leaders, or it must attempt to root them out altogether. Both eastern and western courts were hotbeds of suspicion and intrigue, and the divisions which resulted led to the murder of Rufinus in AD 395 and the fall of Eutropius in AD 399, and were subsequently to lead to the fall and death of Stilicho in AD 408.

Theodosius I had attempted to deal with the barbarians by settling them on Roman land as federates, but this did not remove the danger, and in AD 395 Constantinople had to resort to the traditional policy of using subsidies to buy off Alaric, the leader of the Visigoths who were plundering land dangerously close to the city.[9] Naturally, so short-sighted a policy proved disastrous, and in the following year Alaric devastated the Peloponnese and large parts of the Balkans, an area whose control was disputed between east and west. A major part of the problem lay also in the fact that Gothic soldiers formed a large part of the Roman army itself. But the east was in a better position to buy off the raiders than the west; furthermore, significant voices, including that of Synesius, were raised in favour of expelling the Goths. At any rate, many of Gainas' supporters were massacred (AD 400) and when Gainas himself attacked Constantinople his coup was put down (albeit by another Goth, Fravittas, subsequently made consul for AD 401), and with it the pro-German group within government circles defeated. This result was extremely important for the future of the eastern empire, for though the danger of barbarian pressure was to recur, the influence of barbarian generals on the eastern government was checked, and the east was able to avoid having to make the massive barbarian settlements which so fragmented the western empire. The consequences for the west were also momentous, for Alaric went from the Balkans to Italy, besieging Rome in AD 408–9, demanding enormous payments in return for food and taking the city itself in AD 410 (Zos. V.37–51; Olympiodorus frs 7, 11). The sack of Rome was an almost unimaginable event which caused shivers to run down the spine of St Jerome in Bethlehem and sent rich Christians fleeing to the safety of North Africa.

RELIGIOUS ISSUES

But the violence in Constantinople in AD 400 also had another side to it, for Gainas was an Arian and had demanded an Arian church for the use of his soldiers, much against the wishes of the bishop, John Chrysostom. The situation was further inflamed when 400 Goths were burnt alive after taking refuge in an orthodox church (Zos. V.19). Religious divisions thus contributed to the general tension in Constantinople, while, conversely, the very fact that Alaric and his Visigoths who captured Rome in AD 410 were Christian made it doubly difficult for Christians like St Augustine to explain why God had allowed the sack of Christian Rome to happen.[10]

While by the middle of the fifth century the west was still the target of repeated barbarian assaults and settlements (Chapter 2) and the east was itself threatened by the Huns, the east also had other concerns. Arcadius was succeeded by his son Theodosius II (AD 408–50), only 7 years old when his father died. Theodosius II's long reign provided a stable period of consolidation during which the imperial court was characterized by an extremely pious atmosphere especially connected with the most strong-minded of his three sisters, Pulcheria, who became Augusta and regent in AD 414. Pulcheria chose Theodosius' bride – the intellectual Eudocia, formerly named Athenaïs and allegedly of pagan Athenian origin and selected by means of an imperial beauty-contest – and the relationship between the two women was predictably stormy; but Eudocia too had a strong influence on the church in the east, notably through the patronage she exercised on her visits to the Holy Land.[11] To this period belong the Council of Ephesus (AD 431), at which the title Bearer of God (Greek Theotokos) was officially recognized for the Virgin Mary, and that of Chalcedon (AD 451), when the orthodox doctrine of Christ's two natures, divine and human, was decreed. Each was a landmark in the history of the church, and together they represent an important stage in the working out of the complex implications of the creed agreed at the first ecumenical council at Nicaea (AD 325). It is also to the reign of Theodosius II that we owe the Theodosian Code, a compilation of imperial constitutions since Constantine, and our major source of

Plate 1 A Byzantine empress in her regalia, depicted on a leaf from an ivory diptych, late fifth or sixth century.

knowledge of late Roman law. Theodosius himself may have been weak and easily influenced, as contemporaries suggest ('meek above all men which are upon the face of the earth', according to the church historian Socrates, *HE* VII.42), but his reign was extremely important in the civilianization of the eastern government in the fifth and sixth centuries. Tellingly, Socrates and Sozomen, who composed continuations of Eusebius' *Church History* in Constantinople in the 440s, were both lawyers.

But not all went smoothly. In AD 403 quarrels between John Chrysostom and the Empress Eudoxia, two hot-tempered and outspoken characters, had led to the bishop's deposition by the so-called Synod of the Oak, and, after his return and yet another perceived affront, to a second exile in the following year.[12] Like the events of AD 400, this was a dramatic story: on Easter Saturday, after John's condemnation, 3,000 new Christians about to be baptized when the service was broken up by soldiers, and on the night when he left Constantinople a mysterious fire broke out in the church of St Sophia which burned down the senate house and some of its many classical statues; pagans blamed John's supporters, many of whom refused to communicate with the bishop who replaced him. John had powerful enemies besides the empress, notably the Syrian Severian of Gabala and Theophilus of Alexandria, who objected to John's support of the Tall Brothers, a group of monks who had fled from Theophilus' anti-Origenist activities in Egypt, but it was especially remembered that he had referred to Eudoxia in a sermon as Herodias and Jezebel, and that she had been offended by another he had preached against the vices of women. John had wealthy and influential women among his own following, especially the deaconess Olympias, but the jewels and display of rich ladies were a frequent target of his preaching. The real forces at work behind his condemnation, which was judged illegal in the west by a synod called by the pope, Innocent I, were several and varied, but personalities and personal feelings certainly played a large part.

Similar passions aroused in a religious context can be seen from events at Alexandria, a stronghold of paganism and the seat of the major philosophical school after Athens. Here the aggressively Christian policies of Theodosius I had led to the burning down of the famous Serapeum (the temple of the Egyptian god Serapis) by fanatical monks in AD 391; now the equally aggressive patriarch Cyril raised the emotional tension to such a pitch that Christians were massacred by the Alexandrian Jews when they gathered together on hearing that the church was on fire. In AD 415 Christian fanatics in turn lynched the female Neoplatonist philosopher Hypatia, Synesius' teacher:

> they dragged her from her carriage, took her to the church called Caesareum, where they completely stripped her, and then murdered her with tiles. After tearing her body in pieces, they took her mangled limbs to a place called Cinaron, and there burnt them. This affair brought no small opprobrium, not only upon Cyril [bishop of Alexandria], but also upon the whole Alexandrian church. And surely nothing can be further from the spirit of Christians than massacres, fights, and such-like things.
>
> (Socrates, *HE* VII.15, trans. from Stevenson, *Creeds*)

Alexandria was undoubtedly prone to such outbursts of violence, but every city had its own religious mix, and trouble, stirred up by excitable religious leaders or monks, was common as the urban population in many cities of the east steadily grew during the fifth and sixth centuries.[13]

THE COUNCILS OF EPHESUS AND CHALCEDON

The two great church councils of Ephesus (AD 431) and Chalcedon (AD 451) also have to be seen against this context. It is all too easy for a modern student to dismiss them as somehow irrelevant, but in fact they aroused passions equal to those surrounding any political issue in the modern world, and were just as much influenced by personal, social and local rivalries. Both rank among the seven 'ecumenical' councils recognized by the eastern church, starting with the Council of Nicaea called by Constantine in AD 325 and ending with the Second Council of Nicaea in AD 787. However, many others were held as well, either local and limited in character, or, just as frequently, not recognized for whatever reason as binding by the whole church. On the political level, as the church became more and more influential, and more embedded in society in general, division between the great sees and between individual bishops could and did lead to major splits with long-term repercussions. This was particularly the case with the Council of Chalcedon, for much of the east, especially in Syria and Egypt, refused to accept its decisions and went on to form its own ecclesiastical hierarchy during the reign of Justinian, a factor which had profound implications for imperial security.[14] From the point of view of the state, imperial support for the church necessitated a clear understanding of what the church was as an institution, and was not compatible with quarrelling and division among the clergy. Whether the bishops themselves were as committed to church unity is less clear, but questions of church organization and the authority of episcopal sees were of pressing importance to them, and the many councils and church synods in this period dealt largely with these issues, as well as with other questions of church order. As for the doctrinal issues themselves, despite the numbers of councils and the level of controversy, division continued unabated; indeed, if anything the councils themselves actually increased the tension and inflamed division by polarizing the various groups and forcing them to define their positions ever more exactly. The eventual outcome of a long process was the growing split between the Byzantine empire in the east and the papacy in the west, especially after AD 800,[15] but the eastern empire itself was already substantially divided in the fifth century over the relation between the divine and the human natures of Christ, a question which the Council of Chalcedon failed to settle in the longer term, just as the Council of Nicaea had failed to settle once and for all the question of the relation of Father and Son.

Rather than possessing an original orthodoxy from which a variety of later views ('heresies') were deviations, Christians had interpreted their faith in different ways since its beginning. However, the advent of imperial support, and the consequent public role assumed by the institutional church, gave an entirely new complexion to the process; what had been disagreement became not merely heresy, worthy of the strongest condemnation, but also liable to punishment from the state. The Greek term 'heresy' originally meant simply 'choice'; but each Christian group in turn defined the choices of the rest as heresies, and in the late fourth century Bishop Epiphanius of Salamis in Cyprus composed a 'Medicine-Chest' or list of 'remedies' (that is, arguments, following the medical metaphor) against some eighty such objectionable 'heresies'. The Councils of Ephesus and Chalcedon both carried forward this attempt to arrive at a definition binding on the whole church; both councils took place in a context of bitter rivalry. Again, personalities were much involved; before and during the Council of Ephesus these were led by Cyril, the nephew of Theophilus and bishop of Alexandria since AD 412, a hard and formidable leader. Nestorius, a monk from Antioch, was bishop of

Constantinople from AD 428, and was passionate but clumsy in contrast with the clever Cyril. The issue was whether, and, if so, how, Christ had two natures; the Monophysites held that he had only a divine nature, while Nestorius, and 'Nestorians' after him, emphasized the human. The exact implications of the title 'Bearer of God' now applied to Mary were hotly disputed. But other issues were in play, and behind these divisions lay also the old rivalry between the more literal interpretation of Christianity associated with Antioch and the traditional position of Alexandria. After much argument and counter-argument, imperial manoeuvring, strong-arm tactics and intervention by Egyptian supporters of Cyril, the latter got the better of it and Nestorius was deposed, even though he had the tactical advantage of being bishop of Constantinople.

Roman delegates had supported Cyril, and during the preliminaries to the Council of Chalcedon in AD 451, which was preceded by a second council at Ephesus in AD 449, Pope Leo I (AD 440–61) forcefully intervened, sending a long letter to Bishop Flavian of Constantinople (known as the 'Tome' of Leo), in which he argued for the two natures but questioned the legality of the recent condemnation of a certain Eutyches for denying them. At this the party of Dioscorus, Cyril's successor at Alexandria, was able to overturn the situation, whereupon Leo asked for a second council, calling that at Ephesus the 'Robber Council'. Meanwhile, Theodosius II had died and was replaced by Marcian, an elderly soldier whom Pulcheria chose for her husband. The final definition of the Council of Chalcedon was signed by some 452 bishops, and condemned both Nestorius and Eutyches, adopting a middle way which drew on the arguments of both Cyril and Pope Leo: as a recent critic comments, this was not easy and 'some delicate linguistic work was done'.[16] The Chalcedonian formula is of extreme importance, and despite continuing problems with eastern Monophysites in particular, who refused to accept it, it became and remains fundamental to both the western and eastern churches. It developed and clarified the creed of Nicaea, according to which God was Father, Son and Holy Spirit, by further proclaiming that Christ was at all times after the Incarnation fully God and fully human: 'to be acknowledged in two natures, without confusion, without change, without division, without separation' (Stevenson, *Creeds*, 337 and *passim*).

The definition did not put an end to further theological discussion (which indeed still continues); it did however mean that both the Nestorian and the Monophysite positions were judged to be unacceptable and were officially condemned. The council also legislated about many practical issues to do with church order and discipline, including subsequent marriages contracted by dedicated virgins, and especially on the authority of bishops, also laying down that the bishops in each province should hold formal meetings twice a year (canons of Chalcedon: Stevenson, *Creeds*, 324–33). Importantly, it also continued the previous decision of the Council of Constantinople (AD 381) in enhancing the status of the see of Constantinople, giving it jurisdiction over the dioceses of Pontus, Asia and Thrace, a move which Pope Leo soon attempted to annul in a letter to the Empress Pulcheria (*Ep*. 105.2; Stevenson, *Creeds*, 342–4).

The fifth-century west had been absorbed with its own doctrinal controversies, particularly in connection with the teachings of the British monk Pelagius on free will, against which Augustine fought a long battle; while in North Africa itself the Council of Carthage in AD 411 again condemned the local schism of Donatism and enforced catholic orthodoxy with strong measures.[17] But in the east the Emperors Leo, Zeno and Anastasius continued to wrestle with the aftermath of the Council of Chalcedon, which the Monophysites refused to accept. Their cause was fought by a series of forceful leaders with exotic names – Timothy Aelurus ('the Cat') in Alexandria, Peter the Fuller in Antioch and Peter Mongus.[18] The so-called Henotikon ('Unifier') of AD 481, a letter from the Emperor Zeno to the rebellious church of Egypt attempted to smooth over the differences between Monophysites and those who accepted the decrees of Chalcedon, but only antagonized Rome, which promptly excommunicated Zeno's advisers, Acacius the patriarch of Constantinople and Peter Mongus the patriarch of Alexandria. There were also differences of view in Constantinople itself, and since Basiliscus, who had briefly usurped the throne during Zeno's reign (AD 475–6), had supported the Monophysites, Zeno's letter had political as well as religious aims. His successor Anastasius (AD 491–518) at first tried to pursue a middle line, but later openly supported the Monophysites, deposing a moderate, Flavian, from the see of Antioch and replacing him with Severus, an extreme Monophysite (AD 512). Religious disputes were frequently the starting-point or accompaniment of the violent riots which were a common feature of eastern city life from now on. In AD 493, statues of Anastasius and his wife were dragged through the streets of Constantinople, and also in Anastasius' reign there were serious disturbances after the emperor proposed a Monophysite addition to the words of the liturgy in St Sophia:

> the population of the city crowded together and rioted violently on the grounds that something alien had been added to the Christian faith. There was uproar in the palace which caused the city prefect Plato to run in, flee and hide from the people's anger. The rioters set up a chant, 'A new emperor for the Roman state', and went off to the residence of the ex-prefect Marinus the Syrian, burned his house and plundered everything he had, since they could not find him. . . . They found an eastern monk in the house whom they seized and killed, and then, carrying his head on a pole, they chanted, 'Here is the enemy of the Trinity'. They went to the residence of Juliana, a patrician of the most illustrious rank, and chanted for her husband, Areobindus, to be emperor of the Roman state.
>
> (John Malalas, *Chronicle*, trans. Jeffreys, 228)

We should therefore see the fifth century as a period when some of the basic implications of Christian belief were being hammered out amid a situation of increasing imperial involvement in the church, and increasing power and indeed wealth on the church's side. The question of how to deal with the passionately held differences between Christians was not, as it tends to be today, just a church issue; it was at the top of the imperial agenda.

EMPEROR AND CITY

Theodosius had been succeeded by an army officer, Marcian (AD 450–7), in a political settlement ratified by his marriage to Pulcheria. The latter had acted as regent for her younger brother, whom she brought up 'to be orderly and princely in his manners'; perfectly fluent in both Greek and Latin, she did everything in his name, and never overstepped her position (Sozomen, *HE* IX.1). Marcian proved to be a careful and competent ruler, but he left no heir and the succession was decided by the powerful head of the army, Aspar, in favour of Leo, who was on his staff.

Indeed, imperial succession remained curiously unstable, never having been completely formalized since the early empire; when as now there was no direct heir, it was left to the army, or those elements nearest to the centre of power, and the senate to settle the matter. However, popular assent, in practice that of the people of Constantinople, was also an important factor, the religious role of the patriarch, or bishop of Constantinople, only coming to be formally recognized from the late fifth and sixth centuries on. In such a situation too much was left to chance, especially when, as we have seen, the possibility of rioting was ever-present in Constantinople. It is probably no coincidence that we now begin to have records of something like a formal inauguration procedure, or that the main elements of this were taken from military custom.[19] Leo was invested with the torque, a military collar, in the imperial box in the Hippodrome in full view of the soldiers and people, and then raised on a shield in an improbably Germanic ceremony, only then putting on an imperial diadem. Though the patriarch was also involved, as was appropriate to his new status, there was as yet no religious crowning as such or anointing or any of the trappings associated with medieval coronations, though by the seventh century the ceremony had indeed moved to a church setting.

Imperial inaugurations like other public occasions were accompanied by the shouting of acclamations by the crowd. These might be simple cries of 'long live the emperor' and the like, but they might also be elaborate metrical chants or, at times, doctrinal assertions. Sometimes the emperor in his imperial box would engage in a virtual dialogue with the people; a striking example survives in the so-called *Acta Calapodii*, where such a dialogue is recorded from the Nika revolt of AD 532.[20] As often, these were a chance to air political and other grievances or to appeal to the emperor. The Green faction

> chanted acclamations concerning Calapodius the *cubicularius* and *spatharius*: 'Long life Justinian, may you be victorious; we are wronged, o sole good man, we cannot endure, God knows, we are on the brink of danger. It is Calapodius the *spatharocubicularius* who wrongs us.'
> (*Chronicon Paschale*, trans. Whitby and Whitby, 114)

A surprising license was at times employed: a few days later during the same uprising the emperor went into his box at the Hippodrome carrying the Gospel, and swore an oath to the people in order to pacify them, 'and many of the people chanted, "Augustus Justinian, you are victorious." But others chanted, "You are forsworn, ass"' (*Chronicon Paschale*, trans. Whitby and Whitby, 121).

That the Hippodrome was now the setting for such confrontations followed a precedent from the early empire when emperors and people had also met each other at the games. In Constantinople the practice was formalized, the Hippodrome being linked to the palace by an internal passage, and it was here that the emperor was expected to make his formal appearances to the people as a whole. We can see evolving in the fifth century the ritualized yet turbulent relation of emperor and people characteristic of later Byzantium, in which the 'factions' of the Hippodrome, the Blue and Green sides in the chariot races, played a major role both as participants in state ceremonial and at times, especially in the early period, as instigators and leaders of popular disturbance. Emperors tended to support one 'party' or the other, and it has frequently been supposed that these Blues and Greens also represented the religious divisions of the day; however, though a group in a given city at a particular time (Blues and Greens were prominent in the rioting which took place in many eastern cities at the time of the fall of the Emperor Phocas in AD 609–10) might of course take on a particular cause, there is no evidence to show that either faction was identified with one particular group. The sculpted reliefs on the base of the obelisk set up by Theodosius II in the Hippodrome show the emperor in his imperial box with the performers and musicians in front of him and surrounded by his court. The Blue and Green supporters themselves sat in special places in the Hippodrome (many graffiti with messages such as 'Victory to the Greens' also survive carved on the seats of other theatres and circuses, as at Aphrodisias), and, like partisans of all periods, they dressed in a special way:

the part of their tunic which came to their hands was gathered in very closely round the wrist, while the rest of the sleeve, as far as the shoulder, billowed out in great width. When they waved their hands about while they applauded at the theatre and at the Hippodrome, or while they urged on their favourites in the usual way, this part actually ballooned out, so that unsophisticated people thought that their physique was so fine and strong that they needed garments like these to cover them. . . . Their cloaks and trousers and most of all their shoes were classed as 'Hunnic', both in name and style.[21]

(Procopius, *Secret History* 7)

27

EAST AND WEST

Some important changes were taking place in the east generally during this period. The burgeoning of urban life, in strong contrast to the west, will be discussed in Chapter 8, as will the impact of local cultures, especially in Syria and Mesopotamia, where the border area with Persia acted as a two-way channel for transmission of language, ideas and material culture. A real shift of emphasis takes place within the empire towards the very provinces where Monophysitism tended to flourish, and where Islam was to make its first impact outside Arabia.

But even as the western empire began to fragment, the east still attempted to maintain its relations with the west. We have seen that the developing papacy had to be taken into account in religious affairs, and the idea of an empire of both east and west was not lost. In AD 468 the Emperor Leo launched a massive expedition to free North Africa from the Vandals, who had overrun it and ruled the former Roman province since AD 430. But despite its size (over 1,000 ships) and the fact that it represented a joint effort with the western government, the expedition proved an ignominious and catastrophic failure through incompetence and disunity among the command. The possibility of success slipped away, and the general in charge (the same Basiliscus who later staged a coup against Zeno) barely escaped the anger of the populace at Constantinople, while the financial consequences were themselves disastrous, for the expedition had allegedly cost 130,000 lb of gold (Procopius, *BV* I.6); it is a measure of the underlying prosperity of the east at this period that it was able to absorb such a loss virtually within a generation. It was perhaps characteristic that the eastern government chose to concentrate its military effort on the dramatic target presented by Vandal Africa, just as Justinian did in AD 533, but the failure of the expedition ruled out any thought of similar intervention in Italy itself. When the line of Roman emperors in the west came to an end in AD 476, the east was already resigned to the situation and proceeded to deal by a kind of de facto recognition with the Ostrogothic kings who succeeded them.[22] It was easier to close one's eyes, and it was some time before Constantinople actually realized that the west was in practice divided into several barbarian kingdoms, particularly as the kings for their part tended to adopt a deferential tone towards the eastern emperor.

The memory of the ill-fated Vandal expedition was however still fresh sixty-odd years later when another was undertaken with triumphant success. Another means of maintaining relations with the west was through dynastic marriage; this too could mean military action. On the death of Honorius in AD 423 Theodosius II intervened to support the claims of the young Valentinian, grandson of Theodosius I, against the usurpation of a certain John; in order to do this he had to recognize the position of Valentinian's mother Galla Placidia, widow of Honorius' short-lived colleague Constantius III, whom he had refused to recognize as empress only two years before, and who had now fled to Constantinople.[23] A force was dispatched under the Alan Ardaburius and his son Aspar to instal Galla Placidia and her son, and Valentinian was duly made Augustus and married to Eudoxia in Constantinople in AD 437. For the first part of his reign Placidia acted as regent, and relations between east and west were good. But Valentinian himself proved a fragile reed, and the influence of the general Aetius, whose son was now betrothed to Valentinian's daughter, accordingly grew. The western court made as many marriage alliances with the barbarian peoples as it did with the east, however, and Valentinian himself agreed to betroth his tiny daughter to the Vandal Huneric. Older imperial women sometimes took matters into their own hands: after Galla Placidia's death in AD 450, Valentinian's sister Justa Grata Honoria chose to get herself out of an awkward situation by offering herself to the Hun king Attila, a foolhardy action with dire consequences (Chapter 2), but one to which Theodosius II gave his support. Luckily for Honoria, and certainly for the empire, Attila died first, having just taken a new wife, one Ildico, and his empire broke up:

> on the morrow, when most of the day had passed, the king's attendants, suspecting something was amiss, first shouted loudly and then broke open the doors. They found Attila unwounded but dead from a haemorrhage and the girl weeping with downcast face beneath her veil. Then, after the custom of their race, they cut off part of their hair and disfigured their already hideous faces with deep wounds to mourn the famous warrior not with womanly tears and wailings but with the blood of men.
>
> (Priscus, fr. 24, trans. R. C. Blockley, *The Greek Classicising Historians of the Later Roman Empire*, Liverpool, 1981, 1983)

On the death of Valentinian III in AD 455, the intervention of the eastern emperor was no longer sought, but the idea of an eastern intervention was not lost, and Leo helped to elevate Anthemius, the son-in-law of Marcian. This involved an unequal contest with a rival candidate, Olybrius, who was married to Valentinian III's other daughter and was being promoted by the Vandal king. It was the combination of circumstances in Italy and the growing power of barbarian individuals and groups, rather than any change of policy in the east, which made such interventions less and less relevant from now on. Even so, certain aristocratic families in the west, especially in Italy, remained wealthy and important during Ostrogothic rule, and their voice continued to be heard in Constantinople. For this reason, too, the balance struck in Ostrogothic Italy between Goths and Romans had to be a delicately balanced one.

THE BARBARIAN QUESTION IN THE EAST

Nor, though the immediate danger in AD 399–400 had been averted, was the German danger in relation to Constantinople itself solved in the longer term. Leo himself came to the throne as a member of the staff of a powerful Alan, Aspar, the son of Ardaburius (AD 457), and Aspar seems to have aspired to the same kind of influence exerted by comparable barbarian generals in the west. Determined that this should not happen, Leo tried to counteract the German influence by recruiting heavily for the army among the Isaurians, a mountain people living in Asia Minor. The future emperor Zeno (then called Tarasicodissa) was their chief and married Leo's daughter Ariadne.[24] Though Leo had to make concessions to Aspar by marrying him to another of his daughters, the fact that Aspar was Arian probably helped Leo to take the next step, that of removing Aspar and his father by having them murdered (AD 471). But the promotion of Isaurians also had problems. Contemporary writers are very hostile to them, and refer to Leo himself as 'the Butcher' (Malchus, frs 1, 3, 16, ed. R. C. Blockley, *The Greek Classicising Historians of the Later Roman Empire*, Liverpool, 1981, 1985). Moreover, Zeno himself was deserted by some of the Isaurians, who supported Basiliscus, the brother of his mother-in-law, the Empress Verina, in a successful coup (AD 475), and fled back to the wild mountains. Luckily for him, Basiliscus' Monophysitism so alienated the people of Constantinople that Zeno was encouraged to stage a return and have him executed. But Zeno's problems continued, and Verina's supporters, especially her son-in-law Marcian and his brother, marched against him. Though this too was unsuccessful, Zeno had to face yet another threat from his fellow-Isaurian, the powerful general Illus, which turned into a real war lasting several years, during which Illus proclaimed Marcian emperor and tried to get help from Odoacer in Italy (Chapter 2). Marcian not seeming to Verina to be the best candidate, Leontius was proclaimed in his stead, and crowned by the empress (AD 484). In this context too Zeno was victorious, though the remnants of Illus' party held out in the mountains for another four years. One can imagine the ferment created by such a prolonged period of uncertainty, and the tendency of individuals to switch sides in the tangled network of alliances. Anyone with a grudge against the emperor was liable to see their salvation in opposing him, and indeed Illus' supporters included the pagan intellectual Pamprepius. Zeno also had to contend with other problems from barbarians: on the fall of Aspar in the previous reign, Theodoric Strabo, the Ostrogothic leader, had managed to make Leo buy the safety of the Balkans by extorting political and financial concessions which included his own recognition, and having inherited this situation Zeno's first years were spent in uneasy balancing acts between Strabo and another Gothic leader, confusingly also called Theodoric. The eastern government alternated between promises of payment and threats of war; meanwhile, Thrace and Illyria were the prey of the second Theodoric. This time the east was exposed to the type of barbarian pressure already familiar in the west, and eventually Zeno was compelled to make substantial concessions by giving Theodoric territory in Moesia and Dacia as well as making him master of the soldiers in AD 483 and consul in 484. Naturally the policy failed, and Theodoric marched on Constantinople in AD 487. Fatefully for Italy, and fortunately for the east, an opportunity presented itself: Zeno was able to commission Theodoric, secretly of course, to replace Odoacer in Italy and rule Italy on Zeno's behalf. In this way the east escaped the fate of the west and Theodoric gained control of Italy.

The resilience of the east in the face of these continuous difficulties is remarkable. It was certainly helped by its capacity to pay subsidies in gold, as it had done already to the Hun Rugila and his successor Attila under Theodosius II. Annual payments to Attila amounted to 700 lb of gold and, after a defeat inflicted by him on the imperial troops in Thrace, increased to 2,100 lb, with a payment of 6,000 lb under a treaty of AD 443. The demands made by Attila drove the eastern government to despair, but the Hun king managed to foil an assassination plot made by the eunuch Chrysaphius. On Theodosius II's death, Marcian took the risky line of refusing to give in to this blackmail and ended the annual subsidy. Again however the east was saved from danger, this time by a change of mind on the part of Attila, who now turned towards Italy, where as we have seen he soon met his premature death.

When Anastasius was elevated to the throne in Constantinople in AD 491, Theodoric the Ostrogoth was establishing himself in Italy. Both sides were cautious towards each other, but in AD 497 Anastasius recognized Theodoric, who still held the post of master of the soldiers, as ruler of Italy, though in some sense still within the protectorate of the empire. Theodoric's exact constitutional position was perhaps more a matter of tact and delicate manoeuvring than of hard and fast definition (Chapter 2); there was still a considerable way to go before the shape of Ostrogothic rule was to become clearer. But even if in theory and in sentiment the ideal of a unified empire survived, by the end of the fifth century the barbarian kingdoms which were to be Rome's early medieval successors were coming into being. It was a situation to which Constantinople would have to adapt.

2

The empire, the barbarians and the late Roman army

AD 476

The fifth century saw one of the most famous non-events in history
– the so-called 'fall of the Roman empire in the west', which
supposedly took place in AD 476, when the young Romulus
Augustulus, the last Roman emperor in the west, was deposed and
his place effectively taken by Odoacer, a Germanic military leader.[1]
Odoacer differed from his barbarian predecessors in that he did not
attempt to rule through a puppet emperor; he sent an embassy of
Roman senators to the Emperor Zeno in Constantinople asking to
be given the prestigious title of *patricius*. The emperor's reply was
equivocal, since the deposed Julius Nepos, who was also now
seeking his aid, had been placed on the throne with eastern support
(AD 473); but Odoacer satisfied himself with the title *rex*, and
henceforth the only emperor ruled from Constantinople (Procopius, *BG* I.1.1–8; Anon. Val. 37–8).[2] Thus the date AD 476 has
provided a convenient point at which to place the formal end of the
Roman empire, and Procopius of Caesarea begins his history of
Justinian's Gothic war (AD 535–54) by recounting the history of
Italy from that point. Gradually, though not immediately, the
eastern empire came to terms with the fact that it was left alone as
the upholder of Roman tradition, and invented its own myths of
translatio imperii to justify its new role.[3] But AD 476 has no significance in the context of the economic and social changes that were
taking place in the period; it is doubtful whether even the population of Italy at first noticed much difference. Despite all the vast
modern bibliography which has accumulated about this supposed
'turning-point', the changes which were taking place were long-
term; it is much more helpful therefore to take a more structural
view.

In political terms, the fall of Romulus Augustulus was entirely predictable. Odoacer himself came from the German tribe known as the Scirae, one of several which were by now heavily represented as federate troops in what was left of the Roman army; indeed, he was carried to power by these federates when their demands for a share of the land similar to that enjoyed by barbarian tribes in Gaul was refused. But he was only one in a long line of generals who had held the real power in the western empire since the late fourth century.[4] When one of the first and most powerful of these, Stilicho, the Vandal *magister militum* of Theodosius I and regent for his son Honorius, fell in AD 408, suspected of treason (Chapter 1), he was succeeded by Romans in the powerful positions of *magister utriusque militiae* and *patricius*; but real power still lay with the barbarian generals, in particular Aetius (*c.* AD 433–54). After the murder of Valentinian III (AD 455) (Chapter 1), his successor Avitus, a Gallic senator, was defeated by a Suevian general called Ricimer and an uneasy period followed before Majorian was officially proclaimed emperor in AD 457, only to be killed by the same Ricimer four years later. Again Ricimer was kingmaker, but his undistinguished choice, Severus, who had not been ratified by the eastern emperor Leo, died in AD 465, again leaving the west without an official ruler. When Leo imposed his own choice, a easterner called Anthemius, the rivalry between Anthemius and Ricimer became first a scandal and then the occasion for open hostilities, in the course of which Anthemius was killed (AD 472). Ricimer's final choice for emperor was Olybrius, the Roman husband of Valentinian III's daughter Galla Placidia (Chapter 1); but both Olybrius and Ricimer died before the year was out, and the nominee of the Burgundian Gundobad was deposed by Julius Nepos with the encouragement of the Emperor Leo, only to be deposed in his turn in favour of the ill-fated Romulus Augustulus. It is a dreary and confused story, in which the principal players vary between barbarian or Roman commanders and members of the civilian aristocracy, with the eastern emperor at times invoked for the sake of respectability and at times interposing his own choice. Only occasionally did these power struggles at the top have a direct impact on government itself; Majorian, who did issue reforming legislation, soon fell at the hands of Ricimer. There was no western Leo or Zeno; in fact no western emperor ever succeeded in establishing strong government after the death of Theodosius I, and while the eastern government in the later fifth century under Marcian and Anastasius succeeded in

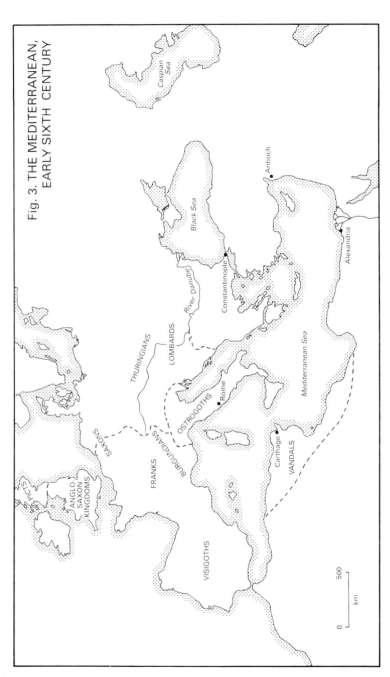

Fig. 3. THE MEDITERRANEAN, EARLY SIXTH CENTURY

Figure 3 The Mediterranean world, early sixth century.

becoming progressively more civilian in style, the exact opposite happened in the west.

But the western government could hardly be said to represent strong military rule; on the contrary, both the territories occupied by the western empire and the Roman army itself had by now suffered fragmentation on a major scale. These processes are closely interconnected, with roots reaching back to the fourth century, but they will be treated separately here for the sake of clarity.

ROMANS AND BARBARIANS FROM THE LATE FOURTH CENTURY ONWARDS

We have inherited a dramatic and overstated view of the Roman empire in the west being submerged by successive waves of northern barbarian invaders. In fact, the movement of barbarian tribes from beyond the Rhine and the Danube had already been a fact of life since the Marcomannic wars of Marcus Aurelius in the late second century.[5] Up to the mid-fourth century, however, it had generally been possible to contain them by a judicious deployment of force and diplomacy. Moreover, these were settled peoples with social hierarchies. However, the arrival on the scene in AD 376 of the Huns, a nomadic people from the north-east, was a decisive moment; it forced the Tervingi under their leader Fritigern to cross the Danube into Roman territory and led to their settlement in the Balkans by the Emperor Valens (Ammianus 31.4f.; Eunapius, fr. 42).[6] The Greek and Roman sources depict the event in lurid colours, but the Goths were no terrified rabble nor part of a great wave of invaders sweeping over the Roman empire. Complex social and economic factors lay behind their appearance in later Roman history, and when they came, they came as an organized military force.[7] Only two years later, at the battle of Adrianople (AD 378), the Goths defeated a Roman army and killed Valens himself on the field. Rome never forgot the blow; the extent of the shock it caused is evident in the account of it given by Ammianus Marcellinus, and by the fact that he chose to end his history at this point (Ammianus 31.7–13).[8] Huge losses were inflicted on the Roman army, and thereafter the Goths were free to roam and pillage freely. Moreover, the Roman defeat was the signal for other barbarian groups to cross into Roman territory. Though in AD 382 a formal treaty seems to have granted the Goths lands along the Danube and in the Balkans (Jordanes, *Getica* 27.141–29.146; Synesius, *De Regno* 21.50),[9] a certain Radagaisus collected a large barbarian army from across the Rhine and Danube and invaded Italy in AD 405; on his defeat by Stilicho 12,000 of them were enrolled in the Roman army (Olympiodorus, fr. 9; Zos. V.26). Almost at the same time the usurper Constantine moved from Britain into Gaul (Zos. VI.2–3). But we meet the barbarians most dramatically as they cross the frozen river Rhine in December AD 406; from then on Alans, Vandals and Sueves were on the move across Germany and Gaul and into Spain (Oros. VII.37).

The story is complex, and the course of events confused by rivalries between different groupings, not to mention the problems presented by the sources themselves; by the late 420s, however, the Vandals under Gaiseric crossed the Straits of Gibraltar into North Africa, reached Augustine's see at Hippo by AD 430, received a hasty land settlement in Numidia in 435 and took Carthage, the capital, in 439. Despite the abortive attempts of the eastern emperor, Theodosius II, to send a fleet to control them in AD 441, Vandal rule of most of North Africa, including Africa Proconsularis, Byzacena and most of Numidia and Tripolitania, received de facto recognition in 442. By 455 Gaiseric had taken over Corsica, Sardinia and the Balearics, and on the death of Valentinian III in that year even entered and sacked Rome, taking Sicily in 468; the further naval expedition sent by the eastern emperor Leo in the 460s was an ignominious failure (see Chapter 1), and North Africa remained in Vandal control until the expedition of Belisarius in AD 533.[10] Though it now seems that Vandal Africa was less isolated economically from the rest of the empire than has traditionally been supposed,[11] the speed and ease by which one of the richest and most urbanized provinces, supplier of grain to Rome, was lost is sufficient indicator of the degree of change which the northern barbarians were to cause from now on.

The situation in the northern provinces was less clear-cut, but just as damaging. In the difficult conditions of the first decade of the fifth century, Zosimus tells us that the defence of Britain was formally abandoned by Honorius: 'Honorius sent letters to the cities in Britain, urging them to fend for themselves' (VI.10); some of the troops in Britain, who had apparently supported usurpers before AD 406, remained in the province, but there was no longer a central authority, and Saxon raids now exacerbated the already confused situation, which is made even more difficult to understand by the disagreements in the few available sources. The rapid disappearance of Roman towns in Britain after several centuries of Roman rule is only one of the many puzzling features of the period.[12] In mainland Europe, the fifth century saw a lengthy jostling for position as different Germanic groups competed against each other and with Rome for land and influence. The west more than once suffered from the greater ability of the east to avert the danger by financial and diplomatic means, most conspicuously in the case of Alaric and the Visigoths, who had been allowed by the eastern government to build up their strength in the Balkans, only to use it against Italy, demand large amounts of gold and silver and eventually to sack Rome in AD 410 (Zos. VI.6–13).[13] The sack itself, while not apparently as destructive as it might have been, caused many leading members of the Roman aristocracy to flee and came as an enormous psychological blow to Christians and pagans alike. But the chance event of Alaric's own death shortly afterwards, like that of Attila, the king of the Huns, in a similar situation later, saved Rome from the possibility of long-term occupation.

The aftermath depended on the changing configurations of the tribal groupings, and their respective success in dealing with the imperial government. Various means were used. Having left Italy in 412, the Visigoths turned to Gaul, where Athaulf, their king, married the captive imperial princess Galla Placidia, only to pass at once into Spain. Not long afterwards the Emperor Honorius was to use the same Visigoths, now under Wallia, against the Alans and Vandals, and to settle them in Aquitaine. Further settlements were made c. AD 440 by Aetius, of Alans in Gaul and Burgundians north of Geneva. Meanwhile, a new threat was being posed by the Hun king Attila, who, having already extracted large subsidies, crossed the Danube in the early 440s, defeated the Roman armies sent against him on two occasions and succeeded in obtaining even higher annual payments of gold. He eventually turned towards the west, accepted the advances of Valentinian III's sister Honoria and demanded half the empire. The battle between the forces of Attila and Aetius on the Catalaunian Fields which followed (AD 451) was a temporary check, but did not prevent the Huns from invading Italy (Jordanes, *Get.* 180ff.). Again, the western empire had a lucky escape: Attila's death (Chapter 1) brought the break-up of the Hun empire and removed the danger.

From now on, however, as the western government became progressively weaker, it became less and less possible to sustain any coherent policy in relation to barbarian settlement. At the beginning

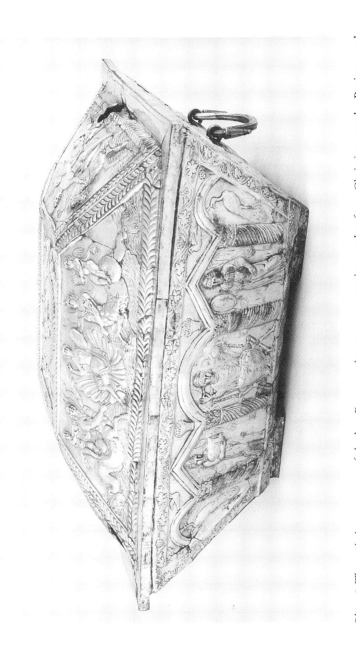

Plate 2 The artistic patronage of the late Roman aristocracy: a marriage casket for a Christian couple, Proiecta and Secundus, from the Esquiline Treasure, Rome, late fourth century.

of the fifth century, even in the vacuum left by the death of Theodosius I in 395, Rome still occupied the centre in the shifting game of barbarian movement; by the end of the century, on the other hand, no Roman emperor was left in the west, and we can see the first stage in the development of the barbarian kingdoms of the early Middle Ages.[14] The first such kingdom to be established was, as we have seen, that of the Vandals in North Africa. However, it was untypical in that it was overthrown by the imperial armies under Belisarius in AD 534 and replaced by well-established Byzantine rule lasting until the late seventh century. North Africa, in fact, represents the success story of Justinian's policy of reconquest; the irony was, however, that in contrast with the long history of Roman Africa before the arrival of the Vandals, the restored imperial province was governed by easterners from Constantinople whose language of administration was Greek.[15] The longest lasting of the Germanic kingdoms was that of the Franks, established by their king Clovis (481–511) after their momentous defeat of the Visigoths at Vouillé in AD 507 and lasting until AD 751. Although it was the Franks who gave their name to modern France, Clovis' descendants are usually known as the Merovingians. They found a vivid chronicler in the late sixth-century bishop Gregory of Tours, whose *History of the Franks* is our main source, remarkable not least for its unrestrained cataloguing of the bloodthirsty doings of the Frankish royal family.[16]

Gregory provides a colourful account of the conversion and baptism of Clovis himself: the king's wife Clotild was already a Christian and tried unsuccessfully to convert her husband, but his reaction when her first son died after being baptized was one of anger:

> if he had been dedicated in the name of my gods, he would have lived without question; but now that he has been baptized in the name of your God he has not been able to live a single day!

> (II.29)

The king was finally converted after successfully praying to the Christian God for victory on the field of battle against the Alamanni, and was then baptized by bishop Remigius of Rheims, who, we are assured by Gregory, had raised a man from the dead. The scene of the king's baptism was spectacular:

The public squares were draped with coloured cloths, the churches were adorned with white hangings, the baptistry was prepared, sticks of incense gave off clouds of perfume, sweet-smelling candles gleamed bright and the holy place of baptism was filled with divine fragrance. God filled the hearts of all present with such grace that they imagined themselves to have been transported to some perfumed paradise. King Clovis asked that he might be baptized first by the Bishop. Like some new Constantine he stepped forward to the baptismal pool, ready to wash away the scars of his old leprosy and to be cleansed in flowing water from the sordid stains which he had borne so long.

(II.31)

More than 3,000 of his army were baptized at the same time.

In Italy, the invasion of the Ostrogoths under Theodoric in 490 marked the beginning of the Ostrogothic kingdom (490–554), whose last king, Teias, was finally defeated by Justinian's general Narses in AD 554 after nearly twenty years of warfare.[17] But again in contrast to North Africa, the invasion of Italy by the Lombards in AD 568 meant that Byzantine control in Italy was not to last for very long, except in an attenuated (though still important) form, limited to the territory of the Exarchate with its base at Ravenna, which lasted from the late sixth until the mid-eighth centuries.[18] After 568 the situation in Italy was confused and fragmented; for this very reason, it was in this period that the popes, especially Gregory the Great (590–604), acquired much of their enormous secular influence and economic power.[19]

Ostrogothic Italy maintained many continuities with the Roman past;[20] among the most important of these was the survival of many of the immensely rich and aristocratic Roman families who continued to hold office under the new regime. It is a remarkable fact that the Roman senate survived during the fifth century, through all the political changes, and its members continued to be appointed to traditional offices and to hold the western consulship even under the Ostrogoths; the consulship was in fact ended by Justinian himself in AD 541.[21] Many of these Roman families were extremely wealthy, and Procopius, who describes the Gothic wars in detail from the eastern point of view, particularly identifies with this class, most of whom lost their land and position, and many of whom were reduced to a pitiable state by the Justinianic war unless they were able to flee to the east where they often also possessed estates.[22] Like many others of this class, Cassiodorus Senator, whose highly rhetorical and bureaucratic Latin letters (*Variae*), many written as Theodoric's secretary, are another of our main sources for the period, went to live in Constantinople during the wars. Before that, he had written a *Gothic History*, used by Jordanes in his *Getica*, and after the wars ended and he had returned to Italy, the *Institutiones*, precepts on Christian learning. Cassiodorus founded the monastery of Vivarium at Squillace, which was to become one of the most important medieval centres for the copying and preservation of classical texts.[23] A traumatic event had taken place in relations between the Ostrogoths and the Roman upper class in Italy in AD 523–4, when Theodoric had unexpectedly turned on and eventually executed two of its most prominent members, Symmachus and Boethius, author of the Latin classic, the *Consolation of Philosophy*. The case was sensational – Symmachus held one of the most prestigious names among the late Roman aristocracy, Boethius' two sons had both been given the consulship and he was himself Theodoric's *magister officiorum*.[24] Boethius' great work, the *Consolation*, was written in prison as he mused on his fate; he imagines himself visited by the Lady Philosophy, and engages in extended discussion of fate and free will, and of the fickleness of fortune, and includes a number of long poems which are of great interest in themselves.[25] But the deaths of Symmachus and Boethius were exceptional; Theodoric himself seems to have shared the general respect for Roman tradition, and the Ostrogothic regime was not in general oppressive.

The defeat of the Visigoths by Clovis at Vouillé in AD 507 put an effective end to their kingdom in Gaul, which had had its capital at Toulouse since AD 418, and to the legitimate descent of the Balt dynasty which had ruled since Alaric I at the end of the fourth century.[26] In the troubled period which followed, the Ostrogothic king Theodoric, whose daughter had married the son of the Visigothic Alaric II, intervened, and Visigothic rule passed temporarily into Ostrogothic hands. More important in the longer term, however, was the movement of the Visigoths into Spain, which had already happened before the end of the fifth century; there, especially from the time of the Ostrogothic Theudis (431–48), they were to establish a kingdom which despite some Byzantine success in the context of Justinian's reconquest lasted until the arrival of the Arabs in the early eighth century.[27]

THE GERMANIC KINGDOMS, THE ROMAN GOVERNMENT AND BARBARIAN SETTLEMENT

With the establishment of the barbarian kingdoms we pass into the traditional realm of early medieval history.[28] But the continuities are such that it is also possible to see the period up to the later sixth century in terms of a still surviving Mediterranean world of late antiquity; despite the obvious changes in settlement patterns in the west, the available archaeological evidence seems to show that long-distance trade and travel still went on, even if the details are still contentious, and that the urban change which has been such a controversial issue in recent historical work was a Mediterranean-wide phenomenon evident in east and west alike in the late sixth century.[29] It can therefore be distinctly misleading to think too much in terms of separation between east and west. The western kingdoms themselves retained many Roman institutions, and even saw their relation with the emperor in Constantinople in terms of patronage; their kings received Roman titles. The former Roman upper classes survived in substantial numbers and adapted themselves in various ways to the new regimes. One such was Sidonius Apollinaris, bishop of Clermont in the later fifth century, who complained bitterly in his elegant poems and letters about the uncouth local barbarian overlords, but adapted nevertheless to the changed situation. Gregory of Tours writes of Sidonius,

> he was a very saintly man, and as I have said, a member of one of the foremost senatorial families. Without saying anything to his wife he would remove silver vessels from his home and give them away to the poor. When she found out, she would grumble at him; then he would buy the silver vessels back from the poor folk and bring them home again.
>
> (II.22)

Both Gregory of Tours, the historian of the Franks, and Venantius Fortunatus, another Merovingian bishop, Gregory's contemporary and friend and the author of Latin poems on political and contemporary subjects, came from this class, as indeed did Pope Gregory the Great.[30] Germanic law existed in uneasy juxtaposition with Roman; the Ostrogothic kingdom had one law for the Goths and another for the Roman population, while successive Visigothic law-codes, beginning with the Code of Euric (c. AD 476) and the Romanizing *Lex Romana Visigothorum* of Alaric II (AD 506) and followed by an extensive programme of law-making in the Visigothic kingdom of the sixth and seventh centuries, gradually brought about a unification of the German and the Roman traditions.[31] The term 'sub-Roman' is sometimes used to designate these kingdoms in this period, and with its denigratory overtones is closer perhaps to the way in which they were regarded by the eastern government. The latter had pursued a pragmatic policy, knowing that it was in no position to impose a western emperor, but not admitting that the regimes were permanent. When the time came, it was very ready to use one against another. The fact that the Goths in Italy, like the Vandals and, at this period, the Visigoths, were Arian was a help to imperial diplomacy, for it made it possible to represent Justinian's invasion of Italy in AD 535 as something of a crusade: seeking aid from the orthodox Franks, the emperor wrote:

> The Goths have seized Italy, which is our possession, by force, and have not only refused to return it, but have committed wrongs against us which are past endurance. For this reason we have been forced to go to war against them, a war in which both our common hatred of the Goths and our orthodox faith dictates that you should join us, so as to dislodge the Arian heresy.
>
> (Procopius, *BG* I.5.8–9)

Prudently, the rhetoric was backed by gold, and by the promise of more if the Franks agreed; not surprisingly, perhaps, they were not to prove very loyal allies.

In studying the process of barbarian settlement in the territory of the western empire, we must try to distinguish between formal grants made by successive emperors and governments and the longer process of informal settlement change. In practice, a continuous process of 'unofficial' barbarian settlement, reaching back at least to the fourth century, had long ago undermined Roman control of the west. Though literary sources give us only a very imperfect and one-sided picture of this, its course can be partly reconstructed from archaeological finds, especially those from graves, though here again the record is still very patchy in geographical terms.[32] The reasons for settlement could vary greatly, from invasion and imperial grants of land to resettlement through service in the Roman army, and it is often difficult to identify the reasons in individual cases. In the same way, it is often impossible to connect known historical events such as invasions, or even in some cases longer-term settlement known from literary evidence with available archaeological remains. In addition, the newcomers often tended to take over the customs of the existing provincial population, making traces of Germanic settlement even harder to detect. Nevertheless, late fourth- and early fifth-century Germanic graves are attested from between the Rhine and the Loire, and in some cases seem to indicate the use of barbarians in the local forces of the Roman army. Strikingly, some of these cemeteries show Roman and Germanic burials side by side. The earliest phase of Germanic settlement in Britain, though on a small scale, nevertheless dates from the early fifth century, before the main wave of invasions.[33] It is true that the remains left in northern Gaul and around Cologne by the Franks, who are much better attested historically, are thin for the fifth century. But even allowing for the gaps in the archaeological evidence, it is obvious that a steady process of small-scale cultural and demographic change had been taking place in the western provinces long before the formation of the barbarian kingdoms as we know them later. By the mid-fifth century the former Roman villas in the western provinces have in many cases been abandoned or gone into decline, and the role of the former Roman landowning class, which will be discussed in more detail in Chapter 4, becomes a major issue in tracing economic and social change.[34]

The study of settlement patterns represents a major advance towards understanding the process of change in the western empire, and especially towards circumventing the problems inherent in the literary sources. Much of the evidence so far collected remains incomplete, and in some cases controversial; interpretation is very much a specialist matter. But there is enough that is clear to show that the Roman government was not so much faced with discrete incursions as with a slow but steady erosion of Roman culture in the western provinces from within. The process was not of course understood in these terms by contemporary writers, who are inspired by ethnographic and cultural prejudice and tend to paint a lurid picture of Romans versus 'barbarians'; contemporary interpretations of highly charged events such as the battle of Adrianople and the barbarian settlements which followed it are thus liable to mislead if taken too literally.[35] Their moral and political explanations are not adequate to explain what was happening on a broader scale, and most of the long-term changes lay outside government control. Yet it was these changes, rather than any political

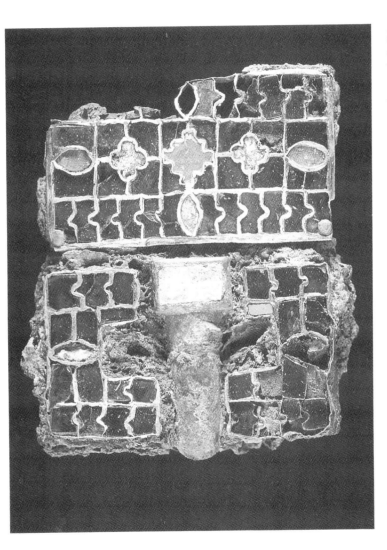

Plate 3 Composite buckle, Ostrogothic style, inlaid with cloisonné garnets, green glass and shell in gold cellwork, late fifth–early sixth century. Found in a female grave near the gate of the church of St Severin, Cologne. Grave goods, of which this is a particularly fine example, are one of the main ways of tracing the movements and settlement of the Germanic tribes.

events, which would in the long run detach these areas from effective imperial rule, and particularly so once that control passed from the hands even of a weak western emperor to those of a government in far-away Constantinople.

The impact of this process on the late Roman economy in general was obviously profound (see Chapter 4); in turn, the cessation of centralized Roman taxation on the former western provinces must have been of importance in stimulating their own economic development.[36] But the possession of wealth also played a direct role in the empire's dealings with barbarians in the fifth century in the form of the 'subsidies' paid by the Roman government to various groups, either as reward for quiescence or as inducements to go elsewhere. Although the eastern government was better placed to make use of this device than the western (Chapter 1), it proved useful at different times to both, and was still a key element in imperial policy in the sixth century when it was scathingly criticized by the conservative Procopius:

> On all his country's potential enemies he [sc. Justinian] lost no opportunity of lavishing vast sums of money – on those to East, West, North and South, as far as the inhabitants of Britain and the nations in every part of the known world.
>
> (*Secret History* 19)

By then (allowing for Procopius' rhetorical exaggeration), the practice was built into Byzantine diplomacy and was indeed in many cases unavoidable – very large sums were paid to Persia, for instance, under the peace treaties of AD 531 and 562.[37] The convenient practice of using barbarian troops as federates for the Roman army, which is a prominent feature of this period, was also expensive, and their maintenance could involve money as well as supplies.[38] An extreme case can be seen in AD 408 when Alaric demanded 4,000 lb of gold for his recent operations on behalf of the imperial government in Epirus. The example of Alaric and his Goths also shows how easily clever barbarian leaders could play off east and west. They are said to have invaded Italy in 401 because the eastern government had cut off their regular subsidies (Jordanes, *Get.* 146). Why this should have happened is not clear, but Thrace was also threatened at the time by Goths under Gainas and other barbarians described as Huns; at any rate, Alaric saw more advantage in moving against Italy, where he was alternately fought and bought off by Stilicho. The latter's dangerous policy of attempting to buy

THE MEDITERRANEAN WORLD IN LATE ANTIQUITY

the service of Alaric and his troops ended when he himself fell in AD 408; but when this happened and Alaric's demands for payment in return for retreating to Pannonia were rejected (Zos. V.36; Oros. VII.38), he besieged Rome itself (AD 408–9) and fixed the price of movements of food into the city at 5,000 lb of gold and 30,000 lb of silver (Zos. V.41). The aftermath of the capture and sack of Rome in AD 410 is highly confused, but enough is clear to show that the situation was quite different from that of the Vandals in Africa twenty years later: long-term occupation was not the issue at this point, and we still find Alaric's successor Athaulf alternately plundering Italy and taking on the role of federates in Gaul. 'When Athaulf became king, he returned again to Rome, and whatever had escaped the first sack his Goths stripped bare like locusts, not merely despoiling Italy of its private wealth but also of its public resources' (Jordanes, *Get.* 31). Athaulf now took Galla Placidia captive and married her, giving both sides a sense of false security:

> when the barbarians heard of this alliance, they were the more effectually terrified, since the Empire and the Goths now seemed to be made one. Then Athaulf set out for Gaul, leaving Honorius Augustus stripped of his wealth, to be sure, yet pleased at heart because he was now a sort of kinsman of his.
>
> (ibid.)

Now, however, grain was demanded rather than gold and silver, and by a momentous step, in AD 418 what remained of the Gothic army of Alaric was settled on Roman land in Aquitaine: 'they received land in Aquitaine from Toulouse to the ocean' (Hydatius, *Chron.* 69).[39] The twenty or more years of plundering, negotiating, bargaining and fighting before the Goths were settled in Aquitaine vividly demonstrate the ambiguities, the cost and the dangers with which the Romans were faced in their attempts to deal with the barbarians.

The settlement of the erstwhile federate Goths in Gaul marks a critical stage in the gradual transformation of landholding in the western provinces. Here, however, we reach highly contentious matters, for the terms on which the land was granted, or on which later settlements were made, are very far from being clear. The traditional view is that the barbarian *hospites*, beginning with the Visigoths, were to be entitled to a share of the land on which they were settled, in the surprisingly high proportion of two-thirds to one-third. Other examples would be the settlements of Alans and

48

Burgundians in AD 440 and 443 (*Chron. Min.* I.660) and Ostrogothic Italy, where, however, the share may have been one-third rather than two-thirds; the rent paid on the share thus received was itself known as 'thirds' (*tertiae*).[40] But there are many uncertainties, arising not least from discrepancies among the sources themselves. W. Goffart has proposed a quite different reading of the evidence from the later German law codes, according to which it was not the land itself, but the revenues from the estates, which were divided between barbarians and Romans.[41] Controversy surrounds the meanings of the Latin terms *hospitalitas* and *sors*. However, our evidence is very incomplete; arrangements probably changed with changing conditions, and while land does seem to have been at issue in the settlement with the Visigoths in AD 418, it may not have been, for example, in the case of the Ostrogoths. By contrast, there is no evidence from northern Gaul, for example, to tell us about the arrangements which were made there.[42]

BARBARIANS AND THE LATE ROMAN ARMY

Why was the Roman army so spectacularly unable to defend the western provinces?[43] R. Collins (*Early Medieval Europe 300–1000*, London, 1991) calls his chapter on the fifth century 'The disappearance of an army', and one must indeed ask what had happened to the Roman army and why it seems to have been so unsuccessful. The very question, however, presupposes (as the Romans did themselves) that the preferred response to barbarian incursions would be to continue to defend the frontiers and keep the invaders out. When they consider the loss of the western empire, therefore, contemporary sources accordingly blame either the poor performance of the army or the weakening of frontier defence, usually attributing the latter to a particular emperor – thus the pagan historian Zosimus lays most of the blame on the Christian Constantine. Soldiers are regularly depicted in the sources from the fourth century onwards as debauched, 'soft' and undisciplined.[44] The late Roman practice of billeting soldiers in towns often lies behind such criticisms; in the early empire, citizens of the more peaceful provinces had rarely seen soldiers at first hand, much less experienced their rough behaviour.[45] The anonymous author of the treatise known as the *De Rebus Bellicis* (late 360s) complains both of the high cost of the army and of the weakening of frontier defence (*De Rebus Bellicis* 5), and the peasant-soldiers settled on the frontiers known as *limitanei*

are frequently blamed for alleged poor performance, although contrary to common assumptions they are not securely attested before
the late fourth century.[46] The fact that these complaints tend to
come in so stereotyped a form should make us suspicious that their
form has much to do with the prejudices of the contemporary
sources. Moreover, as we have seen, the outcome of the barbarian
migrations, in the formation of the Germanic kingdoms, was not
simply a matter of the failure of the Roman army to deal with a
threatening situation, whatever the Romans may have thought
themselves.

Nevertheless, the army of the late fourth and fifth centuries was
indeed very different from that of the early empire. Many of the
changes, such as the stationing of troops in or near cities rather than
in large masses on the frontiers as before, stemmed from the fact that
under the reforms of Diocletian and Constantine the late Roman
army was paid in supplies as well as in cash: there was a simple need
for troops to be near the sources of collection of the taxes in kind
which were now among their chief sources of pay. According to the
sources, Diocletian had strengthened frontier defence installations
throughout the empire, but it appears, perhaps for similar reasons,
that the size of late Roman frontier fortresses and of the legions
which manned them was far smaller than in the early empire. It is
better to view the late Roman army as the product of gradual
evolution than of sudden change introduced by Diocletian and
Constantine, as the sources would have us believe. This evolution in
fact arose from a combination of different reasons, though it is true
that the effects were felt acutely in the late fourth- and fifth-century
west. By the sixth century, however, interruptions in army pay were
also a constant complaint in the eastern sources, and the government
was finding it increasingly hard to keep numbers up and was able to
field only very small forces even for its prestige endeavours in Italy.
Roman/Sasanian military dealings in the sixth century were also
hampered by the fact that the eastern frontier areas were progressively denuded of troops (see Chapter 5).[47] Barbarian bands known as
bucellarii had come very near to being the personal retainers of
individual generals, and the typical soldier of the period was a
mounted archer, part of a trend towards cavalry which had been
taking place gradually over a long period; things had moved a very
long way from the days of the Roman legionary in the early imperial
period.

A major difference was that the Roman army itself now contained a very high proportion of barbarian troops. From the late fourth century federate barbarian troops had constituted a crucial element in late Roman military organization, although they are for the most part not listed in the *Notitia Dignitatum*. This in itself tells us that the *Notitia*, which gives a set of 'paper' figures, is an unreliable guide to the nature of the Roman army as it was in practice. Barbarians could appear in several different guises – as tribal units, in relatively small groups or as mercenaries enlisted by commanders for individual campaigns.[48] In any of these cases, they had to be paid, whether through the *annona*, the official distribution of corn to the troops via the tax system, or directly in money and supplies. Such barbarian troops had frequently in the past been drawn from outside the empire, but with the process of barbarian settlement a fundamental change now took place: the federates came more and more from within the confines of the empire itself, and their numbers increased to such an extent that the army came to be substantially barbarian in composition and was effectively transformed into an army of mercenaries. There was an obvious political danger in this; it has been forcibly argued that the effective replacement of a citizen army whose soldiers fought for their own future by an army of mercenaries drawn from the very peoples against whom the Roman army was supposed to be fighting was a major factor in the fragmentation of the western empire.[49] There was also much contemporary concern in the aftermath of the battle of Adrianople, and the military treatise of Vegetius, probably of this period, reflects the conservative view. But the evidence does not bear out the supposition that the barbarian troops were any less loyal, or fought less well, than Roman volunteers or even Roman conscripts. We have already seen the power gained by individual barbarians holding the highest office of *magister militum*: Stilicho, Ricimer and Odoacer are the most conspicuous examples. Like most of the other drastic changes which took place in the late Roman army, this too had begun in the fourth century, and barbarian officers in general are frequently mentioned in the military narrative of Ammianus, covering the years AD 353 to 378. In the ranks, barbarians held a variety of statuses, including those of *laeti* and *gentiles*, both referring to groups of settlers with an obligation to military service, as well as *foederati*, individually recruited barbarians, and *dediticii*, prisoners of war from beyond the frontiers. It seems that Germans were (as we might expect) most concentrated in the field armies in Gaul. But they were also used in the east, and there is evidence from the fourth century of troops of this kind being supplied to the east. In practice, there were probably barbarian troops in all the many different units of the army. The reasons for this development, which seems at first sight to have been an extremely dangerous one for the empire, are not immediately easy to discern, and cannot be plausibly tied in in all areas with the supposition of a drop in citizen population, which has often been invoked to explain the 'fall' of the western empire.[50] One explanation is simply that it was easy. Barbarians were available in large, if not massive, numbers,[51] and utilizing them in the army was a convenient way of deciding what to do with them. They were easier to recruit than peasants, and the process did not interfere with the interests of the landowners who were emerging as more and more powerful in this period. Besides this, there was also the fact that some tribal groups had the reputation of being good fighters.

THE LATE ROMAN ARMY

Together with internal weakness, barbarian invasion is one of the classic explanations put forward for the fall of the empire. It further implies the ineffectiveness of the late Roman army to contain the situation.[52] One issue is that of size: how large an army was at the disposal of the late Roman state? While calculations based on the *Notitia Dignitatum*, which lists the eastern army establishment *c.* AD 394 and the western one of *c.* AD 420, are difficult to make, they seem to suggest a size well over 400,000 or even more, depending on one's interpretation.[53] The mid-sixth-century Byzantine writer John the Lydian gives a figure of over 435,000 (*De mens*. I.27), and slightly later Agathias gives one of 645,000 (*Hist*.V.13), but the latter must be much too high even as a paper calculation. It is simply incredible that the empire could have sustained so vastly increased an army, and such totals must be treated with extreme caution. As we have seen, the *Notitia* also fails to take into account the very large proportion of barbarian federate troops who actually did much of the fighting. Agathias admits that by his own day the actual overall size had been reduced to 150,000: 'whereas there should have been a total effective fighting force of six hundred and forty-five thousand men, the number had dropped during this period to barely one hundred and fifty thousand' (*Hist*. V.13). Indeed, the armies fielded in Italy in Justinian's wars of reconquest seem to have been very small indeed, while in the fifth century the withdrawal from Britain, the loss of North Africa virtually without resistance and the extent of barbarian penetration in general, all make it obvious that large troop mobilizations were no longer possible.[54] From the fifth century, at least, the western government was simply no longer in a position to control the empire by military means. We must therefore conclude that the high figures tell us little or nothing about actual troop deployment.[55] It is hard enough to believe that the army of Diocletian consisted of as many as 400,000 men; even this would have been an enormous burden, and it is equally clear that it soon became hard if not impossible to maintain. Why that should have been so has to do with political as well as economic factors, and, so far as the west was concerned, also with the increased wealth and power of the great landowners, and the inability of the central government in the west to retain sufficient resources in its own hands (see Chapter 4).

Similarly, the changes in, or, as Roman writers saw it, the progressive weakening of the frontier system should also be seen in the contexts of the long-term transformation of local settlement-patterns and of economic and social change. For contemporaries the concept of the frontier had become an emotive issue; a simple equation was made between failing to keep up the frontier defences and 'letting in the barbarians'. Diocletian was remembered for having strengthened the frontiers by the building and repair of forts, Constantine for having 'weakened' them by supposedly withdrawing troops into a mobile field army:

> Constantine destroyed this security [i.e., Diocletian's alleged strong frontier defence] by removing most of the troops from the frontiers and stationing them in cities which did not need assistance, thus both stripping of protection those being molested by the barbarians and subjecting the cities left alone by them to the outrages of the soldiers, so that henceforth most have become deserted.
>
> (Zos. II.34)

The actual situation was much more complex. Although the literary sources are unsatisfactory and the archaeological evidence hard to assess overall, the latter shows clearly enough the steady development of what are often termed defences in depth, behind the frontier zone itself; by this is meant a whole range of installations such as watch-towers and fortified stores-bases whose functions included ensuring the supply-system to such forward troops as remained, as well as watching and if possible controlling barbarians within Roman territory. It was now impossible to maintain a defensive line which could really keep barbarians outside the empire, and a variety of local expedients recognized the contemporary realities.[56] The expedients chosen differed very much from one part of the empire to another, depending on the terrain and the nature of the threat; in northern Gaul a series of coastal forts had gradually come into being over a very long period; in North Africa the so-called *fossatum Africae* to the south was no help against Vandals arriving from across the Straits of Gibraltar; in the east, where there had never been a fortified line as such, the desert zones, on the one hand, and the powerful military organization and aggressive policies of the Sasanians, on the other, presented a totally different situation. Current research suggests that the many defensive installations in the eastern frontier region in the later empire were designed not only for defence against invaders from outside the empire but also for the maintenance of internal security. The apparently successful defence system of the early empire had worked largely because in most areas there had been no serious threat; once, however, nearly all the erstwhile frontier was under pressure there was no serious chance of maintaining it in the same way, and recourse was made of necessity to whatever best fitted local conditions. The change is best seen in the case of the northern provinces, where the old concentrations of force on the Rhine and Danube can now be seen to have been replaced by a fragmented and complex mixture of ad hoc and often unsuccessful defences.[57] In the confused conditions of the fifth century it must often have been difficult to know exactly not only who was defending and who was attacking but also what was being threatened. Political factors compounded the local ones. Already in the third century, when Gaul had been the scene of a so-called separatist 'Gallic Empire', the line between legitimate rulers and usurpers was a fine one;[58] in the fifth century, when, as we have seen, real power was often held by Germanic military leaders, the official abandonment of Britain by Honorius had been preceded by the suppression of Constantine III, proclaimed by the soldiers in Britain; it was followed by the proclamation of another counter-emperor, Jovinus, at Mainz, whose support seems to have lain among Burgundians, Alans and Franks. In the confused conditions which followed, the elevation in AD 421 of Constantius, who had defeated Constantine III and married Galla Placidia, marked merely another passing event in a situation in which it must for much of the time have been difficult simply to know who was who.[59]

When for some periods in the west, at least, it is hard to see the Roman army as anything other than a hotchpotch of different units without unitary structure or control, it is hardly surprising that the organization, supply and command of the diverse units which made up the late Roman army in the empire as a whole should have proved so difficult. Even if we take a more common-sense view of the actual numbers of troops than has previously been common, the sheer maintenance of the army can be seen to have posed a variety of problems in the fifth century, of which cost was only one. Once barbarian settlement was allowed and encouraged, the frontiers no longer even pretended to keep out barbarians in any meaningful sense, while the growing presence of barbarians within the empire, combined with the activities of barbarian leaders such as Alaric and Gainas, meant that the army itself was in danger of becoming an army of barbarians. Difficulties of recruitment in the face of the mounting power of landowners and their unwillingness to release labour, supply problems and the weakening of government structures, especially in the west, all contributed to make the late Roman army difficult, and in the west impossible, to maintain and control. We can easily see this with the benefit of hindsight, and on the basis of archaeological evidence, difficult though the latter can be to interpret. Moreover, a moment's thought about the political opinions expressed in our own society should remind us that we do not need to take at face value all the complaints about the army which proliferate in our sources, most of which are harked back to supposedly better days which had gone for ever. The literary sources had a rhetoric of their own, of which we need to be sharply aware. When Synesius in Cyrenaica, who had lived with the bitter realities of provincial life for himself, says with tired resignation 'Pentapolis is dead', that is one thing;[60] but when conservative historians like Zosimus and Procopius, who also tended to be the most vocal, fail to understand the depth of the structural change that had taken place, and prefer to lay the blame on moral factors or individuals, we should be fully aware how far such judgements have been conditioned by the nature of their education and cultural background.

It is indeed hard not to conclude that the single most important factor in the so-called 'decline' of the late Roman empire and its failure to retain political control of the west was the totally unforeseen factor of the barbarian migrations. However, to think of this merely in terms of invasion is to miss the point: it was less a matter of military conflict with purposive aims than a gradual and inexorable seepage of barbarian peoples into the former imperial territories, and at all levels of Roman society. As is now realized, it was not a case of enormous numbers of invaders swamping the existing population. Since the reasons for this continuous migration of northern peoples remain obscure, one might be tempted to conclude that the voluminous historical literature on 'decline and fall' has in fact failed in its attempt to explain the end of the Roman empire in the west. But simple explanations are always inadequate for complex historical change. The negative attitudes of the Romans themselves towards barbarians, and their own tendency to see the problem in very black and white terms contributed largely to the problems and made serious integration and acculturation of barbarians more difficult. At the same time the process of barbarian settlement in the western provinces, whether ad hoc or officially encouraged, and the recourse to barbarian troops for the Roman army, brought to social, economic and military structures, which were in many cases already precarious, profound changes, the nature of which was not readily understood by contemporaries and which they had few means of controlling. We can see, as perhaps they could not, that the state was becoming demilitarized; soldiers were now regularly used for essentially civilian tasks, while the state had become dangerously dependent for its security on barbarian mercenaries whom it was not able to control effectively.[61] But we must also remember that the east in the fifth century, even while undergoing similar processes and facing similar dangers, supported a strengthened civilian government and increasingly prosperous economy, and kept its administrative and military structures sufficiently in place to be able to launch offensive wars in the west on a large scale under Justinian; this fact alone should be enough to make us remember the critical importance of local differences in explaining historical change.

3

Church and society

In the eighty or so years which elapsed between the so-called Edict of Milan (AD 313) and the anti-pagan legislation of Theodosius I, culminating in AD 391–2,[1] the Christian church and its bishops had gained a strong position within the Roman state. Most historians would also agree that Christianity itself was by now a powerful factor in society at large, even though it was still very far from universally embraced. An emphasis on Christianization in all its forms – belief, practice, art and architecture, social organization – is very much part of the modern concept of 'late antiquity'.[2] But the ways in which this development has been viewed by modern historians differ widely, ranging from continuations of the hostile attitude of Gibbon, on the one hand, to the triumphalist perspectives apparent in many works whose authors are themselves committed Christians. On a strict materialist view Christianity represents the self-justifying ideology of a new power structure built on even greater inequality than before;[3] A. H. M. Jones, lacking this ideological approach, nevertheless also made the growth of the church an important factor in explaining 'decline'. However, appearing only one year after Jones's *Later Roman Empire*, E. R. Dodds's classic *Pagan and Christian in an Age of Anxiety* (Cambridge, 1965) set a different agenda, asking whether and why the period from the third century on was more 'spiritual' than what had gone before. This question, if not Dodds's own rationalizing and psychological approach, has influenced much of the flood of writing in recent years about holy men and ascetics.[4] However, profound methodological problems are involved in any consideration of the role of religion in this period, and only a multi-faceted approach can do justice to the range of phenomena which need to be considered. In particular, we are now in a better position to realize the power of

57

religious beliefs to exercise a dynamic force in history, regardless of whether or not we ourselves believe them to be true.[5] Whatever the causes we may assign to it, it is a fact that in this period Christianity played a very major role in social change.

CHURCH BUILDING

In the first place, in the post-Constantinian period churches themselves were simply more visible. Once persecution officially ended, the way was opened for the development of ecclesiastical architecture as such. Constantine himself had been a great church-builder, and later emperors followed his example. During the fourth century major churches were dedicated in important city centres such as Antioch, Nicomedia, Milan and Aquileia, some receiving imperial sponsorship which reflected the new idea of emperors as patrons of Christian capitals. The large numbers of bishops attested in the records of church councils must in themselves be some guide to the spread of church building in the empire generally. In some cases, existing buildings were turned into churches, and, in general, Christians used the secular architectural styles that already existed, especially that of the three-aisled basilica, with its long naves leading to an apse, which was to become one of the dominant forms of church architecture for many centuries. The larger and more prestigious of these churches rivalled pagan public buildings in size and splendour and were often commemorated in contemporary sermons or in rhetorical descriptions. This account of the building (under the patronage of the Empress Eudoxia) of the cathedral at Gaza which replaced the destroyed pagan temple, the Marneion, conveys something of the excitement felt by contemporaries:

> The holy bishop had engaged the architect Rufinus from Antioch, a dependable and expert man, and it was he who completed the entire construction. He took some chalk and marked the outline of the holy church according to the form of the plan that had been sent by the most pious Eudoxia. And as for the holy bishop, he made a prayer and a genuflexion, and commanded the people to dig. Straightaway all of them, in unison of spirit and zeal, began to dig, crying out, 'Christ has won!' . . . and so in a few days all the places of the foundations were dug out and cleared.
> (Mark the Deacon, *Life of Porphyry*, 78, trans. Mango, *Art*, 31)

Plate 4 S. Paolo fuore le Muri, an early Roman basilica, destroyed by fire in AD 1823 but captured in this eighteenth-century watercolour by G. P. Panini. The architectural style has many parallels and is based on Roman secular public buildings.

However, the decoration of these new churches took some time to evolve; we have no surviving examples earlier than the turn of the fourth and fifth centuries of the striking later figural mosaic decoration familiar from such churches as S. Apollinare Nuovo (*c.* AD 490) and S. Apollinare in Classe (530s–540s) at Ravenna. S. Maria Maggiore in Rome, built under the patronage of Pope Sixtus III (432–40), is a spectacular example of a consciously classical style of church building where the interior survives intact; the elaborate mosaics on the triumphal arch, including a representation of the Virgin Mary in the dress of a Roman empress, draw on the existing secular repertoire for their biblical scenes. Similarly, the earliest surviving Roman apse mosaic, from the church of S. Pudenziana (end of the fourth century), also uses imperial motifs, showing

Christ surrounded by the apostles in the style of representations of the emperor and the Roman senate.

The other main architectural type followed by church architects was based on the martyrium and used especially for baptisteries, like the famous octagonal Orthodox Baptistery at Ravenna (early fifth century). Many such baptisteries were attached to basilical churches, but the form was not limited to this purpose; Constantine's 'Golden Church' at Antioch, for instance, which does not survive, was also octagonal (Euseb., *Vita Const*. III.50). By the sixth century a much less classicizing architectural form had developed, with many variations ranging from the domed basilica to the so-called double-shell octagon of Sts Sergius and Bacchus at Constantinople.

Justinian's elaborate 'Great Church' of St Sophia (Ayia Sofya) still stands in Istanbul where it was built to replace the earlier building on the site, which had been destroyed by fire in the Nika revolt of AD 532; with its massive dome (dedicated in AD 563 after the original collapsed due to an earthquake in AD 558), it was justifiably regarded by contemporaries as a masterpiece of engineering and design.[6] Justinian's St Sophia was paralleled on a smaller scale elsewhere, for instance at Edessa (modern Urfa in eastern Turkey), where the existing church was rebuilt in the sixth century and itself dedicated to the Holy Wisdom.[7] The more classical basilical form gradually gave way to the cross-in-square pattern familiar from Byzantine churches, whose architecture developed in step with the development of orthodox liturgy. In the fifth and sixth centuries, the public nature of these buildings and the prestige they brought to their builders, emperors or bishops alike, is very apparent; another huge church, dedicated to St Polyeuktos and recently excavated, was built at Constantinople very shortly before St Sophia by Anicia Juliana, a lady from one of the very highest aristocratic families, evidently in direct rivalry with Justinian. Gregory of Tours tells how the gold ceiling of St Polyeuktos was the result of Anicia Juliana's attempt to outwit the emperor's designs on her fortune by using it up first on church decoration.[8] Her church was sumptuously decorated, with a ceiling of pure gold, and elaborately inlaid marble columns, and adorned with a seventy-six-line verse inscription round the nave, in which she celebrated the magnificence of her donation. To judge from the later account of its construction, Justinian's St Sophia, built so soon afterwards, was designed to outdo this church.

There were hundreds of other, less well-known churches, not so spectacular, but just as influential locally in illustrating the impact of Christianity. Their construction did not follow actual need in terms of population size; rather, building or restoring a church was often, as in the case of the Byzantine churches restored and altered during the Vandal and Byzantine period on North African sites such as Sbeitla in modern Tunisia, a measure of local prestige: the expenditure by local well-to-do families which had gone in classical times towards the building or restoration of baths, stoas and other public buildings, was now diverted into churches and their furnishings. This is evident, for example, as late as the seventh century in parts of Syria, where even small village churches possessed elaborate collections of silver plate for liturgical use; these would consist of liturgical vessels, sometimes elaborately decorated with biblical or other scenes such as the communion of the apostles, and frequently with inscriptions giving the names of the donors, in simple formulae such as this one from a silver lampstand in the Kaper Koraon treasure, from a village east of Chalcis: '† Having vowed, they fulfilled their vow to (the church of) Sts Sergios and Bacchos. † Sergios and Symeoni(o)s and Daniel and Thomas, sons of Maximinos, village of Kaper Korao(n)'.[9] Such items were sometimes stamped with official silver marks, which provide an accurate means of dating them. Many of the earlier Syrian churches were extremely simple in style, but here too elaborate buildings soon grew up, most spectacularly at the great pilgrimage centres of St Sergius at Resafa near the Euphrates, where the sixth-century cathedral again replaced an earlier building, and Qalat Siman, the sanctuary of St Symeon the Stylite, where a great church with adjoining monastery and other buildings surrounded the column on top of which the saint had lived for more than thirty years.[10]

THE ROLE OF BISHOPS

But the new churches were not just decorative or cultic buildings; many were the preserve of local bishops, and provided the setting for the moral, social and religious teaching which was a central part of the bishop's role. We know of many powerful bishops during this period. Their influence extended well beyond what in modern terms would be purely church matters; Constantine had set a precedent in giving them secular jurisdiction, and in many individual areas they took on a leadership role which increased in scope in proportion to the difficulties experienced in keeping up the civil administration. In Ambrose of Milan we see an ambitious church-man keen to consolidate his own position, and who was able at times to exercise great influence over the Emperor Theodosius I. Another 'political' bishop was John Chrysostom at Constantinople (Chapter 1), though his ascetic habits allegedly made him unpopu-lar. The church historian Socrates comments on the number of enemies he made through his strict moral teaching and habit of excommunicating backsliders:

> what contributed greatly to gain credence for these complaints was the bishop's always eating alone and never accepting an invitation to a feast. His reasons for thus acting no one knew with any certainty, but some persons in justification of his conduct state that he had a very delicate stomach and weak digestion which obliged him to be careful in his diet, while others impute his refusal to eat in company with any one to his rigid and habitual abstinence.[11]
>
> (*HE* VI.4)

In contrast to Ambrose and John, Augustine, their greatest contem-porary, who had been strongly influenced by Ambrose in his conversion, spent the whole of his bishopric in the obscure town of Hippo on the North African coast, writing, preaching and living under quasi-monastic rule. Christian bishops were highly aware of the importance of communication, and Augustine was a master of the art of preaching and teaching; he wrote treatises about the best techniques of reaching every individual in the congregation, from the educated to the ignorant. We cannot unfortunately assess the impact on his local congregation of this extraordinarily modern understanding of the psychology of audiences, and one might be tempted to conclude that his genius was wasted in such a setting. However, among certain ecclesiastical circles and their upper-class followers the level of travel and letter-writing was such that ideas and influences could spread very quickly, and Augustine was also in communication not only with such figures as Ambrose and Jerome but also with Christian aristocrats in Rome, some of whom fled to his side when Rome was sacked in AD 410.[12] A very different figure was Theodoret, bishop of Cyrrhus in northern Syria in the mid-fifth century, another voluminous writer, theologian and controver-sialist who also led a busy life dealing with the practical problems of his see, which included a majority of Syriac speakers and some exotic ascetics.[13] Theodoret's theology was condemned by a later council (AD 553), and he was a highly controversial figure in his own day, banned by the emperor from travel beyond his own see in AD 448 for disturbing the peace. Nevertheless, energetic though he was in fighting for his doctrinal beliefs, his letters demonstrate the care and attention which he also gave to pastoral matters.

As time went on, bishops became more, not less, important. They were usually drawn from the educated upper classes and had often had a thorough training in the classical rhetoric that still formed the main content of higher education. In the confused conditions of the fifth-century west they often saw themselves as the upholders of civilized values; equally, some bishops, like Martin of Tours, became the objects of cult themselves soon after their deaths.[14] By the sixth century they were adapting themselves successfully to the needs of the new rulers, like Venantius Fortunatus, panegyrist of the Merovingian dynasty and a friend of Queen (later St) Radegund who had retired to a convent at Poitiers, and to whom Venantius wrote courtly poems, like this one on her return from a journey:

> Whence has this countenance returned to me with its radiant light? What delay held you, too long absent? You had taken away my happiness with you, with your return you restore it, and you make Easter doubly a day for celebration. Though the seed just now begins to rise in the furrows, I, in seeing you this day, already reap the harvest. . . .
>
> (Poem 8.10, trans. George, *Venantius Fortunatus*, 197)

Paulinus of Nola is an early fifth-century example of someone from an upper-class background who renounced much of his wealth to settle down at Nola in Campania, where he adopted the role of religious patron and built an ecclesiastical complex celebrating his patron St Felix, just as his friend Sulpicius Severus did in honour of St Martin at Primuliacum in Gaul.[15]

The enhanced importance of the papacy which we have noted in relation to the reign of Gregory the Great (AD 590–604) was another product not only of the contemporary political situation, but also of the kind of personal ability and energy which a good many other bishops also showed. Clearly the see of Rome was likely to occupy a special position, both in terms of secular authority and religious prestige; similarly, the patriarch of Constantinople, though not technically superior to the other eastern patriarchs (of Antioch, Alexandria and Jerusalem), was liable to be both more personally

63

involved in state politics, like John Chrysostom, and more closely connected with the emperor, who indeed might often intervene in appointing or exiling the patriarch. In AD 553, when the existing patriarch died just as Justinian's Fifth Ecumenical Council was beginning, the emperor took care to promote a candidate whom he rightly believed would help to get the imperial view accepted. Having changed his own doctrinal views in AD 565, however, he deposed the same man when this time he refused to go along with them. The relation between church and state was not, however, so straightforward as this might suggest: high-handed actions such as these were not in practice the norm, and theories of so-called 'Caesaropapism', i.e., the supposed control of the church by the ruler, go much too far.

CONFLICTS BETWEEN CHRISTIANS: CHURCH COUNCILS

In general, it is true, emperors did not shrink from involving themselves in religious affairs. These could frequently be turbulent, as when the strong anti-pagan legislation of Theodosius I in AD 391–2 (*CTh* XVI.10.10–12) provoked Christians to besiege and destroy the great temple of Serapis in Alexandria at the instigation of the bishop, Theophilus (Chapter 1). Other important temples were also attacked or destroyed, for instance at Apamea in Syria and at Gaza; this was also the context for the murder of Hypatia, the Neoplatonist and teacher of Synesius (Chapter 1).[16] But there were also many incidents involving violence between rival groups of Christians, of which one example is provided by the clashes between Arians and orthodox in Constantinople in the early fifth century. Monks could be a disruptive influence, like the so-called 'Sleepless Ones' from Antioch who caused such trouble in Constantinople that they were themselves attacked in AD 426 by rival mobs and had to be expelled to preserve the peace. Both the great church councils of the fifth century, the Council of Ephesus in AD 431 and the Council of Chalcedon in AD 451, were preceded by violent scenes between partisans; so great was the furore surrounding the rivalry of Cyril of Alexandria and Nestorius of Constantinople in AD 431 that the bishops themselves nearly came to blows,[17] while the second Council of Ephesus in AD 449 also concluded amid scenes of violence.

As we have seen (Chapter 1), three major church councils took place during this period – Ephesus (AD 431), Chalcedon (AD 451) and Constantinople (known as the Fifth Ecumenical Council, AD 553–4). But though these were the most important, they were by no means the only ones. The sense of a universal faith defined by general councils had grown gradually from the time of the first Council of Nicaea (AD 325), and many different issues were still being fought over, from the central issues of christology to the authority of the major churches and (especially in the second part of our period) that of Constantinople in relation to Rome. Besides the records of their proceedings ('acts'), councils also issued rulings ('canons') on matters of doctrine, ecclesiastical authority and countless details of Christian behaviour, especially in matters to do with the clergy, such as clerical continence and celibacy, on which the west insisted more strictly than the east.[18] The disputes were passionately argued and often resulted in bitter struggles between individual bishops and their supporters. It was the emperor's role to call ecumenical councils, and he could exert strong influence on their outcome, as Constantine had done in AD 325 and as Justinian did in AD 553–4. In the latter case, the proceedings lasted for many months, during which Pope Vigilius refused to attend, even though he was in Constantinople at the time. Eventually, after much harassment, he was prevailed upon to recant his position, but he still did not attend the council, and Justinian's railroading of the council's decisions failed to convince the western church. After the Council of Chalcedon, the Emperor Marcian issued an edict in which he hoped to persuade people that the controversies were finally settled:

> At last that which he wished, with earnest prayer and desire, had come to pass. Controversy about the orthodox religion of Christians has been put away; remedies at length have been found for culpable error, and diversity of opinion among the peoples has issued in common consent and concord.
>
> (Stevenson, *Creeds*, 341)

But as we saw, it was a statement of hope for the future rather than a description of what had actually happened.

It is a mistake to imagine that these doctrinal conflicts merely masked the underlying 'real' issues of power and individual or ecclesiastical authority, for while in our own society religion is relegated by the majority to a separate, and usually minor, sphere, in late antiquity, in contrast, not only was religion – both pagan and Christian – at the centre of the stage, but the Christian church was itself increasingly occupying a leading role in political, economic and social life. In such a situation, Christian doctrines themselves, together with the many permutations on which Christians were divided, aroused the passionate feelings of contemporaries in just the same way as social and political issues do today. Some of the questions were practical ones, as, for instance, when to celebrate Easter, a matter on which local traditions differed; but strictly theological issues such as the question of the divine and human natures of Christ and the status of the Virgin Mary were seen as being even more important. In the early part of the period Arianism, focusing on the relation of the Son to the Father, was still a major issue, particularly in relation to the contemporary barbarian problems, since nearly all the barbarian tribes had been converted to an Arian form of Christianity. By the middle of the fifth century, however, the key issues centred on the divine and human natures of Christ. Nestorius was condemned by the Council of Ephesus (AD 431), but his teachings lived on in the Nestorian insistence on Christ's humanity. The opposite extreme from Nestorianism came to be known as Monophysitism (one wholly divine *physis*, or 'nature'), and it was this belief which, though condemned at Chalcedon (AD 451) in the person of Eutyches, a priest of Constantinople, was to constitute the main obstacle to Christian unity in the next century and a half. When Justinian tried to reconcile the eastern churches by proposing a modification of the decrees of Chalcedon, he succeeded only in offending the west. Some indication of the strength of opinion can be judged from the fact that before Chalcedon, Eutyches had already been condemned by a local synod (AD 448) and immediately reinstated by a rival council (the 'Robber Council', AD 449). It was very much due to the new emperor Marcian and his pious wife Pulcheria that the full Council of Chalcedon was eventually able to issue on 25 October AD 451 a decree affirming the two natures of Christ. Discussion of the so-called 'Tome' ('document') of Pope Leo I, which laid emphasis on two natures (*substantiae*) (Chapter 1), occupied a great deal of the council's time. The Tome was regarded with suspicion by the followers of Cyril of Alexandria, and many easterners regarded the outcome of Chalcedon as a betrayal of the latter's principles. The difference was finally to crystallize into outright schism when only a few years after the Fifth Council Justinian appointed Jacob Bar'adai as bishop of Edessa and allowed the ordination of separate Monophysite clergy throughout Syria, thus paving the way for a separatist church (known as 'Jacobite', after Jacob, or as 'Syrian Orthodox') which was to survive the Arab conquest, and which still exists in certain places today.[19]

Thus despite the enormous effort and intense feelings which went into the councils, religious divisions were not healed; moreover, since the church of Rome and the catholic church of North Africa, which survived persecution during the Vandal period to re-emerge as a strong force after the Byzantine reconquest in AD 534, were strongly anti-Monophysite, the emperors of the late fifth and sixth centuries found it increasingly difficult to keep the ecclesiastical unity which was politically so necessary. Justinian's attempted reconquest of the west, conducted in the name of the restoration of orthodoxy, made these problems even more acute. Meanwhile, the division with Constantinople and the east, combined with the break-up of imperial rule in the west and especially the ultimate failure of Justinian to re-establish lasting Byzantine rule there, set the see of Rome, already granted primacy of honour in the canons of the Council of Chalcedon, on the way towards its development into the powerful and independent medieval papacy.

IMPERIAL INVOLVEMENT IN THE CHURCH

The emperors who followed Constantine were all Christian except for Julian (AD 361–3) and all followed Constantine's example of active participation in church affairs. However, the actual situation was much less clear-cut than this might suggest. Eusebius of Caesarea developed a political theory which saw Constantine as God's representative on earth, and this idea was to become the basis of Byzantine political theory. Emperors could make and depose patriarchs and summon and intervene in ecumenical councils. They could also engage in theological discussion themselves, publish works on doctrinal issues, as Justinian did, and emperors legislated throughout the period on matters concerning the church, attempting, for example, to control access to ordination (which carried tax privileges) and regulating the powers of bishops.[20] But while emperors might also receive relics in formal processions and take part in the increasingly elaborate rituals of the liturgy in St Sophia, where they were accorded special privileges and entrance to the sanctuary, they were not themselves crowned or anointed in a religious ceremony. As we have already seen, bishops could on occasion humble emperors, and the church often resisted the imperial will.

Direct conflict between emperors and patriarchs was to become a regular feature of Byzantine life in later centuries. In practice, the emperor and the church, or churches, stood in an uneasy relationship towards each other, a balance which was rendered still more delicate once imperial rule in the west ended.

The religious involvement of members of the imperial house did not however show itself only in the political sphere. Constantine's mother, Helena, had set a precedent by visiting the Holy Land and founding churches there (Euseb., *Vita Const*. III. 41–6). This did much to establish the idea of Christian pilgrimage, and travellers of all kinds made their way to Jerusalem and the Holy Land during the later fourth century. Some rich Christian ladies founded religious houses there which they ran on the model of their own aristocratic households;[21] Paula, Fabiola, Marcella, Melania all made the pious journey to Jerusalem and Bethlehem. Later in the fifth century the pattern was continued by Eudocia, the Athenian wife of Theodosius II, who left for the Holy Land in AD 438 after Melania's encouragement (Socr. *HE* VII.47; Clark, *Life of Melania*, 56), delivering an elegant speech at Antioch on the way, which she concluded with a quotation from Homer (Evagrius, *HE* I.20). She had Cyril of Alexandria with her, and was received at Sidon by Melania herself, whom she described as her spiritual mother (Clark, *Life of Melania* 58). Eudocia was however a disruptive figure, and her rivalry with her deeply religious sister-in-law Pulcheria showed itself on her return; she found herself again in the Holy Land in virtual exile a few years later, and, once there, her estranged husband forced her to reduce the magnificence of her household. All the same, Eudocia's patronage in the Holy Land in general was of great importance, and included churches, monasteries and hospices, some of which she recorded in her own epigrams.[22] A later empress, Theodora, the wife of Justinian (died AD 548), was remembered by the eastern Monophysites for her paradoxical protection in Constantinople of Monophysite clergy and monks driven to take refuge there by her husband's policies. We are even told that Justinian as well as Theodora would visit the Monophysites in the Palace of Hormisdas, talk with them and seek their blessing, and this was continued by their imperial successors, Justin II and his wife Sophia, who is said to have inclined towards Monophysitism herself.[23] Theodora, surprising though it may seem, had begun life as a variety performer in shows of dubious morality, and after her elevation to pious respectability as empress she included among her charitable acts the foundation of a convent for reformed prostitutes known as 'Repentance' (Procopius, *Secret History* 17.5; cf. *Buildings* I.9.2); her own example made her a figure long revered in the eastern church.

PRIVATE AND PUBLIC RELIGION

Emperors undoubtedly involved themselves in religious matters for reasons of state. But they were as committed as anyone else to the issues involved, and often, of course, personal interest and political advantage went side by side. One of the most striking features of this period is the apparent general increase in religious sensibility, or as it is often termed, spirituality. Another way of formulating what seems to have been happening is to put the question in terms of private versus public religiosity.[24] We certainly now have a great deal of the sort of evidence (saints' lives, monastic anecdotes, ascetic literature) which allows us glimpses of the lives of ordinary people. But it is another matter to deduce that individuals themselves had drastically changed. The type of evidence that we have, being not merely religious in character but also frequently explicitly designed to promote certain ideals of Christian life, suggests a greater conformity to these Christian ideals than was probably the case, to judge from more casual remarks made in passing in the same sources. It is also necessary to remember that it has been in the interest of the church to emphasize the process of Christianization and play down the evidence for a lively continuing paganism (see also Chapter 6); in this, it has been followed by many historians, whether consciously or not. When assessing matters of belief and individual feelings, therefore, we should try to remember that much of the evidence we now have leads of its very nature to a foregone conclusion. The many sermons preached by John Chrysostom in the late fourth century suggest that many among his regular congregation continued happily with practices he regarded as quite unchristian. Even as late as AD 691–2, the Council of Trullo, held in Constantinople, was still condemning pagan practices and trying to regulate the lives of those who called themselves Christians, who were certainly by then the great majority. So while some kinds of evidence, for instance letters and the Christian funerary inscriptions which now begin to appear on the mosaic floors of basilicas, do seem to allow us to perceive the change in personal faith, even here, as in our own experience, individual belief is often concealed under standard formulae, and common sense should tell us not to jump to rash conclusions.

Nevertheless, it is obvious that during this period Christianity became increasingly important, both in terms of practice and – especially through preaching, personal contact and the regulation of membership of Christian congregations – in the personal lives of many people. But this was certainly more evident in the cities, where the church was, as we have seen, highly organized, and it is a commonplace to say that pagan practices continued in the country-side much longer than in the towns; if we are to believe the sources there were still many thousands of pagans in Asia Minor under Justinian when John, bishop of Ephesus was sent out to convert them (John of Ephesus, *HE* III.3.36).[25] 'Conversion' is perhaps not quite the right word; a Greek inscription from Sardis, for instance, records the internment of 'unholy and abominable pagans' there by the *referendarius* Hyperechios (Sardis VII, no. 19). The persistence of pagan cult antagonized aggressive Christians and worried the authorities sufficiently for them to resort at times to violent measures, such as the forcible closure of certain temples by the agency of imperial troops, as happened in the case of the temples at Gaza demolished by the local bishop in AD 402 with imperial permission and with the willing help of the soldiers (Mark the Deacon, *Life of Porphyry of Gaza* 47–50, 63–70, 76). Much of the paganism of intellectuals centred on the philosophical schools of Athens and Alexandria (Chapter 6), but while it is extremely hard to judge the broader extent of pagan survival when so much of the evidence is highly biased, it seems clear that pagan cult also con-tinued in many places long after it was officially outlawed.[26] Many reasons, of course, combined to make people adopt Christianity, including personal advantage for those hoping for preferment from a Christian government, simple convenience and avoidance of the strong anti-pagan measures taken by successive emperors.[27] Very many others, as always, held a variety of conflicting beliefs at the same time and would have been surprised to have this pointed out to them. But there were still pagans among well-to-do families in early sixth-century Aphrodisias, and the student body at Alexandria in the same period contained both pagans and Christians. Trials of pagans were still being held in Constantinople in the late sixth century after a scandalous series of events at Heliopolis,[28] and Justinian conducted purges of pagan intellectuals in high places at Constantinople which led to death and confiscation of property, as well as the effective closure of the Neoplatonic Academy at Athens:

> This caused great fear. The emperor decreed that those who held Hellenic [i.e. pagan] beliefs should not hold any state office, whilst those who belonged to the other heresies were to disappear from the Roman state, after they had been given a period of three months in order to embrace the orthodox faith.
>
> (Malalas, *Chronicle*, trans. Jeffreys, 263)

MONKS, ASCETICS AND HOLY MEN

This was also the age of the holy man and the ascetic. It was now that the monastic movement spread throughout the Mediterranean, first with those who, like Pachomius and Antony in the late third century, retired to the Egyptian desert, then with a multitude of formal and informal religious communities of all types. Some monasteries followed the eastern rule of St Basil or, in the west, that of John Cassian, on which Cassiodorus' monastery at Squillace was based.[29] The numbers of monks could be very large, allegedly amounting to many thousands in Egypt alone: to take a few examples from the literary sources, in the early fifth century Palladius tells us in his *Lausiac History* that there were 2,000 monks at Alexandria, 5,600 male ascetics and hermits at Nitria, and 1,200 monks and twelve women's convents at Antinoe, while at Tabennisi there were 7,000 monks, including 1,300 in the monastery of Pachomius alone, as well as a women's monastery of 400 nuns. Despite the large monasteries mentioned here, however, it is important to emphasize the actual variety of the religious life at this period, which did not by any means always involve living in the type of community familiar from the Middle Ages and later. Many dedicated religious, especially women, still lived in small groups or even in their own homes,[30] while in the desert many communities adopted the form of the laura, where individual monks lived in their own cells around the central church, to which they typically returned weekly for common worship.[31] It can hardly be doubted that by the fifth century many who did not adopt the religious life themselves were also deeply influenced both by the ideals of asceticism and by the example of individual ascetics, or that they had thus taken these ideals into their own lives and their own faith. Ascetic aims were not limited to organized religious communities, nor indeed to Christianity; they were preached with equal fervour by the Neoplatonic philosophers of the fourth and fifth centuries, who advocated abstinence from sex, rich food and luxury of all kinds (Chapter 6). But while there were many similarities between pagan and Christian asceticism, especially at more intellectual levels, Neoplatonic teaching advocated a bodily regime based on prudent restraint (*askesis* – 'training'), including sexual continence, following the precepts of the early Greek philosopher Pythagoras, who had been revived as a model, for instance by the early fourth-century philosopher Iamblichus in his treatise *On the Pythagorean Life*.[32] Some Christians at least went further, following the pattern laid down in the narrative of the temptations of Antony, directing more of their attention to the avoidance of sexual lust and adopting exotic forms of self-mortification.[33]

It has been argued that monasticism was a kind of 'protest' movement against the institutionalized church, but the ascetic ideal in general (renunciation of bodily comfort, including warm clothes, adequate diet, cleanliness and especially sexual relations) had become prominent in early Christianity from a very early date.[34] For our understanding of the particular ways in which it was taken up in late antiquity the *Life of Antony*, attributed to Athanasius, is extremely important. It set the pattern for the classic ascetic life, with its opposition between the world and true spirituality, its lurid scenario of temptation overcome and its desert setting, where lions are tamed by the spiritual power of the holy man. In addition, it became required reading for educated Christians. Augustine heard of the powerful effect it could exert shortly before his own conversion to the ascetic Christian life in Milan in AD 387: he and his friend Alypius were visited by a Christian called Ponticianus, who:

> told the story of Antony, the Egyptian monk, a name held in high honour among your servants [Augustine is addressing God], though up to that time Alypius and I had never heard of him. When he [Ponticianus] discovered this, he dwelt on the story, instilling in us who were ignorant an awareness of the man's greatness, and expressing astonishment that we did not know of him. . . . From there his conversation moved on to speak of the flocks in the monasteries and their manner of life well pleasing to you and the fertile deserts of the wilderness. (*Conf.* VIII.6.14, trans. H. Chadwick, *Saint Augustine. Confessions*, Oxford, 1991, 192)

The monks at times engaged in highly political activity, and there could be sharp tensions at times between them and the civil authorities. But it is a mistake to separate 'monasticism', still extremely fluid at this period, from the ascetic movement in general, and there is no doubt that ascetic ideas and practice percolated through society as a whole. By the fifth century, some ascetics, especially in Syria, were practising spectacular forms of renunciation, such as the stylites, who lived for many years at a time on platforms on the top of specially erected pillars. The most famous of these were the two Symeons (the first died in AD 459 having lived on a pillar at Qalat Siman in Syria for nearly forty years; the second (sixth-century) had his pillar near the city of Antioch) and Daniel (died AD 493), a disciple of the first Symeon, who lived on a pillar near Constantinople for thirty-three years.[35] Then there were the 'grazers' who lived only off grass and shoots, and some who chained themselves up and lived in cowsheds. Others so renounced worldly pretensions that they pretended to be mentally defective. These included both men and women; one example is the sixth-century ascetic known as Symeon the Fool, who defied conventions to such an extent that on one occasion at Emesa (Homs) he tried to take a bath in the women's baths, only to be roundly beaten and ejected by the indignant women bathers (Leontius, *Life of Symeon the Fool* 14). Other forms of asceticism, however, involved practical charity, as with Euphemia and her daughter in Amida, and Euphemia's sister Mary in Tella, recorded by John of Ephesus, who spent their lives caring for the sick and needy, but who were not afraid when they felt the need to embark on a pilgrimage to Jerusalem.

As with most historical phenomena, there are several reasons for the popularity and prevalence of such holy men and women in this period. The classic discussion by Peter Brown suggests that they should be seen, especially in Syria, in anthropological terms as a type of rural patron, defusing the tensions and difficulties felt by the villagers.[36] While Brown's article acted as an enormous stimulus, it was quickly pointed out not only that holy men were often to be found in or near cities, where they might attract the attention of the wealthy élite, or even the emperors (the stylite Daniel is such an example), but also that functional explanations are only part of the story – in particular they do not explain how the ascetics were seen by contemporaries or necessarily how they viewed themselves.[37] There were in fact many different sorts of holy men and women; we should certainly not see them as an exclusively rural phenomenon, even though the ascetic idea of retirement from the world might make a rural or desert environment seem particularly appropriate. Fleeing into the farther desert is a *topos* in the monastic literature. When most would-be ascetics fled to the desert, however, whether in Upper Egypt, Judaea or Syria, they usually settled in practice not very far away from the settled areas on which they depended for food and sustenance. Archaeology reveals that the Judaean desert was crossed by a network of paths linking the monasteries together, and we know that in many cases the monks retained close relations with the organized church and the patriarch in Jerusalem. Moreover, the staple diet of the monks seems to have been bread, for which it was necessary to buy wheat, sometimes from far afield since it could not be grown in the desert environment. Other activities of the monks, such as their basket-weaving, also involved them in market transactions with the outside world, while the actual building of the monasteries implied a major investment and had a considerable effect on the local economy. In effect, the monasteries of the fifth and sixth centuries in the Judaean desert north and south of Jerusalem were themselves part of the process of settlement of population on marginal land which is a striking feature of Palestine and Syria in that period (Chapter 8).

Hospitality was in fact seen as a central part of monastic duty, and the coenobitic monastery of Martyrius not far from Jerusalem had a large hospice for visitors, with its own church and stables. In order to escape the numbers of visitors who seem to have pursued them, some solitaries adopted the tactic of moving from place to place, but it was part of the holy man's role to interact with the rest of society, as indeed Antony had done; thus, like many others, Amoun, an early monk at Nitria in Egypt, received visitors and performed miracles. The monks needed other people on whom to practice their charity, and hospitality was an important part of their way of life. The *Lives of the Desert Fathers* record many such visits:

> We also put in at Nitria, where we saw many great anchorites. Some of them were natives of that region, others were foreigners. They excelled each other in the virtues and engaged in rivalry over their ascetic practices, struggling to surpass each other in their manner of life. Some applied themselves to contemplation, others to the active life. When a group of them saw us approaching from a distance through the desert, some came to meet us with water, others washed our feet, and

others laundered our clothes. Some of them invited us to a meal, others to learn about the virtues, and others to contemplation and the knowledge of God. Whatever ability each one had, he hastened to use it for our benefit.[38]

(Russell, *Lives of the Desert Fathers*, 105)

We can see from the literature that asceticism of this kind was a matter of theory as well as practice, so that it suited the monks to complain about the visitors who disturbed their prayer, while actually encouraging them to come. Similarly, though ascetics did often enough live in towns, it was debated whether one could in fact practise holiness while living in the city. But it is a mistake to pose the issue too much in terms of urban versus rural life, for in the monastic discourse the 'desert' and the 'city' stood for individual spirituality and external ties respectively rather than for actual locations. And while the holy man needed other people, every community, large or small, also needed its own holy man; he might not be called upon very often, but his presence and his holiness were essential. All sections of society came to take this for granted; thus even the sophisticated Procopius relates how when Hephthalite archers in the Persian army of King Cavadh tried to shoot at the holy man James their arrows would not leave their bows. James had taken himself to a retreat two days' journey from Amida where he lived on seeds; the local people had built a rustic shelter around him, with gaps allowing him to see out and to converse. Cavadh asked him to restore the firepower of his archers, but when James complied, and the king offered him anything he asked for, the holy man asked for the safety of any who chose to take asylum with him from the present war (*BP* I.7.5–11).

Like much of the material used in Peter Brown's original article, this example relates to Syria, and it is clear that though Antony had retreated to the Egyptian desert, asceticism took a particularly striking form in Syria. This is certainly in part because the ascetic ideal was already well established there, and was not confined solely to Christianity – Gnostics, Marcionites and Manichaeans all preached renunciation. But it is also the case that from the time of the first great Christian writer in Syriac, Ephrem of Nisibis (died *c.* AD 373), the Syriac ascetic tradition adopted an especially severe form.[39] The more general questions of the development of Syrian Christianity, often seen as highly distinctive, and its subsequent influence on the rest of the empire are also important (Chapter 8).

CHRISTIAN ART AND SOUVENIRS; PILGRIMAGE AND PILGRIMAGE ART

Another new phenomenon whose development can be traced in the latter part of the period is the increasing use of and attachment to religious images, portraits of Christ, the Virgin and the saints. Despite the prohibition on figural images which Christianity had inherited from Judaism, icons, portable images, often painted on wood in the style familiar from the Byzantine period begin to be attested in the later sixth century, but similar subjects were already familiar in many different media, including small items such as ivories as well as larger embroideries and mosaics in churches.[40] Again, and especially in view of the many stories which record the miraculous intervention of an icon in the life of an individual, this has been seen both as a manifestation of popular religion and as a reflection of private and personal piety. However, the first major public icons are attested in the context of the wars against Persia in the later sixth century, when they are paraded round as military standards; moreover, it is clear that the court and the official church were as quick to commission and adopt them as were individual citizens, and while women feature in many of the stories, it by no means follows that men were less likely to worship icons than women.[41] Their proliferation had profound implications for the nature of artistic patronage and for attitudes to secular and classical art, and was to stimulate a prolonged period of religious division in Byzantium in the eighth and ninth centuries.[42]

Even in the sixth century and into the seventh, however, classical styles and subject-matter are still found alongside Christian ones. In general, it is misleading to think either of a linear development from classical (equated with 'pagan') to Christian, or of a series of classical 'revivals', though the latter has been a favourite theory among art historians. Rather, different styles and subjects existed side by side, and are more easily explained in terms of patronage and function than, as still commonly, in terms of increasing spirituality.[43] The relation between religious affiliations and taste and the choice of classical subjects is a difficult one, but recent work makes it clear that one cannot argue for pagan connections or a pagan user simply on the basis of the classicizing themes used, for example, on many examples of late antique silverware or on late antique ivories: Christian patrons liked classical themes too.[44] The interpretation and dating of such themes and styles has been

Plate 5 Pottery pilgrim token (*eulogia*) showing St Symeon Stylites the Younger (late sixth century) on his pillar at the Wondrous Mountain near Antioch. Together with bottles (*ampullae*) containing holy oil or water, such tokens were regularly taken home as souvenirs from pilgrim sites.

extremely contentious, particularly in relation to items connected with the late Roman senatorial aristocracy, and which have been taken to demonstrate its continuing paganism into the fifth century, but the problems of interpretation are felt no less acutely later in the period. We shall have more to say on this in relation to the reign of Justinian, who has often been seen as having sponsored a classical revival himself (Chapter 5).

There were other ways in which Christianization affected artistic production too, for example in the manufacture of souvenirs – lamps, bottles for water from the River Jordan and the like – which pilgrims could take home with them. In this period one might say that pilgrimage was booming, whether to the holy places themselves, or to the shrines of saints or holy men, especially those which housed famous relics. The many surviving examples of pilgrim souvenirs from the Holy Land are often dated to around the sixth century, and are an indication of the extent of the pilgrim trade experienced in Palestine at that period, but their equivalents could be obtained at other pilgrimage sites such as that of Thecla at Seleucia in Asia Minor.[45] One can observe from the fifth century onwards the desire among pilgrims for a souvenir of their visit, whether in the form of a lamp or bottle of holy water, or a specially manufactured token, such as the sixth-century clay tokens from the shrine of St Symeon the Younger, south-west of Antioch, and many similar examples. We have already observed the proliferation of churches and their impact on architectural development. A pilgrimage centre would typically have one or more churches, with other buildings for the reception and care of pilgrims; such sites were also often the location for the major market and fair held in the area. Monasteries, too, began to be built all round the Mediterranean, some of them on a big scale; as well as those which belonged to the religious houses themselves, many other hospices for travellers (*xenodocheia*) and hospitals for caring for the sick were founded by wealthy Christians who adapted the traditional practice of public benefaction to serve the aim of Christian charity.[46]

THE CHURCH AND WEALTH

Almsgiving had been a principle of the early church, and widows and orphans had been maintained by individual congregations since the second and third centuries. This was now continued, and takes concrete form in the foundation of buildings financed for the very purpose. Through almsgiving, and through the financing of such institutions, the church, bishops, or, as often, individual wealthy Christians were effective in redistributing wealth; at the same time, through church building and other forms of patronage, these agencies took a major part in changing the appearance and the economic basis of urban life (Chapter 4).[47] But though there was a clear relation between classical benefactions and Christian patronage, the aims and motivation of the latter also drew on other roots, in particular the Scriptural injunction to renounce wealth and give to the poor (Matt. 19.21). Unlike classical benefactions, Christian charity was, at least in principle, aimed at the poor themselves, of whom indeed the Roman élite had been barely aware.[48] Naturally, not all rich Christians were inclined to give up their luxurious lifestyles, as we learn from the sermons condemning them for continued ostentation, and a considerable literature built up which attempted to soften the Gospel saying by arguing that a rich man could indeed still be saved. But we also hear of many cases of individual renunciation of wealth, such as that of Paulinus of Nola, or the even more famous example of the Younger Melania (died AD 438), who with her husband Pinianus sold up her vast estates in order to live a life of Christian renunciation.[49] Acts of renunciation such as these may however actually have been somewhat less dramatic than they seem, in that the donors took care of their own family first, and rather than giving their wealth directly to the poor, tended to give it to the church for further distribution, thereby increasing the latter's wealth. It must also be said that the monasteries which many subsequently founded were often run on somewhat aristocratic and privileged lines. All the same, there is no doubt that spectacular giving did occur.[50] In the late fourth and early fifth centuries, when there were still many pagan members of the aristocracy – sometimes even in the immediate family of the giver – the practice caused them serious concern about the maintenance of family property.[51] The tension between the demands of Christian renunciation and celibacy and the need for procreation and, in a traditional society, for the retention of wealth within families for the maintenance of society, became a real issue.[52] But even if we need not suppose that the average Christian took the drastic measures of renunciation of wealth, or sexual abstention, it cannot be doubted that a large proportion of wealth did seep away from production and towards the church. The poor certainly benefited to some extent from the process, and some monasteries, for instance in Palestine, themselves contributed to the local economy, but the main beneficiary was surely the church itself, which was now able to lay the foundations of the vast wealth which it enjoyed in the later Middle Ages. The extent of this wealth, which had flowed into the church in the form of gifts and legacies ever since Constantine gave the church the power to inherit and took away the Augustan prohibition on celibacy among the wealthy classes, can be judged from the *Liber Pontificalis* (based on a sixth-century original), which lists the extraordinary riches endowed on the Roman churches, including estates whose revenues would provide for the upkeep of the church in question.[53]

Even though, as we have seen, there were still a number of dramatic 'purges' of pagans under Justinian, and even as late as AD 579–80, it is clear that by the sixth century Christianity was firmly established within the fabric of the state. The fragmentation of the western empire, combined with the conversion of all the invading barbarian tribes (something which was not at all a foregone conclusion), allowed the church to assume a leading role, even when the surrounding kingdom was Arian, or even, as with the Vandals in North Africa, persecuted catholics. In the east, the church, while itself profiting from the growing prosperity of the fifth century, also played an active role in the redistribution of wealth which was changing the late Roman empire into a Christian medieval society.

This process was hastened by the fact that the emperors, even if not always the leading members of society, took an active lead. We are still left with the difficulty of judging the extent to which this institutional Christianization was also internalized by the average citizen, and have noted that the sources may give a somewhat misleading impression. But it was of the nature of early Christianity not just to provide a cultic framework but to teach, discipline and regulate the lives of its members to an exceptionally high degree. Pagan practice and pagan beliefs might continue, as they have done into modern times, but the post-Constantinian church knew well how to win hearts as well as minds.

4

Late Roman social structures and the late Roman economy

Understanding the late Roman economy presents a particular challenge. Because of the deep-seated disposition to think in terms of 'decline', attention has traditionally been focused on the supposed negative indicators. Certain topics, such as slavery, taxation and the so-called 'colonate' (see pp. 85ff.), have occupied a special place in the secondary literature. All have undergone re-evaluation in recent years, and many other older assumptions have been questioned as well. In addition, the increased interest in this period shown by archaeologists in the past two decades or so, and the vast amount of new evidence that is becoming available mean that the old questions can be looked at in new ways. This has meant that the late Roman economy in general is now one of the most lively areas of current research. It is not too much to say that the large volume of new material is dramatically changing the look of the subject.

THE OLDER MODEL

As I have suggested, the whole subject of the late Roman economy (which involves also the consideration of groups such as landowners, tenants and slaves) is closely tied to conventional historiographical models of decline and collapse, and economic collapse, or at the very least severe strain, has been adduced by many historians anxious to explain Rome's fall. The resulting scenario is however more a convenient myth than a realistic analysis.

In the first place much of the evidence is impressionistic. Complaints about tax collectors or soldiers billeted in towns are indeed extremely common, but similar examples can be found in almost any society, and need to be read with caution. Whether things had really changed significantly for the worse is equally hard to establish; it is possible to find plenty of evidence from the Principate which suggests that the condition of the peasant then was hardly better.[1] Individual instances of peasants taking evasive action at the tax collector's approach (see p. 98) do not necessarily add up to a general picture of flight and collapse. A more fundamental problem is posed by the legal evidence, especially the often repeated laws in the Theodosian Code, by which successive emperors legislated to keep decurions in place in their towns and *coloni* on the estates in which they are registered (see p. 86). The picture of oppression and authoritarianism which these laws seem to suggest has been endorsed by many scholars, who have represented the later Roman empire as virtually collapsing under its own weight, and described it in terms such as 'totalitarian' and 'repressive'.[2] But when laws are constantly repeated they must be presumed to be ineffective; moreover, laws need enforcement. Where the necessary apparatus for the latter is lacking, it may be comforting for those in authority to repeat the law itself, but it does not necessarily follow that it was actually carried out in practice.

The literary sources may also distort the picture, and taking them at face value can lead to equally overstated conclusions. Many modern discussions take literally the apparent statement by the Christian Lactantius (*De mortibus persecutorum* 7), a biased and hostile source, that Diocletian quadrupled the size of the army, and then used this as the basis for a highly negative view of the economy in general. Similarly, despite Diocletian's measures to ensure better collection of revenue, it is far from certain that the level of taxation itself increased, as many scholars have assumed.[3] The few general statements that we have on such matters as taxation tend to come from writers as biased and as unsubtle as the pagan Zosimus or the fifth-century Christian moralist Salvian, and must be treated with considerable caution. Finally, in considering these methodological issues, it is also necessary to consider the relative weight of internal factors versus external ones like the impact of barbarian invasion and the question of east versus west. After all, if the structure of the state in the late fourth and fifth centuries was as top-heavy and as liable to collapse from its own internal contradictions as many scholars assert, why is it that the eastern empire seems to have gone from strength to strength?

AN ALTERNATIVE APPROACH

It is the contribution of archaeology in particular which has led historians to question the older view, and it is worth noting that A. H. M. Jones published his great work, *The Later Roman Empire*, in 1964, well before the current interest in late Roman and early medieval archaeology. Such a book would look very different today. But it is also a matter of new ways of looking at the subject. While the older assumptions of decline are still very much with us,[4] many historians have been influenced by different approaches, especially comparative ones. Perhaps most interestingly, the lively debate about the ancient economy in general which has been going on since the publication of M. I. Finley's *The Ancient Economy* in 1973,[5] has taken in the later empire as well as the Principate, thus to some extent bypassing the supposed great divide that came with the third century and the reforms of Diocletian.[6] The older model depends on the view of a massive tightening up of government control and consequent increase of government expenditure, generally attributed to Diocletian. If, however, those reforms were actually merely revisionist in character, this in turn should cause us to question the general model, and in particular to pay more attention to the underlying economic structures which held good throughout the long history of the empire.[7]

EAST AND WEST

There are of course certain obvious issues which do affect the later period specifically, including that of the increasing divide between east and west. Here it is important to remember that the basic administrative, economic and military structures of the Roman state established in the early fourth century were still in place in the eastern empire at least up to the reign of Justinian, and often beyond. We must therefore look for special factors, such as those described in Chapter 2, to explain why the west should have been different.

The late Roman tax system was designed to cope with a situation in which continual debasement of the coinage had led to near collapse and revenues had to be collected and payments made to the troops in kind; the regular census and the five-year indiction aimed at ensuring reliable collection of tax revenue for the state, and the scheme also involved elaborate matching of need and supply. The main item of expenditure as before was on the army, who were now paid in kind as well as money (Chapter 2). Certain obvious consequences followed: army units (themselves far more varied in type and organization than previously) now tended for instance to be stationed near to the sources of supply, and thus in or near towns, instead of on the frontiers. While by the end of the fourth century more payments were made in cash, the central role of the state in collecting and distributing the *annona* (the army supplies) remained an important feature of the economy, both in terms of organization and stimulus to production; the cessation of this state function in the fifth century was a major factor leading to economic fragmentation, as was the end of the grain requisitions for the city of Rome (Chapter 7).

In contrast, basically the same system was in force in the east as in the west, but apparently with more success. A number of factors contributed to this. The east, for instance, had been much earlier and more successfully urbanized than the west and, despite the ceaseless complaints of municipal councils and their spokesmen, most of these cities continued in existence or were even flourishing during the fifth and sixth centuries. We hear a great deal about their problems, not least because our written sources tend to come from just this kind of milieu; thus Ammianus Marcellinus, Libanius, Julian and later Procopius all took up the cause of the cities versus the central government (see Chapter 7). But many of their complaints had an ideological basis; in practice, the fifth and early sixth centuries seem to have been a time of prosperity for many eastern regions, especially parts of Syria and Palestine (Chapters 1 and 8). Another obvious difference between east and west in economic terms relates to the constant and in the end more serious barbarian incursions suffered by the west in the fifth century; not only was the economic base itself weaker than in the east (see p. 95), but the demands on it were greater. As we have seen, the western government had great difficulty in maintaining military forces adequate for their task. But a deeper and more structural difference lay in the growth of an immensely rich and powerful class of senatorial landowners in the west during the fourth century, whereas wealth in the east was by comparison more evenly spread. The combination of a weak government and wealthy and powerful landowners was crucial in determining the shape of the western economy.

Thus east and west were both similar and dissimilar in this period. Local factors are increasingly important from AD 395 onwards, yet many shared features remain and some similar trends can be observed, even though the rate of change may differ. The standard accounts of decline and collapse obscure these real differences. In contrast, the present lively state of archaeological investigation invites us to compare one site or area with another, and encourages the broader view; it also invites the question of how the traditional textual evidence and the increasing amount of material evidence relate to each other. By the end of our period, while it is still possible in some ways to speak of a Mediterranean world,[8] the west has largely fragmented, while the eastern government and its provincial and defensive structures are clearly in a far weaker position than before. It is possible to argue, as we shall see, that Justinian's wars of reconquest (Chapter 5) actually contributed to this weakness, as did the catastrophic plague which first hit the empire in AD 541. In addition there were also structural factors which we can see reflected in the gradual metamorphosis of many cities in the eastern empire either into medieval towns or (more often) into villages, a process which had begun before the end of the sixth century (see Chapter 7). In many areas, the signs of prosperity evident earlier were already beginning to tail off when the Persian invasions of the early seventh century dealt another severe blow to the east, and made it unable to resist the first Arab conquests of the 630s (see Chapter 8). Taking a long view, it is possible to argue that the east and west underwent similar processes, but at different times, the speed of change being regulated by the operation of local factors.[9]

THE ORGANIZATION OF LABOUR

It has been argued, notably by M. I. Finley, that large-scale slavery declined in the Roman empire for a variety of reasons, of which the most important was a drying-up of the main supply of slaves when the more or less continuous wars of conquest ceased in the early empire. Yet the sources for the late Roman empire make it clear that slaves continued to exist;[10] sometimes indeed they existed in very large numbers, for example on the vast estates of senatorial landowners. When such landowners became Christian, they sometimes sold their property in order to use the wealth for Christian purposes, in which case the slaves were sold too; we know that this was the case with certain estates which belonged to Melania the Younger in the early fifth century (see p. 78). Legal sources also demonstrate the continued existence of slaves on the land and elsewhere, and the church itself soon became a major owner of slaves. We can assume that part of the labour force on the land and in many forms of production will still have been servile. However, it is less clear what this meant in practice, or how slaves related to *coloni*, technically free tenants who were, in many areas, theoretically tied to their particular estates by imperial legislation, and over whom the landlords had rights which can look very like the rights of owner over slave. It was for instance possible to be described as *servus et colonus* (both a slave and a *colonus*), and it is clear that slaves could themselves be tenants.

This apparent confusion illustrates very well one of the basic problems we have in understanding the late empire. Are we to take the mass of imperial legislation at face value? How reliable a picture does it present of the way in which society really worked? As we can see from the *Codex Theodosianus* under Theodosius II, and from the *Codex Justinianus* a century later, late Roman emperors passed repeated laws which on the face of it sought to restrict the freedom of movement of *coloni* and tie them to the land; if these laws were really successful, we would have to conclude that the late empire was a time of real repression, in which the population was reduced to virtual serfdom.[11] In law, this was certainly the case. The difference between slave and free may often have been slight or nonexistent in practical terms: by the time of Justinian, for instance, tenants who are *adscripticii* (bound to the soil) were treated in the legal texts more or less as if they were slaves (*CJ* XI.48.21.1; 50.2.3; 52.1.1). Yet the impression we get of these classes from saints' lives and other more popular sources is far from being one of total repression and alienation, and social mobility was surprisingly common at slightly higher levels. There was thus evidently a large gap between theory and practice.

It is very important to realize that late Roman law often followed, rather than led, social practice. The frequently repeated and often contradictory pronouncements of emperors do not signify authoritarian intrusions on the lives of individuals so much as vain attempts to regulate a situation which was in practice beyond their control. Once this is fully recognized it is easier to understand why there is so much confusion and inconsistency between the laws themselves, and to discard the idea of Diocletian as the initiator of some kind of rigid and repressive regime. Rather, the legislation on *coloni* grew out of the difficulties experienced in collecting the poll-tax (*capitatio*), for tax due from *coloni* could only be collected if their whereabouts were known. Thus the state legislated essentially to help landlords to control and trace the labour force on which the tax was due. Not surprisingly, given the ways of late Roman government, this legislation developed only gradually and piecemeal during the fourth century, and uncertainty as to the relation of slave and *colonus* in individual areas, and inconsistency between geographical regions, were among the results of the untidy process that was adopted.

Legislation on the apparent reduction in the status of *coloni* was thus introduced at differing rates in different geographical areas, in Illyricum and Palestine not until the end of the fourth century. Furthermore, as the evidence of the Egyptian papyri suggests, there were many possible variations at the level of actual arrangements between landlord and tenant; loans, effectively mortgages, from large landowners to small were common, and defaulting borrowers were subjected to coercive measures from the lenders which were of more immediate concern than any imperial legislation.[12] The 'colonate' itself is thus an institution more theoretical than real.[13] In general, it seems doubtful whether conditions for the lower classes had in practice significantly deteriorated since the early empire. The condition of the poor, whether urban or rural, remained hard at all times. There had indeed been over the imperial period a progressive intensification of penalties applied to those convicted under the law, with an ever-widening division between the treatment of the rich and powerful and the cruel treatment (torture, chains, mutilation) meted out to the poor.[14] But the same process coincided during our period with a new consciousness of 'the poor' as a class, no doubt inspired by Christian teaching, which found some expression, as far as the urban poor were concerned, in various forms of Christian charity. Moreover, a number of saints' lives attest the role of the local bishop in alleviating economic distress in the country areas, and especially in providing food in times of famine (Chapter 6).

The economic changes which took place in the late empire were not of a revolutionary nature. This was still a basically agrarian society, and much of the land was owned by large landowners and worked by tenants, whether slave or free; for slavery as such certainly continued into our period. Again, though comparisons with medieval feudalism are tempting, especially for Marxist historians, they can be very misleading: there was no simple chronological transition from late Roman *coloni* to medieval serfs, and the institutions of late antiquity and of the medieval kingdoms need to be examined separately from each other. It would also be a mistake to suppose that peasants in earlier centuries had had much possibility or inclination de facto to move away from their area, or that they had not been dependent before; terms like 'serf' are liable to carry value judgements with them, and for this and the other reasons given should only be applied to the late empire with extreme caution.[15] As for the lower classes in the towns, it is equally difficult to get a fair picture of their lot when so much evidence is anecdotal and when so many of the literary sources are liable to exaggerate for their own purposes. Naturally it is very easy, as in most periods, to find evidence in the sources of both urban and rural poverty, especially in relation to tax debts.[16] But again one should be cautious about generalizing too much on the basis of this evidence. In the same way we hear many complaints in this period from the town councillors, the *curiales* or decurions, about their difficulties in continuing to finance urban life. But while we can certainly detect a slow process of increased imperial intervention in the affairs of cities, especially their financial affairs, and, at any rate towards the later part of the period, a degree of weakening of the traditional ways of urban government (Chapter 7), it is not until the later sixth century that the city structures of the eastern empire suffer real change. When they do, it is often the local bishop who steps into the breach, and even then, with the exception of the not inconsiderable part now played by Christian charity, one may suspect that the condition of the people remained much the same. On the whole the economic role of towns remained similar to what it had been during the early empire.

But if there was no economic revolution, certain new factors did become operative – on the one hand, barbarian settlement on a large scale; on the other, the growth of the church as a major economic institution in its own right, with the profound implications which we have already seen, ranging from the role of bishops as urban and rural patrons and the diversion of resources into church building, to the growth of monasteries and their potential impact on the local economy. It was factors such as these, together with the severe damage caused in some areas and to some towns by invasion and war, which severely disturbed the balance of landholding and wealth and which inevitably brought profound change with them.

THE CLASSES OF LATE ANTIQUE SOCIETY

The senatorial class of the west had been a major beneficiary of the disturbances which took place in the third century, and was, more-over, at least in part itself a product of the patronage of Constantine and his successors. One of the main features of the early fifth-century west is the enormous wealth, by which we mean the enormous landholdings, of the western senatorial class. Perhaps because of unsettled conditions in many areas, it had become poss-ible to acquire vast estates – the size of towns, we are told. A landowner would also expect to have at least one town house in which he lived in extreme luxury, as we learn from Ammianus' famous (and scathing) description of the fish ponds and table delica-cies of the Roman nobility of the late fourth century (14.6, 28.4). Owning estates on this scale was a business in itself, even if the landlord was an absentee. According to Ammianus, 'a journey of fair length to visit their estates or to be present at a hunt where all the work is done by others seems to some of them the equivalent of a march by Alexander the Great or Caesar' (28.6). None the less, upkeep of these estates required armies of retainers and an elaborate system of production and supply of goods. Owners were naturally interested in profits, and had perforce to devote a good deal of time simply to keeping things going. Much of it was occupied not as it might be nowadays by arranging how to sell surplus produce, or how best to invest in their estates, but in dealings for mutual benefit with others in a similar position, transactions which reinforced the gift element and the importance attached to display which were typical features of the late Roman economy. Sulpicius Severus and Paulinus provide evidence in their writings of typical gifts from one landowner to another of such commodities as oil and fowl, a practice continued by Sidonius, and indeed by bishops and kings in the Merovingian period; Pope Gregory the Great was no different in this respect from a secular landowner of earlier times.[17] While therefore a landlord might well become involved in production and engage in long-distance transport, both might take place within an exchange system involving either simply his own estates, or those of himself and his friends; this is less an economic activity than a patronal relationship. Even the widespread appearance overseas of African pottery during our period may be partly a product of this mutual exchange rather than the result of new market or production systems.[18] Emperors and the church, not surprisingly, behaved in essentially the same way. If then it is true that the amount of land in the hands of great proprietors (the *potentes*) increased, it may also be the case that overall markets – never greatly developed – were correspondingly diminished as a result of this increase in reciprocal exchanges between the estates of the rich.

During the same period the enlargement and transformation of the senatorial class, greatly increased in numbers from the time of Constantine on, as well as by the creation of a senate at Constantinople as well as Rome, rendered the old equestrian class otiose; the latter eventually disappeared as its former offices were progressively renamed and redefined as senatorial. Nor was it enough to be called simply *vir clarissimus* (the standard senatorial rank in the early empire). Valentinian I in AD 372 laid down a hierarchy of *clarissimi*, and above them *spectabiles* and (at the top) *illustres*; these grades were attached to the holding of particular offices, and other privileges of rank, such as the seats allotted at the Coliseum in Rome, also followed. The senate of Constantinople, on the other hand, differed from that of Rome since it was an artificial creation; while the Roman senate comprised families of vast wealth and pretensions to aristocratic lineage (even if in many cases they did not go further back than the third century), that of Constantinople was filled with new men. However, this feature in the long run helped its future continuance; being based on Constantinople itself, and lacking the enormous estates of its counterparts in Rome, the eastern senate was also likely to be able to avoid the tensions which developed between the Roman senate and the imperial government.[19] But eastern senators too enjoyed substantial privileges, and their role as members of the traditional landowning class, allegedly preyed upon by the rapacious emperor, is emphasized by Procopius, who himself identified with their interests, in his *Secret History*.[20] Like their western counterparts, eastern senators were not only undertaxed but also no doubt in a good position to evade the special tax (*collatio glebalis* or *follis*) which had belatedly been imposed on them by Constantine. In the example of the senatorial class we can in fact see the combination of tradition and innovation which is typical of the late empire; for while, on the one hand, the late Roman senate was essentially a service aristocracy which differed considerably from the senate of the early empire, it did not occur to anyone not to maintain existing social patterns, so that many of the outward signs of senatorial status and privilege were retained or even enhanced. In such circumstances, the Christianization, and in particular the conversion to asceticism, of members of leading senatorial families, which began to occur in Rome in the late fourth century, could seem to present a threat to status, wealth and tradition, and therefore met with considerable opposition.[21]

The later Roman empire is characterized by a high degree of competition for status and access to wealth and privilege, which we can see operative also in the centralized bureaucracy. Since posts in the imperial service could be highly lucrative, and released the holder from burdensome existing obligations, the bureaucracy drew off talent from the ranks of the *curiales* in the cities even as imperial legislation, conscious of economic and administrative needs, sought to keep them in their places. One of the most persistent of modern myths about the late empire is that of a top-heavy and rigid bureaucracy which wielded the hand of repression, yet whose size made it unsustainable from the existing resources of the empire. In fact the empire was engaged in a constant balancing act between what was perceived to be necessary and what was in fact possible. Paradoxically, there was in practice a high degree of social mobility, and the court and the office-holders had a natural tendency to proliferate in view of the attractiveness of the posts. The nomenclature and emoluments of the imperial service paralleled those of the army; office-holders held titles of military equivalence and received military stipends. This had little to do with modern concepts of efficiency, though the government had at least an interest in filling the administration with people it deemed suitable; at the same time however it also needed to maintain the numbers of *curiales* in each city (the obvious candidates for openings in the imperial service), since on them fell financial responsibility and tax obligations at local level.[22] Jones rightly emphasizes the very large number of posts (*dignitates*) that had to be filled on a regular basis, and the law-codes make it very clear that *curiales* were constantly endeavouring to escape their lot and better themselves, in the administration, the church or the army. This class as a whole was the subject of what Jones calls 'a vast and tangled mass of legislation', whereby the state attempted ineffectually to prevent the seepage and maintain the councils on whom the cities depended.[23] Earlier attempts to return *curiales* to their cities if they had managed to secure a post in the administration failed, and in principle after AD 423 individuals could no longer escape their obligations in this way. Similarly, the fifth-century emperors were still attempting to stop the loophole opened by Constantine when he freed clergy

from curial obligations, as was Justinian, when in AD 531 he allowed
ordination of *curiales* only if they had spent fifteen years in a
monastery first, and were willing to surrender a substantial part of
their estate (*CJ* I.3.52). The double bind in which the government
found itself was further complicated by the willingness of individuals effectively to buy their way into the administration, and that
of the government to sell offices within it – the attraction for the
purchaser being the emoluments that went with the position, and
often the possibilities for favour and extortion that it carried in
addition. To a modern observer this is not likely to seem an
acceptable way of going about things, but we should remember that
for all its impressive state apparatus, the late Roman empire was still
a very traditional society. The 'government' lacked both more
sophisticated means for coping with these problems, and an understanding in modern terms of where the problems lay.

The practice of selling offices in the imperial administration
provides a particularly delicate example; on the one hand, the late
Roman and Byzantine governments were concerned to stop the
abuse of the practice, while at another level each used it as a financial
tool and mechanism for selection. In AD 439 an oath was exacted
from all those appointed to provincial governorships that they had
not paid to secure office:

> we ordain that men appointed to provincial governorships
> should not be promoted by bribe or payment but by their
> own proven worth and your [i.e., the prefect's] recommen-
> dation; let them testify on oath that in gaining their responsi-
> bilities they have neither made any payment nor will they
> make any subsequently.

> (*CJ* IX.27.6 pr.)

Yet later emperors actually sold offices: Zeno for instance, raised the
price for the governorship of Egypt from 50 lb of gold to nearly
500 (Malchus, fr. 16, Blockley). Justinian again tried to stop the
practice, repeating the earlier demand for an oath from those
appointed; again, however, Procopius claims that Justinian himself
was selling offices again within the year (Just., *Nov.* 8; Procopius,
Secret History, 21.9f.).[24] The example illustrates both the weakness
of the government and the lack of effective remedies at its disposal.
The corollary, and the underpinning of the sale of offices was,
of course, extortion by the officials themselves in order to recoup
the moneys paid, the prospect of which had been a powerful

attraction to purchase in the first place. Corruption, both in the sense of buying favours in a more or less blatant way and of rapacious behaviour by office-holders, was evidently all-pervasive, just as it is in any similar society where more overt procedures are lacking. It does not however follow, as is sometimes argued, that corruption in itself was a major element in the decline and fall of the Roman empire, and we should be careful not to import modernizing (and moralizing) assumptions into the study of a traditional system.

One of the hallmarks of the late Roman administrative system was patronage. Recent work has increasingly emphasized the importance of patronage in understanding ancient society as a whole, especially in the context of the Roman empire,[25] and this should make understanding the late empire somewhat less daunting. Patronage, in the sense of a more or less systematized protection of the poor, has existed and does exist in many – perhaps even all – societies, but is present typically where the protection offered by the state is weak, as here, where the social bonds are loose or where there is change and competition for place in the new scheme of things. In late antiquity, 'traditional patrons found themselves supplanted as patrons, but also impeded as landlords – and as tax collectors – by men with local authority, secular or religious. Their protests were echoed with legislation representing the fiscal interests of the central government.'[26] For when new actors – bishops, state officials – entered a stage on which patronage already operated on every level, and when the interests of the poor, the landlords and the state diverged, any existing equilibrium was broken. In such conditions the poor and the helpless looked where they could for protection. The state for its part made repeated attempts to declare this form of protection (*patrocinium*) illegal, representing as it did an evasion of the responsibilities of those who were its subjects, and an illicit appropriation of authority by those who took it on, not to mention the extra tips which they doubtless imposed. A law of AD 415 allowed the churches of Constantinople and Alexandria to retain villages which had come under their protection, provided that all taxes were paid and other obligations fulfilled (*CTh* 11.24.6), but later emperors such as Marcian and Leo continued to try to end the practice, and Leo attempted to forbid all patronage contracts from 437 in Thrace and from 441 in the east (*CJ* XI.54.1, AD 468). Again, the practice itself and the government's inability to deal with it demonstrate not so much endemic corruption as the weakness of the bureaucratic system in comparison with the vast and fragmented areas which it was attempting to control.

FINANCING THE STATE

Behind many of the problems which the state experienced, and which gave rise to these social difficulties, lay the need for tax revenue and the difficulties of collection. Many scholars have believed that late Roman taxes were higher than before – so high in fact as to contribute substantially to increased extortion and consequent decline. Before considering this question a brief excursus is necessary on taxation and the ancient economy in general.

Fortunately there is no shortage of guides; indeed, the nature of the ancient economy was one of the liveliest topics of research in the 1970s and 1980s, and the increased interest in late Roman archaeology is guaranteeing that the later period is not neglected.[27] It is probably fair to say that since the early 1970s the model of the ancient economy associated with Moses Finley's *The Ancient Economy* (Berkeley and Los Angeles, Calif., 1973) has been modified but not essentially given up. According to this model, the ancient world was basically an agrarian society in which towns were not centres of industrial production and in which markets and profit were comparatively undeveloped, as were notions of 'economic rationality' in general. More recently, scholars including Finley himself have laid more emphasis than this model would allow on the extent of monetarization, and on the level of trade, while Keith Hopkins in particular has argued for a slow degree of economic growth, at least up to the end of the second century AD. Some recent archaeological work in our period now suggests both a surprising degree of prosperity in the east and more long-term exchange than had previously been supposed. One is therefore led to ask how far if at all the arguments put forward in the general debate apply to the later empire. This section will therefore focus on issues relating to taxation, money and state revenues and expenditure, while the next will take up the questions of production, rural prosperity or decline and long-distance exchange.

Certain premises about the ancient economy have been generally accepted, and there is no reason to doubt that they apply equally to the later empire. These are (in the case of the Roman empire) that the wealth of the empire came largely from its land, which also provided the bulk of the state's revenues; that the army, or at least the defences generally, constituted by far the biggest part of the state budget;[28] and that other state expenditure was extremely limited by comparison with that of modern states. The extent of monetarization has been seen as low on this model, and the state's purpose in issuing coin as political or military rather than economic or commercial, though this has indeed been strongly challenged of late.[29] Hopkins has usefully listed the factors which in his view may have been conducive to a certain degree of economic growth. Taking these as a base we may ask how many of them were present in the late empire, and whether there is likely to have been growth or recession, assuming these concepts to be applicable at all.[30] They include: an increased amount of land being brought under cultivation; a greater population size, with more division of labour and consequent growth in non-agricultural production; and higher productivity per capita (including the increase attributable to the fact that in peacetime some of those who would otherwise have been engaged in warfare are available as part of the labour force). Finally, two propositions important for the late empire are the suggestions, first, that increased government exaction acted as a stimulus rather than a damper on productivity and, second, that government expenditure of the money raised by taxation itself in turn benefited the economy.

If we apply these suggestions – which have been derived largely from the period *c.* 200 BC to AD 200 – to the period covered here, certain points are immediately apparent. In the west, the available land from which the state was able to collect taxes actually diminished through the processes of war and settlement. Further, the population itself may already have dropped during the period of crisis in the third century, and at any rate the Roman population in the western provinces was partially displaced during the later fifth century by new barbarian settlers with whom it was forced to share its land on terms which were heavy whichever interpretation of the evidence we may adopt (Chapter 2). The question of peace versus war also raises the question of the difference between west and east; thus the east could prosper at least during much of the fifth century and into the sixth, while the wars with the Sasanians were enjoying something of a lull, but as we have seen, the west saw continuous warfare and fragmentation of territory, with all the obvious consequences of damage to land and urban centres as well as the cost in manpower.

On several of Hopkins's criteria, then, it looks as though the western empire must have suffered a degree of economic decline even before the main period of barbarian settlement. Some other indicators point in the same direction. Both the smaller units and the stationing of the late Roman army within the empire rather than in large numbers on the frontiers will have reduced its former role in the circulation and redistribution of coin through army pay and expenditure, even without the large element of its needs now supplied in kind. If correct, the postulated trend towards exchange within the network of large estates rather than via the open market should have operated in the same direction. And finally, the disruption of so much of the land-base of the empire, combined perhaps with other natural factors, may in itself have led to a reduction in available raw materials.[31]

Added to these factors is the sheer cost of maintaining the late Roman army (Chapter 2). If it were true that Diocletian had really doubled, let alone quadrupled, the size of the army, as well as increasing the bureaucracy, the economic problems of the later empire would indeed have been insuperable. Jones put the problem neatly in his famous statement that the late empire had too many 'idle mouths', that is, non-producers, who therefore had to be paid for out of the diminishing resources of the empire.[32] But few historians today would be as confident as Jones was in 1964. As we have seen already (Chapter 2), Diocletian is more likely to have regularized the status quo than actually doubled the army in size, and it must be regarded as doubtful whether even that figure could be maintained after the late fourth century. At 400,000 plus, the late Roman army was still an extremely large force, notably bigger than the Augustan army of the early Principate, and such an army must certainly have represented a great drain on resources.

Yet historians may have got the issue the wrong way round when they emphasize the contribution of this military expenditure to eventual collapse. What is remarkable is rather that the system continued as long as it did. One might equally argue that while the cost was indeed heavy, the empire's most intractable military problems lay in the sheer size of its borders and the difficulty of maintaining defence on such a scale. Had the west not had to endure decades of barbarian attack, the story there might have been very different. As for the east, Justinian did indeed encounter severe financial problems in conducting his wars, which he passed on in turn to his successors, but here too it was a combination of external factors which was operative in causing his most severe problems

(Chapter 5). The state had already found partial answers to the difficulties of cost in that by the sixth century much of the defence of the south-eastern part of the frontier area from Transjordan to Arabia had been left to Arab allies, and, even in the regular armies, barbarians were regularly used.[33] Finally, the equation worked both ways: the presence of the army in a particular area, with all that it required for its maintenance – not just the pay and supplies of the troops, but also a good road system and transport and local support systems – could in itself be a powerful economic stimulus. This was no doubt one of the factors behind the undoubted prosperity and density of settlement in the fifth century in the south-eastern frontier areas even in barren and difficult places such as the Hauran and the Negev, where there were many small military settlements in addition to the major fortresses.[34]

From all this it is clear that generalizations about the late antique economy as a whole are likely to be misleading, and that we must always allow for regional variations and the intervention of external factors. The difficulty of computing the cost of the army, as of its size, is also partly a matter of methodology, in that while we have in the sources a number of figures for tax revenue and budgetary expenses, it is far from clear whether they are reliable or not, or how far they may have changed over the two centuries we are considering.[35] There was at least in the late empire a regular tax period (indiction) for which levels were fixed, and the system had been changed to take into account both labour force and quality of land. Constantine had imposed special taxes on senatorial wealth and on commerce, and had thus at last brought these sectors into the tax net. Basically, however, the taxes still fell mainly on the land and on agricultural production; the government had little recourse in response to loss of land and shortage of manpower apart from often repeated legislation such as that seeking to restrict movement of *coloni* and thus help landlords to keep their tenants:

> whereas in other provinces which are subject to the rule of our serenity a law instituted by our ancestors holds tenants down by a kind of eternal right, so that they are not allowed to leave the places by whose crops they are nurtured or desert the fields which they have once undertaken to cultivate, but the landlords of Palestine do not enjoy this advantage: we ordain that in Palestine also no tenant whatever be free to wander at

his own choice, but as in other provinces he be tied to the
owner of the farm.

(CJ XI.51.1)

The tax collector indeed looms large in contemporary literature as a
hated and dreaded figure, and the danger to those who could not
pay was very real. Paphnutius, a hermit near Heracleopolis in the
Thebaid, met a former brigand who told him how he had once come
upon a woman who had suffered in this way, and asked her why she
was crying:

> she replied, 'Do not ask me, master; do not question me in my
> misery but take me anywhere you wish as your handmaid. For
> my husband has often been flogged during the last two years
> because of arrears of taxes amounting to three hundred gold
> coins. He has been put in prison and my beloved three
> children have been sold as slaves. As for me, I have become a
> fugitive and move from place to place. I now wander in the
> desert but I am frequently found and flogged. I have been in
> the desert now for three days without eating anything.' 'I felt
> sorry for her,' said the brigand, 'and took her to my cave. I
> gave her the three hundred gold coins and brought her to the
> city, where I secured her release together with that of her
> husband and children.'

(Russell, Lives of the Desert Fathers, 95)

The repeated laws show, however, how little the government could
actually do to enforce collection of revenue. The taxes were highly
regressive: small peasant proprietors paid the same as great landlords for the same amount of land. And despite Constantine's
reforms, the traditional emphasis on the land still meant that they
failed to tap major sources of wealth, whether from trade or,
importantly, from senatorial incomes. In the latter case, especially,
it was in part the nature of the tax laws themselves which enabled
senators to amass colossal fortunes while the government went
short. Emperors themselves shared the traditional view that exemption from taxation was a privilege to which rank and favour allowed
one rightfully to aspire, and thus their grants of exemption were an
expression of this traditional attitude as well as a way of gaining
popularity. Cancelling arrears was another common device, either
in the face of real inability to enforce the law, or in response to these
traditional attitudes, and there was little conception of budgeting

for the future. On the other hand, as Jones points out, the eastern government at any rate seems to have been able to collect very substantial sums on a continuous basis;[36] this was despite the outflow of large sums of gold to buy peace with Persia, or for 'subsidy' payments to barbarian groups.[37] As for commerce, the so-called *chrysargyron* (gold and silver tax, so-called because it had to be paid in gold and silver, usually, in practice, gold) was consistently unpopular; it was actually abolished in AD 499 by the Emperor Anastasius (*CJ* 11.1.1), as the *collatio glebalis (follis)*, levied on senators, had been by the Emperor Marcian (*CJ* 12.2.2). Then, as now, taxation was an ideologically charged issue, and emperors who raised taxes, even if like Justinian they did so for military purposes, are uniformly criticized in contemporary sources.

The late Roman taxation system was thus a complicated and unwieldy affair, full of inequities and far from perfectly administered. Its most important part, the *annona*, the supplies for the army, was also the most difficult to organize. From the later third century much of the *annona* had been collected in kind, by means of a cumbersome system which one is surprised to find working at all; even so, while the method of calculation varied from province to province, it was possible from time to time to reduce the demand on a particular province, as with Achaea, Macedonia, Sicily, Numidia and Mauretania Sitifensis in the fifth century. However, the regular censuses necessary to keep the registers of land and population accurate tended not to be held, and great discrepancies could arise. Once collected, finally, the goods had to be transmitted to the necessary unit – a further process requiring complicated organization. Other forms of taxation were also of great importance throughout the imperial period, especially the grain requisition for the food supply of Rome, a system Constantine also extended to his new foundation of Constantinople (Chapter 1). Since the Republic, the Roman government had considered it a priority to ensure the food supply for the capital, and had maintained free bread doles for the purpose.[38] The corn came in the main, though not only, from North Africa and Egypt, where in each case its provision had a major impact on the local economies;[39] equally, its eventual cessation as conditions changed in the west must have exercised a material effect. At Rome, the loss of North Africa to the Vandals caused severe disruption, but the distributions went on and were eventually taken over by the church. In the east, Egypt continued to supply Constantinople, but the link was abruptly broken by the

Persian invasion of Egypt in the early seventh century. Before this, however, the tickets on which the actual distributions were made had come to be passed on by sale or inheritance; the government tried at times to regulate these practices too, but as time went on, as with other late Roman taxes, the match between those theoretically qualified and those actually receiving the dole had already become less and less close.

By the beginning of our period payment in kind was beginning to be commuted into gold, especially in the west, at varying rates of commutation which at times had to be regulated by the government, and in the sixth century payment in gold (pounds or *solidi*) was the norm. Though Constantine was able to introduce the gold *solidus*, which remained standard henceforth, later emperors were unsuccessful in their attempts to reintroduce silver coinage on a stable basis. Inflation itself also continued, as can be seen from prices given in papyri, probably because the government minted far too much of the small base-metal coinage, but the *solidus* remained stable throughout the period and for long afterwards. By the fifth century, however, there was effectively nothing between the gold *solidus* and the tiny copper denominations, whose rate, valued against the *solidus*, was constantly changing. The later fifth-century emperors, in particular Anastasius (AD 491–518), were more successful in introducing some stability; here it is interesting to find that Anastasius' reform continued trends already to be seen in the Vandalic and Ostrogothic coinages of the west.[40] It is extremely difficult to assess the economic consequences of this state of affairs. On a priori grounds alone, the collection and distribution of taxes in kind, which continued in part well into the fifth century, and the constant fluctuation of value against the *solidus* of the base-metal/copper coinage (*pecunia*) cannot but have had a depressive effect on the existence of a market economy. But the roots of third- and fourth-century inflation lay with the monetary policy of the state rather than with the economy itself, and we have seen that revenue levels in our period were apparently maintained, at least in the east. One must conclude that shaky though its control may have been, so long as the late Roman government continued to operate well itself, as it did in the east during our period, the economy as a whole also continued to function. Local and unforeseen factors such as famine, pestilence or the like constantly threatened a traditional agrarian economy with no obvious technological advances, but were also part of the expected range of possibilities and could therefore be contained, whereas external factors such as invasion, settlement and demographic change were another matter altogether.

TRADE AND TRADERS

Given its date, the 'Pirenne thesis' (see p. 4) was necessarily based mainly on literary evidence; now, with the growth of interest in this period by archaeologists, far more material is available, and this, together with the more sympathetic approach to the role of trade in assessing the ancient economy to which we have referred above (p. 94), puts a new light on the old controversy. We shall return to the theme later (Chapter 7); for now, we can conclude this chapter with some brief comments on the controversy concerning the role of long-distance trade in our period.

Much of the question turns on pottery evidence, in particular the diffusion of African Red Slipware and African amphorae outside North Africa, which continued even during the Vandal period. On this base an extensive hypothesis about trading patterns has been built, especially in relation to the fifth to seventh centuries.[41] A clear curve is evident from the finds: first, between the second and fourth centuries, African pottery gradually comes to dominate sites in the west in a striking way, while the former exports from Gaul and Baetica diminish;[42] next, with the growth of Constantinople and the diversion of Egyptian grain to the eastern capital, an eastern axis, Carthage/Constantinople, comes into being; export along these two lines, north and east, continues into the fifth century, with no break at the Vandal conquest of North Africa in 439;[43] however, decline can be seen by the early sixth century, along with certain changes in production, the former to be connected not only with circumstances in North Africa itself but also with the reduction in markets as a result of the establishment of the barbarian kingdoms – nevertheless, the eastern axis continues in existence throughout the period, as the importance of Constantinople reaches its peak; finally, further and clearer decline is evident in the seventh century, where however evidence is also much more sparse.

Many questions suggest themselves as a result of these conclusions, of which the following are only the most obvious. For example, whether these findings actually represent trading links at all (the evidence of pottery will not tell us the *why* of transmarine exchange, only the *how*). What if anything can these results tell us about the impact of the barbarian kingdoms on the Mediterranean economy? Finally, how far does this evidence tally with that of urban change to suggest that a significant weakening of the Mediterranean system of classical antiquity can best be located in the later sixth to early seventh centuries, that is, after the Justinianic attempt at reconquest and before the Arab invasions?

It is important to note that all these issues are still the subject of ongoing debate and considerable disagreement, not least because they raise ideological issues about trade and the nature of the ancient economy. Carandini, Panella and their colleagues see the evidence as reflecting trading patterns in a market economy. This emphasis may need to be qualified. Among the questions still to be settled is that of the economic impact of the Vandal conquest, including that of the effect on North Africa (and the other conquered areas) of the cessation of Roman taxation. Wickham rightly underlines the importance for North Africa of the grain requisitions for Rome, which would have had the effect of requiring a highly developed navigation and export system from which other products could also benefit, and whose cessation was therefore likely to have serious and widespread effects. According to this argument, while the enforced grain exactions for Rome and Constantinople called forth a considerable level of production that was itself non-commercial, their ending, in the case of Rome, with the collapse of Roman government in the west, should have had serious repercussions on such market economy as did exist. And since North African wares were so completely dominant previously, a major change of this kind which affected North Africa directly will have had widespread effects in other regions.

CONCLUSION

There is no simple way to characterize the late Roman economy, or the actual effect on society of the government's attempts to control it. Certain trends are evident, not simply the profound impact of barbarian invasion and settlement during this period, but also more general developments such as the tendency towards the amassing of vast amounts of land by individuals, the return to taxation in coin (gold) instead of in kind, the growing gulf between east and west and the difficulty experienced by the government in ensuring the collection of revenues and staffing its own administration. Not surprisingly, the existence of the barbarian kingdoms in the west and the effects of the wars of reconquest had major economic repercussions; these will be discussed in Chapter 5. In the east, by contrast, there is evidence of population increase and of intensified agriculture and cultivation in areas such as the limestone massif of northern Syria and even in such unpromising areas as the Hauran and the Negev; this evidence will be discussed further in Chapter 8. On the other hand, by the late sixth century, following the effects of war and perhaps also plague, the Roman military presence in the east was clearly becoming harder and harder to maintain.

Clearly it is misleading if not impossible to generalize over so wide an area and so eventful a chronological span. Unfortunately, however, modern historiography abounds in confident value-judgements about the decline or the end of antiquity, many of which rest on unacknowledged assumptions about the late Roman system itself. That system was certainly cumbersome and had many defects. Lacking modern communications, it could neither operate efficiently nor respond easily to change. The government resorted all too easily to empty and hectoring legislation; the officials did what they could; the people learnt how to cheat the system. There is nothing surprising in that, and the power of inertia was also great. What *is* surprising, in such a context, is rather that this highly traditional society did manage to survive so comparatively well.

5

Justinian and reconquest

INTRODUCTION

Besides pointing to differences between east and west, we have also emphasized the pervasiveness of broad economic and social patterns throughout the Mediterranean world. Under the Emperor Justinian (AD 527–65) a dramatic intervention occurred, in the shape of an attempt by eastern armies – at first spectacularly successful – to recover the lost territories of the western empire. This was the so-called 'reconquest' policy of Justinian, which began with the dispatch of an expedition against Vandal Africa in AD 533 and continued for over twenty years of military action and many vicissitudes until the settlement known as the 'Pragmatic Sanction' of AD 554 signalled the hoped-for return of Ostrogothic Italy to Roman rule.

This episode is important for a variety of reasons, among which the question of Justinian's own motivation plays only a minor role. For one thing, it is fully and dramatically reported by a major writer, Procopius of Caesarea, who has provided both a nearly complete military narrative in his *History of the Wars*, and a sensational deconstruction of the same events in his *Secret History*.[1] In Procopius' works we have a body of historical writing in Greek as important and interesting in itself as that of any historian in antiquity and a wealth of detailed information on military matters, topography, finance, buildings, and all kinds of other things. Procopius was a participant in and eyewitness of some of the campaigns which he describes, and although that does not guarantee his accuracy as a reporter, it does give his work an immediacy and an authority which strike anyone who reads it. More broadly, the wars of Justinian raise the issue of east and west in particularly sharp form: here, after all, is an emperor in Constantinople using eastern

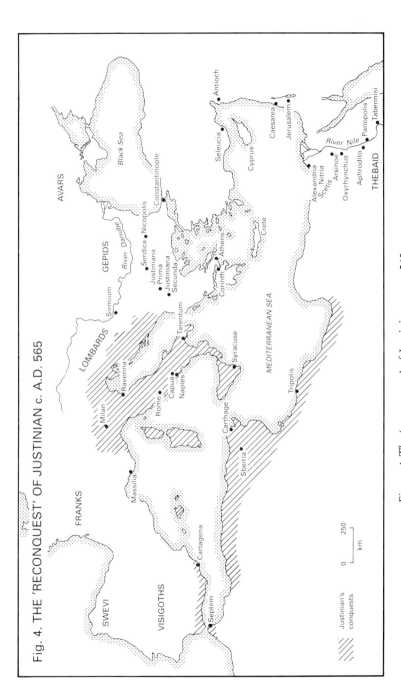

Fig. 4. THE 'RECONQUEST' OF JUSTINIAN c. A.D. 565

Figure 4 The 'reconquest' of Justinian, c. AD 565.

armies to reclaim what he still thinks of as Roman territory. In North Africa, where the reconquest was most successful and over which the general Belisarius celebrated a magnificent triumph in Constantinople in AD 534, we have the spectacle of a Greek administration, imposed from Constantinople in the name of Roman restoration, being set up in a province which was tradition-ally a bastion of Latin-speaking Christianity. An equally ironic effect of the long years of war against the Goths in Italy was the effective destruction of the Roman senate and the departure of many of the remaining Roman aristocratic families to the east, where some of them formed a Latin-speaking colony in Constantinople. Finally, it can be argued that the cost and the effort of this huge and prolonged military initiative, coinciding as it did with a major plague and continuing and expensive wars against Sasanian Persia, actually weakened the eastern government and made it less able to deal with the military challenges of the late sixth and early seventh centuries.

Justinian's wars are as susceptible to contradictory judgements as the rest of his policies. Procopius himself, for personal or other reasons, has left a highly ambiguous, indeed contradictory, picture. Apparently giving the official view in the *Wars*, yet undercutting it with his own mounting criticism, as is clearly evident in *BG* III–IV, he praises the same emperor in his panegyric on his building policy, and viciously attacks him in his 'secret' history, which he did not intend to be made public until after Justinian's death.[2] But other contemporaries too, such as the retired official and antiquarian known as John the Lydian, were unsure whether to praise or criticize.[3] Justinian himself enunciated high-sounding claims that he was restoring the Roman past while issuing such severe laws against pagans and all other dissidents that they have led one recent writer to compare him with Stalin.[4] It was Justinian whose laws forbidding pagans to teach had the effect of closing the 1,000-year-old Academy at Athens, which had been founded by Plato in the fourth century BC. Yet it was also Justinian whose law commission, within only a few years of the emperor's accession, had codified Roman law in the *Digest* (AD 533) and the *Codex Iustinianus* (AD 534), and whose great legal collections were to become the foundation of the Roman legal systems of European states.[5] The emperor is often depicted as a patron of letters and as one who inspired a classicizing artistic renaissance.[6] Both judgements need to be treated with cau-tion. Yet the reign did see a notable amount of literary activity in

Plate 6 The Barberini ivory. An emperor (probably Justinian) is shown in traditionally classicizing style and in triumphant pose with conquered peoples below, but with a bust of Christ above.

classical genres and much spectacular imperial art, even if little has survived. But Justinian was also an avid theologian who enjoyed debating even with clerics exiled by his own policies, and who wrote his own highly technical theological treatises.[7] Perhaps because of these contradictions and others like them, he aroused violent reactions among contemporaries, something in which he resembles most other strong rulers in history.[8] Procopius condemned him for greed and for overreaching himself, and the fiscal demands of his policies placed a heavy burden on the empire, especially on the wealthy classes. In a sense his reign was a splendid anachronism, the final reassertion of Roman military and imperial traditions before the end of classical antiquity; in another sense, it precipitated the decline.

There were many motives at work in the programme of reconquest, taken as a whole, but those most commonly overtly expressed and emphasized by contemporaries were the twin aims of imperial restoration and the championing of Christian orthodoxy in the territories ruled by Arians. These objectives, which to a modern observer may seem to fit oddly together, in fact run through the politics of Justinian's reign as a whole; in the same way the emperor seemed to be at one and the same time a conservative and an innovator – something which contemporaries found hard to understand or, often, to tolerate.[9]

Whether or not Justinian already had in mind the long-term objective of reconquest of the west (which is by no means certain), the expedition against the Vandals in AD 533 was despatched with a great sense of style. On board the ships was a force of 10,000 infantry and 5,000 cavalry, with the general Belisarius and his wife Antonina and the historian Procopius, Belisarius' right-hand man; they were seen off from Constantinople by the emperor and empress and the patriarch, who said prayers for the expedition's success. Remembering the ignominious failure of the expedition sent by the Emperor Leo (Chapter 1), nobody had been in favour of the emperor's idea, says Procopius, but the only one who dared to speak against it to the emperor was his minister John the Cappadocian, whose long speech the historian records. However, a mysterious 'bishop from the east' conveniently reported a dream in which God had promised his help, and confirmed the emperor's enthusiasm to proceed (*BV* I.10–12).[10] Within an amazingly short time, Belisarius was back in Constantinople celebrating a triumph, and Justinian was thinking of Italy, where Belisarius was soon despatched via Sicily, reaching Italy itself in the summer of AD 536, and where the emperor had a pretext for war in the murder of his protégée Amalasuntha, the daughter of the Ostrogothic king Theodoric and mother of the dead Athalaric, who had misguidedly offered the throne to Theodatus (*BV* II.9; *BG* I.4–5).[11] However,

Justinian also had good political reasons at home for mounting such an attempt, even against the prudent opinions of his advisers, for he had only recently weathered with extreme difficulty a great riot in Constantinople, known as the 'Nika revolt' from the cries of 'nika' ('victory') by the rioters. During the uprising the emperor had allegedly only been prevented from fleeing altogether by the resolve of the Empress Theodora, who rallied the imperial party by declaring in ringing tones that she would never flee – 'empire is a fine shroud'.[12] The immediate danger was averted and, as Procopius points out, it was felt that since the situation on the eastern front against Persia was satisfactory after the treaty of AD 533, a successful expedition might restore the emperor's reputation. This impression is reinforced by Procopius' emphasis on the opposition to Justinian's scheme, which he shared himself, and the role played in his narrative at this point by prophetic dreams – he even claims to have had a dream himself of Belisarius' future success. The unexpectedly quick and easy success of this first expedition, combined with the murder of Amalasuntha, made similar action against the Goths in Italy seem equally feasible. The reforming laws of this period have an optimistic and energetic tone which fits Justinian's confident expectations of imperial success.[13] He was not to know that the Italian campaigns would drag on for nearly twenty years, or that the price of the final settlement in AD 554 would be a devastated Italy.

THE EASTERN PROVINCES: WAR AND PEACE WITH PERSIA

But the motivation for the wars is less important than what actually happened. As in all such cases, whatever the original intention may have been, ideas and policies changed with changing circumstances and the hopeful beginning soon met with problems. Moreover, the Persians presented a major military problem which lasted throughout the period of the western campaigns and beyond, passing in turn to Justinian's successors. The story of Justinian's wars with Persia dramatically illustrates the actual lack of the necessary resources to pursue major campaigns in the eastern frontier area, or even to resist Persian raids, while simultaneously campaigning elsewhere, as well as the enormous cost to the eastern empire of securing temporary peace.

The two powers had remained in competition over the border territory and its population since the Sasanians first came to power in the third century (see further, Chapter 8). Now, a series of not-so-glorious campaigns on the Mesopotamian frontier in the first years of Justinian's reign, as a result of which the future historian Procopius first became the intimate of Belisarius, came to a temporary end in AD 531 with the death of the Persian shah Cavadh and the accession of Chosroes I. A major treaty between the two powers was concluded in AD 533 (*BP* I.22);[14] the terms included a payment by Byzantium of 11,000 lb of gold, but apart from forcing a certain degree of retreat on both sides, left things essentially unchanged. It was not likely that a strong ruler like Chosroes I, who was fully a match for Justinian, would rest content with this. Moreover, his timing was fatal for the Byzantines; after making hostile noises for some time, he invaded Roman territory again in AD 540, the very year when Belisarius was recalled from Italy.[15] The second Persian war, in the 540s, was a very different affair from the first. The lack of an adequate Roman defence system is now painfully obvious in the ease with which the Persian armies could approach towns like Edessa and Apamea in Mesopotamia and Syria, and extort large payments of silver. The local bishops were the unfortunate middlemen in these transactions; the Persians took and burnt Beroea (Aleppo) while its bishop, Megas, was away appealing to the Roman command at Antioch for assistance, only to find that Justinian had given orders for no payments to be made for the safety of eastern cities, and that Ephraem, patriarch of Antioch, was under suspicion of being willing to hand over his city to the Persians. Returning to Beroea, the hapless Megas expostulated with Chosroes, but let out that he had received no funds for the safety of Antioch, whereupon the Persian king at once made for Antioch (*BP* II.7).[16] Those citizens who could, immediately left, and Chosroes besieged and sacked Antioch, second city of the eastern empire, a catastrophe which provoked Procopius to exclaim:

> I shudder when I describe so great a disaster, and pass it on to be remembered by future generations, and I do not know what God's will could be in raising up the affairs of a man or a place, and then casting them down and wiping them out for no apparent reason.
>
> (*BP* II.10.4)[17]

We have a telling glimpse of the real situation at Antioch before the Persian siege when we see the patriarch, local bishops and Byzantine envoys from Constantinople all in urgent conference about what best to do. Since the Persians demanded payments in silver, the local population did its best to rid itself of as much silver as possible before they arrived. When the Persians did start the siege, the population was unwise enough to indulge in taunting the enemy from the walls, only to be subjected to a massacre when the Persians entered the city. After this example, Chosroes was able to ask an even higher price in silver for the safety of other cities such as Apamea, Chalcis and Edessa.

The early 540s also saw one of the greatest plagues in history. The disease, a form of bubonic plague, struck Constantinople and the eastern provinces in AD 542 and is vividly described by Procopius, who was an eyewitness (*BP* II.22–3). Even allowing for exaggeration in the literary sources (the plague is also described by the Syriac church historian John of Ephesus), the level of casualties was clearly extremely high, perhaps approaching that of the Black Death. The church historian Evagrius, who was a child at the time, movingly describes its effects at Antioch, which fell heavily on his own family. The plague, he says, fell upon the east two years after the sack of Antioch, and was in some respects, though not all, similar to the Athenian plague of 430 BC described by Thucydides:

> I too, the writer of this history . . . was afflicted in the early stages of the plague with the so-called buboes, while I was still just a schoolboy. In the various attacks of the plague many of my children died, as well as my wife and other members of my family, servants and countrypeople, for the attacks returned up to my own day, as it were in cyclic progression. I lost my daughter, as well as the earlier ones, and her child, two years before the time of writing, when I was in my fifth-eighth year, the plague having returned four times to Antioch and this being the fourth attack in the cycle.
>
> (*HE* IV.29)

Though it is hard to demonstrate it directly from archaeological evidence (see Chapters 7 and 8), the plague must have had a disastrous effect on the overall population size; at any rate, the death toll had an immediate effect on imperial tax revenues and military manpower which can clearly be seen in subsequent legislation to recover taxes from the estates of those who had died intestate, and from the great difficulties now experienced in sustaining the war on two fronts simultaneously.[18] It was not just a matter of numbers, however: a large Byzantine army gathered to defend

Armenia in AD 543, but thanks to confusion and mismanagement on the Byzantine side a small force of Persians was able to kill the general Narses and inflict a heavy defeat at the fortress of Anglon near Dvin (*BP* II.24f.). Eventually a five-year treaty was concluded in AD 545 at a cost to the empire of 2,000 lb of gold. Even during this period, operations continued between the Arab allies of Byzantium and Persia, the Ghassanids and the Lakhmids respectively, and a substantial Byzantine force, having previously laid siege to Petra in Lazica, which was held by the Persians, was able to destroy the Persian forces in Lazica twice in the course of the year AD 549. A further five-year treaty was concluded in AD 551 in Constantinople, the empire paying on this occasion 2,600 lb of gold; but hostilities dragged on in Lazica, where a complex local situation exacerbated the difficulties caused by the rival powers. By AD 561, however, both sides had reasons for concluding a more solid peace, and the end of that year saw a fifty-years' peace agreed at Dara between the Byzantine Master of Offices, Peter the Patrician, and the Persian ambassador Yesdegusnaph, with the Persians renouncing their claims to Lazica, but exacting from the empire the large annual sum of 30,000 gold *nomismata*, of which ten years' instalments would be paid in advance. Existing frontiers were confirmed and trade across the borders was limited to those cities where there were customs facilities. A long and detailed account of the negotiations, which provides interesting information about contemporary diplomacy, and a complete text of the treaty itself, is given by the historian Menander Protector, who also records the letters sent by both rulers to ratify what had been agreed by their envoys:

> The letter of ratification from the Roman Emperor, bearing the usual superscription, is well known to us. The letter from the Persian king was written in Persian and the following is a Greek translation: 'The divine, good, father of peace, ancient Khosro, king of kings, fortunate, pious and beneficent, to whom the gods have given great fortune and a great kingdom, giant of giants, formed in the image of the gods, to Justinian Caesar, our brother.' Such was the superscription, while the meaning of the text was as follows (I use a word-for-word translation, a procedure I felt absolutely necessary lest, if I changed the phraseology, I be suspected of distorting something of the truth). . . .
>
> (fr. 6.1 Blockley, *Menander the Guardsman*, lines 175–87)

Among the clauses agreed was one relating to the movements of the Arab tribes allied to each side, who were now becoming a more and more important factor in maintaining the security of the east (see Chapter 8), and another guaranteeing the status of the Nestorian Christians in Persia.[19]

THE WAR IN ITALY

The continuous drain of resources, manpower and indeed gold on such a large scale to the east helps to put the 'reconquest' of the west into a more realistic perspective. One of the striking features about the conduct of the campaigns is the small number of troops dispatched from Constantinople, which evokes constant complaints from the generals that they are being starved of resources. Belisarius, for instance, found himself defending Rome with 5,000 men against a Gothic force of possibly 20,000. It is true that the Byzantine cavalry, as mounted archers, were more mobile and thus had an advantage over the Goths, who were armed with spears and swords, but their small numbers constituted a major problem, especially in the early 540s after Belisarius' recall to Constantinople, and Totila's accession as king of the Goths in AD 541. Sieges played a major role in Ostrogothic success in these years, and the Gothic superiority in numbers gave them the capacity to starve out the inhabitants of the towns, the resulting loss of Byzantine control leading to Belisarius' second Italian expedition in 544.[20] Even then he was consistently left without enough troops to give battle effectively, as Procopius scornfully reports:

> when he arrived in Italy, there was not a single day when things went right for him, because the hand of God was unmistakably against him . . . in spite of five years' effort he never once succeeded in disembarking on any part of the coast, unless there was a fortress handy: the whole of that time he sailed about, trying one landing-place after another.
>
> (*Secret History* 4.42, 5.1)

There were however other factors besides financial ones that delayed a final victory, including, it would seem, the emperor's own suspicions of his generals, especially Belisarius. Though in fact he remained entirely loyal to Justinian, Belisarius was often recalled, and even after the inopportune death in AD 550 of Germanus, newly appointed general for the Italian campaign, he was kept in

Constantinople doing nothing, if we believe the disappointed Procopius (*BG* III.38). After his return in AD 549, and the fall and occupation of Rome for the second time by Totila, it had still taken the latter's attack on Sicily and lobbying by prominent Italians now living in Constantinople to persuade Justinian to pursue the war with real force.[21] That the eunuch Narses was able to win the final battles, beginning with a naval battle in AD 551, owed much to his having insisted on being given enough silver to raise sufficient troops and pay the soldiers' arrears; in the encounter at Busta Gallorum (AD 552) the Byzantines for once outnumbered the Goths, whose weakness in archery again told against them. The Gothic king Totila was fatally wounded in this battle, before which he performed a dramatic war-dance 'wearing armour plentifully covered with gold, and the decoration on his cheek-plates as well as on his helmet and spear was of purple – indeed a wonderful display of regal splendour' (*BG* IV.31.18). A few months later his successor Teias was also defeated in battle at Mons Lactarius.[22] But even before this Procopius' account had become more and more disillusioned about Justinian and imperial policy generally, and he left the closing stages of the war to be told by his successor Agathias, writing in the early 570s.[23]

In taking on the task of reconquering Italy, Justinian clearly underestimated the power of the Ostrogoths to mount a long-term and serious resistance, as well as the consequent costs to the empire of keeping up the military effort year after year. He may have thought in terms of an offensive as short-term as Belisarius' spectacular campaign against the Vandals. No one could have foreseen the devastation caused by the plague of AD 542, not least its drastic impact on the capital, and the relative quiet of the situation on the eastern frontier at the start of the Italian campaign was to prove illusory. Once conquered, North Africa and eventually Italy each required a new administrative organization – also costly. In the case of Africa, in particular, this meant a massive investment of men and resources for the province's defence, which added to the difficulty of carrying on the wars elsewhere. But in addition to all these factors, Justinian himself turned out to be an uncertain commander, suspicious of his subordinates and jealous of allowing them even the forces they needed for the task in hand.

Moreover, the military problems went hand in hand with those of maintaining religious unity. The closing stages of the Gothic war coincided with a tense period in ecclesiastical politics which led up to the Fifth Ecumenical Council held in Constantinople in AD 553–4, by which Justinian hoped to find a formula acceptable both to the Monophysites in the east and to the church of Rome. Passions ran very high on all sides. The Latin-speaking North African bishops, who were strongly on the side of Rome and against the emperor, went to Constantinople *en masse*, while Pope Vigilius, having tried to hold the reins, spent a good deal of time under virtual house arrest and for a long time refused to attend the council altogether, only recanting in its final stages. The crisis had been sparked off in the first place by Justinian's own religious initiative in AD 543, known as the affair of the Three Chapters, because of his decree ordering the condemnation on doctrinal grounds of the works of three theologians allegedly of Nestorian tendency (Theodore of Mopsuestia, Theodoret of Cyrrhus and Ibas of Edessa), and was raging throughout the later 540s, just when the war in the east and in Italy was itself going badly. The degree of disturbance caused by this – only one of the doctrinal issues causing division during the reign – was very great, even in the provinces where the military campaigns were pursued, and it coincided with the general political difficulties which Justinian was experiencing, and which are graphically recorded in book III of Procopius' *Gothic Wars*. Given all these problems and adverse factors, it is less surprising that the military campaigns ran into difficulties than that they could actually be sustained for so long; this which can only be explained in terms of the generally prosperous and healthy condition of the eastern empire when Justinian came to the throne in the early sixth century. On the other hand, as we shall see, the signs of decline in population and defence, and the indicators of urban change begin to become apparent from the end of Justinian's reign (Chapters 7 and 8), which suggests that his ambitious programme of military reconquest and imperial reconstruction was actually a contributory factor in that process.

THE COST OF RECONQUEST: NORTH AFRICA

The speedy, and no doubt to contemporaries surprising, capture of North Africa from the Vandals provides a striking example of the continuing cost of conquest, even after the initial fighting was over. The emperor claimed the titles *Vandalicus* and *Africanus* with almost indecent haste, even before the final victory, and already in April AD 534, before Belisarius' return, Justinian had legislated for the future civil and military government of the newly reconquered province (*CJ* I.27). Africa was placed under a praetorian prefect and soon had its own *magister militum*. Much was made of the victory. In a grandiose imitation of earlier Roman triumphs, Gelimer, the last Vandal king, was taken to Constantinople to walk in chains in Belisarius' procession (Proc., *BV* II.9; John the Lydian, *De Mag.* II.2). As befitted a commoner, the victorious Belisarius himself walked to the Hippodrome, where he prostrated himself before Justinian, who sat in the imperial box wearing the special triumphal garment known as the *loros*, to underline the lesson that victory belonged to the emperor. The scene was depicted on the ceiling of the Chalce, the entrance to the imperial palace, and even on the funeral pall of Justinian himself (Proc., *Buildings* I.10.16f.; Corippus, *Iust.* I.276ff.).[24] But the next two decades were to prove much more difficult than could have been anticipated. A new and more recalcitrant military threat immediately presented itself from the Berber tribes, together with a mutiny in the Byzantine army; and while the eunuch general Solomon, and then a certain John Troglita fought successful, if hard, campaigns, the problem of dealing with the raids of nomadic tribes did not go away.[25] The condition of Africa is painted in gloomy terms by the African poet Corippus who had meanwhile come to Constantinople and composed a Latin panegyric on the accession of Justinian's successor, Justin II, in November AD 565,[26] but by the later sixth century the province seems to have attained both peace and prosperity, and the expedition which was to overthrow the tyrant Phocas in AD 609–10 and put Heraclius on the throne was dispatched to Constantinople from Carthage.

Africa was rich and fertile; the reconquest made its grain available for Constantinople, and its oil production reached a height in the seventh century, when it was described by the later Arabic sources as immensely rich. Justinian's regulatory law laid down provisions for a civil administration of 750 persons (staffed from the east), whose salaries amounted to over 17,500 *solidi* per year. In addition there was the cost of the military hierarchy, perhaps 500 strong, and the army itself (*CJ* I.27).[27] Added to this regular expenditure was the special cost of defensive and other building works (see p. 118); these were necessary after 100 years of Vandal rule.[28] The imposition of immediate taxation was obviously a priority, as Procopius recognizes.[29] Thus having got rid of the Vandals, the 'Roman' inhabitants, still Latin-speaking and with their religious loyalties centred on Rome, found themselves faced not only with heavy taxes and military rule, but with a situation in which the army billeted in their towns was not always by any means able to defend them against the increasing threat of Berber raids. If Procopius' picture of Africa in the *Wars* is somewhat mixed, that in the *Secret History* is one of unrelieved gloom: 'Libya, for instance, in spite of its enormous size, has been laid so utterly waste that however far one went it would be a remarkable achievement to find a single person there' (*Secret History* 18). In addition to their military and economic impositions, the newcomers used Greek instead of Latin, as the many surviving official seals make clear. Justinian had embarked on the war against the Vandals under the banner of restoring orthodoxy, yet very soon after the conquest the emperor in Constantinople began imposing a religious policy which the African church, traditionally linked with the church of Rome, found totally unacceptable. Thus the price of reconquest was high on all sides, and both the conquering power and the local populations got more than they had bargained for. Africa was atypical, however, in that despite all this, and despite the hard fighting which ensued between the Byzantine army and the Berbers, it eventually did well under Byzantine rule, thanks to various local factors – its own bountiful natural resources, the speed of the original conquest, which spared it from the lengthy war and frequent sieges which so devastated Italy, and perhaps also the situation under Vandal rule, which seems in fact to have been better than was once thought and to have profited in turn from the prosperous condition of the late Roman province of North Africa.[30] The real puzzle of Byzantine Africa lies in the severe lack of literary source material for the more peaceful second half of the sixth century, which makes a closer assessment of the economic and social effect of Byzantine reconquest extremely difficult. Yet the province was not subject to the kind of invasion and consequent fragmentation experienced by Italy, or for example Greece, where Justinian's defence system failed to halt the Slav invasions of the late sixth century. It remained a Byzantine province much longer than Egypt, indeed until the eventual fall of Carthage to the Arabs, which came only at the end of the seventh century.

FORTIFICATIONS AND OTHER BUILDINGS

To judge from Procopius' account, much of Justinian's extensive building programme in the provinces was dedicated to defence. However, its overall scope and impact are extremely hard to assess for a variety of reasons. The first has to do with the fact that our main literary source is indeed Procopius' *Buildings*, a panegyrical work written explicitly to praise Justinian, which makes extravagant claims for the emperor's achievements. Since the work is also incomplete as a record, and since individual statements often cannot be checked, this is a difficult text on which to base a fair assessment, especially as in those places where checking is possible from archaeological or other evidence Procopius is quite often found wanting.[31] In addition, especially in the case of the forts and fortified sites in the northern provinces, many sites remain unexcavated, or, if they have been excavated, there is nothing in the material remains (for example, inscriptions or coins) by which they can be securely dated. It may well be that substantial parts of the programme which Procopius ascribes to Justinian were actually begun by Anastasius; as for the *Buildings*, it is entirely in the nature of panegyric to seem to claim the credit for building anew when in fact the work in question is a work of restoration.[32] But even if Justinian was the restorer rather than the initiator, the sheer amount of building suggested by Procopius was enormous, implying 'capital investment in military installations on a massive scale'.[33] How effective it was in terms of defence is another matter. In some areas the building took the form of long walls, as at Thermopylae and the Isthmus of Greece; elsewhere it was a question of fortified refuges or, less often, actual fortresses. Some at least of these installations needed to be properly manned if they were to be effective, but, as we have seen, there were few available soldiers and much was left to the local inhabitants.

Ambitious or not, the scheme was unable to keep out the Huns in AD 558–9. Yet even allowing for exaggeration, it represents an extraordinary outlay of resources, even during the years of the reconquest. Nor was it confined to defence: there were also works of social welfare, and Procopius makes it clear time and time again that the military and the religious aims went hand in hand. Churches were built as often as forts, especially in newly reconquered territory, and indeed they could serve as demonstrations of Roman power. The position of the fortified monastery

Plate 7 The walls of the monastery of St Catherine beside Mt Sinai, built by Justinian and described by Procopius. The fine mosaic in the apse of the church depicts the Tranfiguration; the dedication to St Catherine came considerably later.

which still stands at the foot of Mt Sinai where Moses saw God, and is itself built over the traditional site of the burning bush and in a location already inhabited by many monks and hermits, clearly shows such a diplomatic and religious function, in contrast to Procopius' claim that it was built to keep Saracen invaders from entering the province of Palestine (*Buildings* V.8.9). This it could hardly do, positioned as it is in a cleft between two mountainous peaks; on the other hand, the Justinianic walls which surrounded the monastery itself remain one of its most striking features.[34] This raises the question of the nature of reconquest itself – military or diplomatic? For together with the military policy went a determined missionary activity. This can be seen in several areas, for instance in Nubia and in the case of King Tzath of Lazica, whose conversion was the price of clientship, while the Ghassanids, the Arab tribal group closely associated with the Byzantines as against the pro-Persian Lakhmids, were Monophysite Christians.[35] Justinian was even willing to entrust the conversion of pagans in Asia Minor to a Monophysite, and to allow the wholesale ordination of Monophysite clergy in the eastern provinces. Even in the case of the provinces which were subject to military offensives, the wars were given the appearance of crusades undertaken to restore orthodoxy, although the reality of the situation often looked different when the local Roman population was faced with the choice between the Arian rulers to whom they had become accustomed and the harsh actuality of the Byzantine intervention.[36]

THE EFFECTS OF THE WARS

The length and the implications of the process of reconquest were surely unforeseen at the start, and the effects of the attempt were profound. For the eastern empire the drain in gold, men and other resources was immense, especially when combined with the similar demands made on imperial funds by the wars and the treaties with Persia. There was a cost in public opinion too: the early euphoria could hardly be maintained, and as things became difficult, whatever the reason, the emperor lost popularity. Two works reflect the doubts and criticisms of the later part of the reign:[37] Procopius' *Secret History*, with its violent tirades against Justinian and Theodora (who died in AD 548) and its catalogue of complaints and accusations against the abuses which Procopius claims had taken place, and John the Lydian's *De Magistratibus*, where an attempt is made to save the emperor's reputation by blaming everything on his ministers, especially the praetorian prefect, John the Cappadocian:

> Our emperor, gentlest of men, knew nothing of these affairs because everyone, though abused by the Cappadocian's unrestricted exercise of power, spoke in defence of that wicked man. . . . Only the emperor's wife and helpmeet, who was most vigilant in her sympathy towards those suffering injustice, found it intolerable to ignore the destruction of the state. . . . Naturally, then, the emperor, being a good man though slow to requite evil, was in the grip of a baffling situation.
>
> (*De Mag*. III.69, from Maas, *John Lydus*, 95)

Blame is also attached to Justinian's ministers by Procopius, but his account of the eventual fall of John the Cappadocian spares neither Justinian nor Theodora, who emerges as both vindictive and manipulative (*BP* I.25; *Secret History* 17.38f.).[38] Justinian was indeed hesitant, especially in his handling of his ministers and generals; nevertheless, remarkably, he was able to keep the momentum going. Only with hindsight do we see so clearly that the changes already taking place in the Mediterranean world would combine with the sheer size of the endeavour to prevent his military successes from lasting. The truce with Persia was bought at a high price and could not last, and new invaders in the shape of Lombards, Huns, Avars and Slavs soon reached Italy (AD 568) and the Balkans. North Africa remained a Byzantine province, and a prosperous one, but much of Italy was soon lost to the sub-Roman kingdom of the Lombards, and Byzantine control reduced to the exarchate of Ravenna and the duchy of Rome, which facilitated the development of a strong territorially based papacy.[39] On the other hand, the coastal territories gained by the expedition sent to Spain in AD 552 under the aged patrician Liberius, to help the pretender Athanagild, were in the main kept by Byzantium until AD 624 and their defence put under a *magister militum* appointed by Constantinople.[40]

With the important exception of North Africa, then, the net effect of the supposed reconquest of the western provinces was that the eastern empire regained and retained a portion of Italy and a much smaller portion of Spain during the ensuing period when the early medieval western kingdoms were taking shape. In itself this was a significant achievement, but it did not constitute the restoration of the Roman empire, as Justinian had perhaps at times hoped it would. On Italy the effects of the Gothic wars were destructive in the extreme. A law known as the Pragmatic Sanction imposed a settlement on the model of that given to North Africa twenty years before. But Pope Pelagius I (556–61) complained in his letters that agriculture was devastated; the senatorial aristocracy had had its fortunes undermined if not destroyed, and many members had left for the east; the senate itself collapsed as an institution; many towns, including Rome, suffered greatly during the hostilities.[41] Even if Italy's capacity for recovery is often underestimated,[42] Ravenna especially showing evidence of growth and vitality, profound underlying changes in urban structure, municipal organization and settlement patterns were already under way. The future Pope Gregory I spent some time in Constantinople in the 580s, where he established excellent relations with the family of the Emperor Maurice and the Italian senatorial exiles in the eastern capital which survived into his tenure of the papacy, as his letters show. But, as T. S. Brown points out, this group suffered severely from the attack made on the supporters of Maurice by the usurper Phocas (AD 602–10), and with it, valuable connections between Constantinople and Italy were broken. Another factor which made for difficulty in relations with Constantinople was the opposition of the Roman church to the Three Chapters decree and the Fifth Ecumenical Council of AD 553–4. This was to continue: in the seventh century, too, Rome was the centre of opposition to the imperial policy of Monothelitism, and attracted African as well as eastern participants to the Lateran Synod held there which condemned the policy in AD 649. The African church was equally opposed to Constantinople, and looked to Rome throughout this period as its natural ally.[43] The church in Italy also gained economically and in other ways from the political changes in the later sixth century, in effect stepping into the shoes of the old senatorial aristocracy and acquiring both wealth and political influence.[44] In this way, Justinian's own ecclesiastical policies, however much they, like the ill-judged Monothelite formulation of a century later, may have been aimed at the near-impossible task of achieving unity between the eastern and western churches, in practice proved a major difficulty in Byzantine relations with Rome and contributed to the growth in power of the Roman church.

In considering the effects of the reconquest policy on the provinces and on the empire generally, three factors need to be remembered: first, of course, the immediate effects of war and of the subsequent administrative, economic and military settlements; second, Justinian's own energetic interventions in religious policy, which so far as the western provinces were concerned cut across the process of reunification; and third, the backdrop of steady urban and rural change which can be perceived in all areas throughout the period (Chapter 7). As for the eastern provinces, the wars with Persia resumed after Justinian's death; and archaeological evidence in many places shows decline setting in by the second half of the sixth century, either for local reasons or as a result of reduced investment from Constantinople (Chapter 8). Here too, the unfortunate Justinian failed to conciliate eastern religious feeling – indeed, it was his unsuccessful attempts to do so which led to the alienation of the western churches after the Fifth Council. In the 540s, even as Monophysite exiles were housed in the palace at Constantinople, a certain Jacob Bar'adai was made bishop of Edessa and licensed to ordain Monophysite clergy, a fateful step which thus created a dual hierarchy in the east, especially Syria and Mesopotamia, and allowed the development of the Jacobite church, so named after Jacob himself.[45]

JUSTINIAN AS EMPEROR

Even though it is usually more helpful in understanding the late Roman empire to think in terms of processes and structures than of reigns of emperors, Justinian's reign was clearly extraordinary. Not only did it last for thirty-eight years (AD 527–65), but it was also commonly agreed that he had been the effective ruler during the reign of his uncle Justin I (AD 518–27).[46] The reign itself opened with a grand imperial gesture, the idea of codifying the whole of previous Roman law; amazingly, the work was completed in record time, the situation on the eastern frontier looked hopeful and the trauma of the Nika revolt was surmounted by Belisarius' astonishingly successful expedition against the Vandals. Italy followed as the next imperialist objective, and a high point was reached with Belisarius' entry into Rome in AD 540. The plague of AD 542, which affected the emperor himself, came as a severe blow; besides the laws of the early 540s which attempted to solve the resulting problems of intestacy (Justinian, *Edict* IX.3), there was an immediate rise in prices (*Nov.* 122, AD 544), showing how quickly the fiscal effects were felt by the imperial treasury. Many historians tend to play down the effects of this plague as a major factor, especially in relation to urban decline, and its effects are certainly hard to quantify and to trace archaeologically. But the population of Constantinople may have suffered a sudden drop of as much as a third, and the losses among the rural population in the eastern provinces must have been dramatic, with severe consequences for the imperial tax revenues:

> when pestilence swept through the whole known world and notably the Roman Empire, wiping out most of the farming community and of necessity leaving a trail of desolation in its wake, Justinian showed no mercy towards the ruined freeholders. Even then, he did not refrain from demanding the annual payment of tax, not only the amount at which he assessed each individual, but also the amount for which his deceased neighbours were liable.[47]

> (*Secret History* 23.20f.)

The ensuing phases of both the Italian and the Persian campaigns were, not surprisingly, difficult, and command problems were added to those of supply and manpower. However, we have to use common sense in reading the abundant contemporary sources, for Procopius, with his traditional mentality, tends to ascribe all difficulties to personal or class motives, and there were certainly enough examples of bad ministers under Justinian to make such accusations plausible.[48] As the reign drew on, with the death of the Empress Theodora in AD 548, the spectacular imperial initiatives of the early years gave way to other concerns, such as religious unity and the building of a longer-lasting peace with Persia. Justinian's later years were gloomy by comparison with the early part of the reign, with new barbarian threats and the emperor himself turning more and more to theological speculation. The Fifth Council had solved nothing, and Justinian continued to be embroiled in the wranglings of the different eastern religious groups. In his last years he made yet another unsuccessful attempt at conciliation by adopting the Julianist formula according to which Christ's body (being divine) was incorruptible, an old subject of controversy relating to the deeper question of the relation of God to matter in the Incarnation which was to go on to be a central issue throughout the seventh century. Justinian's edict on the subject (AD 564) resulted in the exile in the following year of Eutychius, the patriarch of Constantinople whose appointment the emperor had himself contrived in order to get his way at the Fifth Ecumenical Council.

Eutychius was replaced by the ultra-orthodox John Scholasticus, a great supporter of Justinian's orthodox nephew and successor, Justin II, but Justinian's action and Eutychius' deposition left many loose ends, and the latter was briefly reinstated after the death of John Scholasticus in AD 575, only to relaunch himself deep into theological dispute.[49]

Events and policies during the reign, and their effects, were thus deeply contradictory, as were the verdicts of contemporaries. Justinian was regarded both as a great and strong emperor and as a dangerous reformer, sometimes indeed by the same writer; this is particularly obvious in the case of our main source, Procopius, but also applies to John the Lydian, who had been an official in the praetorian prefecture and knew what he was talking about.[50] Similarly, Justinian has featured in modern works as a Christian humanist, as the giver of Roman law to Christian Europe, as an intolerant and authoritarian persecutor of pagans and heretics and as a prototype for Stalin.[51] All these judgements suffer from the tendency to confuse the man himself with the events of his reign. The tendency is reinforced by the temptation to read off the personalities of Justinian and Theodora from two very striking surviving works: the *Secret History* of Procopius and the well-known mosaics of Justinian and Theodora in the church of San Vitale at Ravenna – especially as the rather podgy appearance of Justinian and the distant look of Theodora in the mosaics both seem to fit Procopius' descriptions of the emperor and empress:

> [Justinian] showed himself approachable and affable to those with whom he came into contact; not a single person found himself denied access to the Emperor, and even those who broke the rules by the way they stood or spoke in his presence never incurred his wrath . . . with a friendly expression on his face and without raising an eyebrow, in a gentle voice he would order tens of thousands of quite innocent persons to be put to death, cities to be razed to the ground, and all their possessions to be confiscated for the Treasury.
>
> (*Secret History* 13.1–2)

To her bodily needs she [Theodora] devoted quite unnecessary attention, though never enough to satisfy herself. She was in a great hurry to get into her bath, and very unwilling to get out again. When she had finished her ablutions she would go down to breakfast, and after a light breakfast she would take a rest. But at lunch and supper she indulged her taste for every kind of food and drink. Again and again she would sleep for hours on end, by day until nightfall and by night till sunrise.

(ibid., 15.6–8)

To set against this, we have utterances from Justinian himself, who was a great legislator and an author of theological treatises. But even accepting that the words are Justinian's own, works like these are inevitably written in a rhetorical mode which masks the personality of the author. It is similarly difficult to assess the emperor's contribution as patron to the culture of his age, especially in relation to visual art, for despite the mass of public works to which Procopius' *Buildings* testifies, very little official imperial art has actually survived. What little there is, such as the Barberini ivory, which is probably, though not certainly, Justinianic, shows what we would naturally have expected – a mixture of classicizing and traditional motifs; the same goes for the ivory of the Archangel Michael in the British Museum, one of the masterpieces of the period. As for the famous mosaics of Justinian and Theodora at Ravenna, however, they are not certainly imperially sponsored, nor are the great Sinai icons of Christ, the Virgin with angels and St Peter universally agreed to be Justinianic, even though the monastery itself was a Justinianic foundation.[52] The church of St Sophia in Constantinople, described in detail by Procopius in book I of the *Buildings* and by Paul the Silentiary in his long hexameter poem on the rededication of the dome in January AD 563, after it had been damaged by earthquake, is a masterpiece, but it is not classical at all.

Similar problems arise with the literary texts. In one sense, the reign is rich in classicizing literature, from Procopius' own works to the clever classical epigrams by Paul the Silentiary (a palace official) and several other office-holders such as Macedonius the consul and Julian the prefect, which were collected by Agathias and eventually passed into the *Greek Anthology*.[53] Both the technical expertise and the reading public were evidently still present. Procopius claims that the *Buildings* was an imperial commission, and Paul the Silentiary's poem on the restored St Sophia, written in formal hexameters, is a formal panegyric composed for an imperial occasion.[54] On the other hand, imperial themes were also addressed in the elaborate rhythmical *kontakia* (liturgical hymns) by the deacon Romanos, performed as part of the liturgy in St Sophia and influenced by Syriac poetry and homiletic, and Justinian's reign saw the composition of the first important Byzantine chronicle, that of John Malalas.[55] All these writers used Greek, but Latin should not be forgotten, even in Constantinople. Not only did Corippus compose his panegyric for Justin II in AD 565 in Latin, but Cassiodorus, one of the great figures of early medieval Europe, who had been the secretary of Theodoric, came to Constantinople in AD 550 with other Italian exiles from the Gothic war and spent some time there before returning to Italy to found his monastery at Squillace which subsequently became one of the most important medieval centres for copying manuscripts.[56]

Much more could be said about the cultural changes taking place during the reign of Justinian,[57] but it is already evident that no simple formula and no simple appeal to imperial character or policy will do justice to them. Justinian was a strong emperor who initiated a series of extraordinarily ambitious policies, and carried most of them through in the face of great obstacles. But it is very doubtful whether even without these obstacles the eastern empire would have been sufficiently strong in economic and administrative terms to sustain the extra burdens it was taking on. And at the same time processes of social change were taking place throughout the Mediterranean world of which contemporaries were barely aware, yet which were conditioning the outcome of the policies which they adopted.

6

Culture and mentality

Was there a specifically late antique 'mentality'? What kind of cultural life went on in this period? More important, in what ways were culture and society changing?

Questions like these tend to hide unexpressed comparisons with the classical world, or with the medieval west, or (but less often) with Byzantium. In the past the later Roman empire has particularly suffered from unflattering comparisons with the supposedly superior and more 'rational' centuries that went before, in contrast with which late antiquity has been seen typically as superstitious, irrational, totalitarian or all three together (see Introduction and Chapter 1). This period of supposed decline has been seen both as the end of antiquity and as the beginning of the Middle Ages. But late antiquity has also been seen more sympathetically, even sometimes nostalgically, as a supremely religious or spiritual age.[1] And finally, Byzantinists have discussed at length the question of when Byzantium began, and whether the period from Constantine to the seventh century should count as late antique, early Byzantine or simply Byzantine. But while dividing history into periods is usually necessary on practical grounds, and may be illuminating, it can also be a barrier. In our case it also depends on whether one is considering the life of a monk in northern Syria, an aristocrat in Rome or a peasant in Greece. For late antiquity was not a unified society. Geography and social class are variant factors which tell against generalization, quite apart from equally significant variables like religion and ethnic background.

'Cultural studies' now amounts to a discipline in itself. But while questions of culture and 'mentality' are familiar enough when applied to other periods of history, they have only recently begun to impinge in their current form on the study of the later Roman empire. As we have seen, Marxist and materialist approaches have been, and still may be, important in the historiography of this period, though with the present emphasis on 'culture', several other approaches may also come into their own. There is, for example, no feminist history of the end of antiquity, even though the proponents of decline all too often posit a fall from a previous norm defined wholly in masculine terms. Even Peter Brown, who rejects decline in favour of change or transformation, defines the latter's starting point as lying in a 'model of parity' which existed among the (male) urban élites of the High Empire, with their civic paganism; what emerged from the upheaval of the third century was, in this view, 'Late Antique man'.[2] I cite this example, no doubt unfairly, because Peter Brown himself has also suggested that late antiquity saw a distinct shift away from traditional public values towards the private sphere, and, with it, a significant step towards the growth of individual identity.[3] Whether this was really the case, and how far the process may have been connected with Christianization, is a matter for further discussion (see p. 148). As for the argument from decline, like the arguments from corruption and superstition, it proceeds from within a historiographical discourse which is itself highly authoritarian, reminiscent indeed of the discourse of contemporary traditionalists like Procopius, when he writes about groups such as women, the lower classes or barbarians.[4]

THE SURVIVAL OF TRADITIONAL STRUCTURES

First, however, we must ask to what extent the traditional culture was still maintained.

Until the end of our period, much of the territory round the eastern Mediterranean, at least, was subject to a single administrative and governing system, paying taxes and expecting to be defended by works of defence and military power. In many areas culture was still largely urban, just as it had always been. For Procopius, as for Justinian, the idea of civilization went hand in hand with that of cities; new cities were founded in the reconquered territory, while others were restored, and as long as the cities survived, the apparatus of culture – baths, education, municipal institutions – had a chance of surviving as well. It was the decline of these cities, preceded by, or rather, manifested in the decay of these institutions, that marked the real transition from antiquity to Middle Ages (Chapter 7). Even in the barbarian kingdoms of the west, titles and institutions recalled imperial models, and kings showed themselves deferential to the emperor; Amalasuntha, the daughter and only child of the Ostrogothic king Theodoric, and learned herself, wanted a Roman education for her son (Proc., *BG* I.2), and defended what was to prove an unfortunate choice of Theodahad for her husband to the Roman senate in terms of his education:

> to these good qualities is added enviable literary learning, which confers splendour on a nature deserving praise. There the wise man finds what will make him wiser; the warrior discovers what will strengthen him with courage; the prince learns how to administer his people with equity; and there can be no station in life which is not improved by the glorious knowledge of letters.
>
> (Cassiodorus, *Var.* X.3, trans. S. Barnish, *Cassiodorus: Variae*, Liverpool, 1992)

The other institution which gave a sense of unity of custom, if not of belief, was the church. From east to west bishops enjoyed a local authority and prestige that was temporal as well as spiritual, and preached sermons on similar themes, while holy men and women, whether living in monasteries or independently, were an important part of the social scene. And if the higher forms of culture belonged to the towns, many sources from this period, especially saints' lives, allow us to see into the lives of villages, which perhaps did not differ too much between east and west. Despite a more centralized legal system, and threats of harsher and harsher punishment, the government of the later Roman empire was probably no more totalitarian, or ordinary life more brutal, than in the early empire. The state structures characteristic of the earlier Roman empire still to a large degree survived, and the church, the main rival of the state for social power, still shared the stage with secular authority. Long-distance travel and exchange continued, even after the loss of the western provinces in the late fifth century. This was still a pre-modern and pre-industrial society, as it had always been, but in the east – and in many parts of the west too – it was still recognizably Roman; it was not yet the Middle Ages.

HIGH CULTURE – LITERATURE

As long as the apparatus of state and cities lasted, the old-style classical education remained available, if sometimes in diluted form. Indeed, the availability of rhetorical training was essential to the functioning of the political and social structure, and was provided by the state itself in Constantinople and the main urban centres. Books were still available, and while expensive, had also been expensive in classical times. Acquiring this training, which was based firmly on the classical authors, was a matter of being well-to-do and, usually, male. Thus Synesius, from a well-to-do background in Cyrenaica, was highly educated in Greek prose, poetry and philosophy. Only a few particularly favoured women gained access to these skills, like the Empress Eudocia, who composed Greek verses. Greek verse composition was highly valued; many poets flourished in Egypt in the fifth century and were able to sell their services as panegyrists. As late as the late sixth century a certain Dioscorus from Aphrodito in Upper Egypt was still writing Greek verse on traditional subjects.[5] A whole series of historians wrote classicizing histories in Greek in the fifth and sixth centuries,[6] and though the approach of the ecclesiastical histories of such writers as Socrates and Sozomen in the fifth century or Evagrius Scholasticus at the end of the sixth may have been somewhat different, these too were works written from the basis of a thorough training in rhetoric.[7] A similar training continued to be available in Latin in the west. Servius' commentary on Virgil, Macrobius' *Saturnalia* and Martianus Capella's *De nuptiis Philologiae et Mercurii*, in nine books, belong to the first half of the fifth century,[8] while the North African poet Dracontius composed lengthy hexameter poems in the Vandal period, from which we also have the collection of short Latin poems known as the *Latin Anthology* and the epigrams of Luxorius.[9] From the first part of the Byzantine period we have the panegyrics of Corippus (Chapter 5), and it seems that Virgil went on being taught in North Africa after the reconquest as he always had, at least for a while. Everyone learning to write Latin seriously learned it from Virgil: papyrus finds from the small town of Nessana in a remote spot on the Egyptian border show that this continued in the late seventh century, long after the Arab conquest. In Ostrogothic Italy, as elsewhere, elaborate rhetoric was highly admired, as we can see from the works of Cassiodorus (Chapter 2), and the many learned western bishops, from Ambrose

of Milan in the late fourth century to Caesarius of Arles, Avitus of
Vienne, Ennodius of Pavia and, under the Merovingians, Venantius
Fortunatus, all drew on a rhetorical training in the classics. Indeed,
the tensions which naturally arose when classical forms and language were progressively put to different uses were among the most
productive factors in the evolution of 'medieval' literature.

Turning to Greek literature, we have seen that the difficult art of
writing classical Greek epigrams still flourished under Justinian, and
at Gaza in Palestine in the sixth century there was a lively school of
accomplished Christian rhetoricians and poets.[10] A rhetorical training might be a prelude to law school, for example, at Berytus
(Beirut), the centre of legal studies until the city was destroyed by
an earthquake in AD 551. The early sixth-century writer Zacharias
Rhetor has left us a vivid picture of student life in the late fifth
century both here and at Alexandria, where Christian and pagan
students, among them Severus the future patriarch of Antioch,
studied together and sometimes fought each other.[11] It was possible
to study both rhetoric and philosophy there, and Severus had
among his fellow students Paralius, a pagan from Aphrodisias in
Caria, a small and remote city from which we happen to have good
evidence of the educational possibilities available for the young men
from its better-off families.[12]

HIGH CULTURE – PHILOSOPHY

In the fifth and sixth centuries philosophy was also vigorously
practised, particularly at Athens and Alexandria, the two main
centres where it was taught; we know much more about it now than
previously, thanks to a recent renewal of interest in later Greek
philosophy among specialists.[13] Many elements of the Platonic
philosophical tradition had been absorbed into Christian teaching
and had thereby become available to a wider public in a different
guise.[14] The Neoplatonist teaching of the fifth and sixth centuries,
however, was often identified with paganism. It took a highly élitist
form, and among certain sections of the upper class it still enjoyed
considerable prestige; as we saw, the family of Paralius in
Aphrodisias sent its sons to Alexandria, and a number of important
mosaics from Paphos in Cyprus and Apamea in Syria, home of a
flourishing school especially notable for the early fourth-century
philosopher Iamblichus, also suggest the diffusion of Neoplatonic
ideas in the fourth century.[15] Athens was the particular home

of Neoplatonism, the late antique version of Platonism associated in the first place with Plotinus, active in the third century, and in our period especially with Proclus. The latter arrived in Athens in AD 430 and became head of the school there at the early age of 25 or 26 in AD 437. He remained head of the school until his death in AD 485, when his *Life* was written by his successor Marinus.[16]

The Neoplatonists evolved their own system of philosophical education, in which the teachings of Aristotle and of the Stoics were harmonized with those of Plato to form an elaborately organized syllabus. The 'Aristotelian' philosophers of late antique Alexandria were in fact as much Neoplatonists as the Athenians, while in turn Simplicius, one of the last and greatest of the Athenian philosophers of this period, wrote a series of important commentaries on the works of Aristotle. But Neoplatonism was also deeply religious; indeed, it almost amounted to a religious system in itself. Neoplatonists sought to understand the nature of the divine and to evolve a scientific theology, practised asceticism (Chapter 3), contemplation and prayer, revered the gods and adopted special ways of invoking them ('theurgy'). They believed in the possibility of divine revelation, especially through the so-called 'Chaldaean Oracles' (second century), which claimed to be revelations obtained by interrogation of Plato's soul. Indeed, for Proclus and his followers, Plato himself and his writings acquired the status of scripture.[17] Naturally such teachings came to be identified with paganism, but many of the greatest Christian thinkers, such as Gregory of Nyssa and Augustine, were also deeply influenced by Neoplatonism. Certain of Plato's works, especially the *Timaeus* and the *Phaedrus*, were deeply influential on many Christian writers, including Augustine, and there was much common ground between Neoplatonism and Christianity.[18] In Athens in the fifth century, Proclus headed a 'school', not so much in the sense of buildings or an institution (the teaching of the Academy seems still to have been conducted in a very informal way by modern standards), as in the fact that he had a group of pupils, on whom he seems to have exercised a charismatic influence and with whom he celebrated a variety of forms of pagan cult which included prayer, meditation and hymns and even extended to healing miracles. When the father of a little girl appropriately called Asclepigeneia, who was desperately ill, asked for Proclus' prayers,

Proclus took along with him the great Pericles of Lydia, a man who was a great friend of wisdom, and together they went to the Asclepieion, to pray to the god there, on behalf of the ailing girl. In fact, at the time, the city still had the good fortune of benefiting from the presence of the god and the temple of the Savior [i.e., Asclepius] had not yet been pillaged [i.e., by the Christians]. And while Proclus prayed, according to ancient rite, a sudden change took place in the little girl, and she immediately felt easier: the Savior, inasmuch as he was a god, had truly cured her with ease.

(*Life of Proclus* 29, from Saffrey, 261–2)[19]

When, in AD 529, Justinian forbade the teaching of philosophy in Athens,[20] the seven Neoplatonist philosophers then active there, led by the great Damascius, are said to have made a voyage in search of Plato's philosopher-king to Persia, where the new king, Chosroes I, was thought to be interested in Greek philosophy to the point of commissioning translations of Plato. If they ever actually reached the Persian court (this romantic story has several suspicious features) they soon became disappointed in him and returned, though not before securing a safe conduct for themselves under the terms of the peace treaty of AD 533. The story is told by Agathias, *Hist.* II.30–1, in the context of a denunciation of Chosroes and a certain Uranius who had, according to Agathias, absurdly encouraged the king's philosophical pretensions. It has given rise to much discussion, both as to the fate of the Athenian Academy itself and as to that of the philosophers, in particular Simplicius, who went on to conduct a vigorous polemic against his rival John Philoponus in Alexandria. A recent theory suggests that he spent the rest of his active life and founded a Platonic school at Harran (Carrhae) in Mesopotamia, known as a home of paganism until a late date. If correct (apart from possible local references in Simplicius' commentaries, it depends largely on a single statement in a tenth-century Arabic writer, which may suggest the presence of Platonists there), this would have important consequences for the transmission of Greek philosophy into the Islamic world.[21]

For our present purpose it is the intensity of philosophical debate even in the mid-sixth century that is so notable. John Philoponus, the leading philosopher at Alexandria at that time, was himself a Christian. He wrote a long series of works in the course of which he argued against the view of Proclus that the world had had no beginning, though his own views were not fundamentalist

Plate 8 The shape of the world, modelled on that of the Ark of the Covenant, according to a MS of the sixth-century *Christian Topography* by Cosmas Indicopleustes.

enough for some Christians. Philoponus also espoused a particular form of Monophysitism known as Tritheism,[22] but he was an individualist, and a controversialist, and there seems to have been room for a considerable range of approaches within the philosophical circles of Alexandria. Unlike Athens, which succumbed to the Slav invasions of AD 582 onwards, and where, if philosophical teaching continued at all, it had no chance of doing so on a scale remotely comparable with its long past tradition, Alexandria weathered the Justinianic legislation and was able to preserve its philosophical tradition until the Arab conquest.

A CHANGING SOCIETY

Quite apart from philosophy, who would have read the high-style works of literature? If anything, the literary culture of late antiquity was even more class-based than previously. It required a specialized training, not only from writers but also from their audiences, and by the sixth century at any rate the spoken language in Greek was diverging markedly from this high literary language.[23] The traditional literary culture was still available in Constantinople under Heraclius (AD 610–41), but once cities declined it became much less accessible for the majority, and a sharp decline set in also in the availability of books and the knowledge of classical authors, which did not begin to be restored in the Byzantine empire until the ninth and tenth centuries.[24] But so long as that educational system still prevailed, works written in the classical manner, such as the ones mentioned above, continued to be produced. Teachers were needed to perpetuate the system, while in turn a training in classical rhetoric was regarded as an essential qualification for the imperial bureaucracy and indeed for any secular office. We can see the process clearly in the mid-fourth century, when Constantine's new governing class was very much in need of a brief tutorial in Roman history,[25] and again a generation or so later, when the provincial rhetor Ausonius shot to prominence as praetorian prefect and consul, and the Egyptian poet Claudian became chief panegyrist of Stilicho and Honorius. Other literary figures who became prominent in the fifth century included the historian Olympiodorus from Egyptian Thebes, who describes himself as 'a poet by profession' (fr. 1 Blockley), and who was a pagan, well educated in the classical tradition and much-travelled, distinctly more enterprising than most of his peers. Priscus, another fifth-century Greek historian and more of a classical stylist than Olympiodorus, based his history on both Herodotus and Thucydides. He went on a mission to the Hun king Attila in AD 449 and expressed his admiration for him in his history, while criticizing Theodosius II for his policy of trying to buy Attila off.[26] Yet another colourful character was Cyrus of Panopolis, also in Egypt, a poet who rose to the positions of prefect of the city, praetorian prefect and consul under Theodosius II, only to be accused of paganism in court intrigues and sent into exile as bishop of the small town of Cotiaeum in Phrygia.[27] The very persistence of and approval given to classicism in literature could however certainly cause problems in the effort to adapt it to contemporary conditions.[28] Such a system perpetuated traditional attitudes, as indeed it was intended to do; not least, it imposed fixed categories of thought, and in particular impeded realistic perceptions of relations with barbarian peoples who were by definition seen as lacking in culture.

Yet the actual cultural system which had produced and sustained this very élitist literature was in fact changing fast. One can read the ensuing effects both vertically, in terms of 'high' and 'popular' literature, and horizontally, in terms of religious affiliation. Both distinctions can at times be misleading: thus Christian saints' lives may sometimes be 'popular', or they may embody highly literary qualities;[29] similarly although Christian world chronicles, running from Adam to the writer's own day, often seem credulous and simple through their apparent lack of critical judgements, the genre began with the great Christian scholar Eusebius and the surviving examples have much more in common with 'classical' historiography than used to be supposed.[30] Finally, very many Christian writings are themselves extremely rhetorical in character, and use all the panoply provided by a classical education. Augustine, perhaps the greatest Christian writer of the period, had been a teacher of rhetoric himself, and did not hesitate to use his skill to the utmost when he later came to write religious works. But, as we have seen (Chapter 3), unlike most classical writers he was also supremely conscious of the techniques necessary in addressing himself to an uneducated audience, and kept returning again and again to the problems of reconciling intellectual and rhetorical aims with religious faith. His great work, the *City of God*, written in the aftermath of the sack of Rome by Alaric in AD 410, is less an extended meditation on the reasons for that event than on the place of the classical world and classical culture in the scheme of Christian providence.[31] Other Christian writers, like Synesius or Sidonius Apollinaris, both landowners who became bishops (Chapter 2), composed classicizing poems which are at first sight not obviously Christian at all.[32] But the impact of Christianization also changed reading practices, especially through the availability of the Bible. A specifically Christian learning developed, with the early monastic communities in the west, for example on the island of Lérins, leading the way in the late fifth century for the great medieval monastic centres of learning. Bishops and writers such as Paulinus of Nola combined secular learning with Christian expression, not least in the form of letters, which constituted a particularly flourishing genre among educated Christians in the early fifth century; a large number of these survive, testifying to a close network of shared culture and common interests stretching between Gaul, Italy and North Africa.[33]

CHRISTIANITY AND POPULAR CULTURE

There has been a persistent assumption among scholars that Christian literature constitutes a form of popular culture. Such a view, however, tacitly denigrates the importance of Christian writing, and, it has to be said, is closely associated with the idea that late antiquity was a time when there was a kind of general softening of the intellect.[34] The examples given above show that it cannot be accepted as it stands. But unlike classical culture, which was essentially élitist, Christianity did indeed consciously direct its appeal to all classes of society, explicitly including slaves and women. While it is true that St Paul's famous declaration that 'there is neither Jew nor Greek, there is neither bond nor free, there is neither male nor female; for ye are all one in Christ Jesus' (Gal. 3.28) did not, and was probably never meant to, lead to the abolition of social differences, nevertheless, along with such sayings as that about the difficulty of the rich man in entering the kingdom of heaven, Christianization did bring with it something of a change of attitude towards those groups who had been barely considered at all in the pagan Roman world, chief among whom were the poor.

The process eventually made itself felt in cultural life also. The breakdown of the old classical cultural and educational system has sometimes been associated with a 'new, popular culture', more universal in character and based less on the written word and more on the visual and the oral.[35] There is at first sight much in this view in relation to what was happening to the towns and the educational structure in both east and west; all the same, one needs to be cautious in ascribing the change to Christianity. For one thing, the nature of the available evidence is heavily biased in the direction of an identification of 'pagan' and 'classical' with higher social levels, whereas such Christian sources as saints' lives, and the monastic literature in particular, are weighted in the opposite direction. In other words, we simply know more about the poorer sections of society from Christian texts than we do of the same social groups in the pagan world. If there is really a difference, it may have come as a result of a social change of which Christianity was only one part. The Fathers indeed sometimes referred to sacred pictures as a way of educating the illiterate, which again may suggest the equation of 'Christian' and 'popular' culture, and it has been common to appeal to 'popular beliefs' as the explanation for the increase in the evidence for religious images in the sixth century.[36] The problem here is that with the Byzantine icon we seem to be in a specially 'spiritual' and unclassical world:

> the visual image, the stylized portrait, was a concentrated and potent symbol that spoke directly to the man in the street. The average man had lost touch with the erudite, literary symbolism that had encrusted the public life of the empire.[37]

This is, however, to mistake the symptom for the cause: in practice, the educated upper class was just as enthusiastic about icons, saints and holy men as the ordinary people. Their priorities had changed too; in other words, the very cultural system which had supported the urban culture of classical antiquity was rapidly being transformed. Even secular historians from the late fifth and sixth centuries, such as Zosimus (who was actually pagan) and Procopius (who is certainly not a 'popular' writer), seem to show a greater receptiveness to miracle and other religious factors as part of historical explanation.[38]

It does not seem then that Christianization necessarily went hand in hand with a weakening of élite cultural norms, though of course the latter themselves underwent change. Nevertheless, even basic social structures were in many cases in a state of flux by the later part of our period, especially on the periphery of the empire. We can see something of this in the relation between language and local culture. Latin remained the official language of law, the administration and the army until the mid-sixth century, and a good deal of

Latin was used in consequence, even in Constantinople. In the barbarian kingdoms of the west Latin also retained its place alongside native languages, eventually to develop into the romance languages. But in the east, not only was Greek itself changing as a spoken language; in addition, the relatively peaceful and prosperous development of the east in the fifth century brought with it both a significant increase in settlement and therefore population, and an increase in the importance of local languages. Georgian, Armenian and Coptic all took written form during this period, and we see the phenomenon most clearly in the case of Syriac, the dialect of Aramaic which now emerges as a major literary language, especially used by Christian writers. The increased emphasis on the eastern provinces and the eastern frontier areas from the fourth century onwards, and the cosmopolitanism of the population of those areas, made for a high frequency of translations between Greek and Syriac, even for practical purposes. Many literary works were also quickly translated from Greek into Syriac, a process which also happened in reverse, perhaps more often than we usually realize.[39] One result was that Syriac gained many Greek loan words and expressions, another that Greek literature in turn (we are talking of Christian works) became influenced by Syriac.

Palestine in late antiquity was also the centre of contact between the Christian and the Jewish traditions. We have seen that Constantine's Holy Land churches set in motion the transformation of Palestine into the busy centre of Christian pilgrimage (Chapter 3). In the course of the fourth and fifth centuries, Jerusalem itself was transformed from Roman colony (after the Jewish war) into Christian holy city.[40] But Christians also needed to engage with the continuing Jewish presence in Palestine, where the mass of material in Aramaic known as the Palestinian or Jerusalem Talmud (rabbinic interpretations of the earlier Hebrew Mishnah, or commentaries on the Law) was nearing completion at the start of our period.[41] Tiberias in Galilee was the centre of the rabbinic Judaism from which the Talmud appeared, and until AD 429 there were hereditary Jewish patriarchs based there, among whom Gamaliel (early fifth century) was particularly influential. However, progressive Christianization produced increasingly hostile attitudes towards the Jews on the part of Christian writers such as John Chrysostom,[42] and this trend steadily intensified and found expression in discriminatory legislation.[43] But the Jews in Palestine were still prosperous and Hellenized as late as the sixth and seventh centuries, as is shown by many magnificent synagogue mosaics, like that depicting David as Orpheus found at Gaza, or the several representations of the zodiac and Helios, as at Hammat Tiberias. Jews used both Greek and Aramaic in their funerary and other inscriptions; a very long inscription in Aramaic (fifth century) comes from Rehob, and sets out the Talmudic regulations about the land of Israel.[44] A few Christians, like Jerome, learnt Hebrew; however, Jerome himself studied the Hebrew Scriptures, which he translated afresh into Latin (the Latin Bible in use in his day had been made from the Greek translation known as the Septuagint), chiefly in order to argue against Jewish interpretations.

It is clear even from these limited examples (and similar cases could be made for many areas in the west) that cultural change in our period followed the mixing of population and settlement in given areas at least as much as it went along religious lines. The fifth and sixth centuries in the west are obviously a prime example of settlement change, while the case of Palestine in the sixth century, on the eve of the Persian and Arab invasions, also provides very clear evidence for the juxtaposition of different social and religious groups. Difficult though it is, the recent change of emphasis in archaeology towards studying the archaeology of settlement in given areas offers the best way forward for understanding cultural change in late antiquity and superseding the older models based on literary sources or simply on the preconceptions of scholars.

CHRISTIANITY AND PAGANISM

In considering the secular literature of the period it is hard to draw the line between what is classical and what is actually pagan, and indeed 'Hellene' itself became the regular Greek word for 'pagan'.[45] The distinction was also seen as a problem by Christians themselves, some of whom attacked Greek classical literature and 'Hellenes' in no uncertain terms.[46] The modern controversy about the secular Latin literature and classicizing art produced in Rome in the late fourth and early fifth centuries is also in part about a matter of definition.[47] As for the actual process of Christianization within late antique society, it took place much more slowly than is often realized. It is hard to judge the reality of religious conviction in a society from sources which are often polemical or exaggerated. It was a regular feature in Christian literature to compile catalogues of pagan cults and heresies, each with its Christian counter-argument,

Plate 9 The large refectory of the monastery of Martyrius in the Judaean desert near Jerusalem. The monastery was built in the late fifth century, but the refectory dates from a century later.

142

and this has led to a general caricature of paganism in the Christian sources. As we have seen (Chapter 3), the state officially claimed to be imposing Christianity from the reign of Theodosius I onwards; Christians were encouraged by imperial legislation to attack pagan temples and statues, and occasionally the violence was carried out by soldiers at imperial command. However, attempts to carry out the orders were often greeted with violence from the local population, and clashes could also arise from personal grievances and rivalries, as they did among the students at Alexandria in the time of Severus.[48] Well over a century after Theodosius, Justinian was still legislating against pagans and issuing laws against dissidents including heretics, Manichaeans and homosexuals, particularly those who were teachers.[49] But while Justinian certainly pursued a strongly pro-Christian policy, this legislation should also be seen in relation to the generally repressive attitude of the state in this period towards all minority groups, including, for instance, Jews and Samaritans, and it is difficult to know whether the charges are not actually political. The general situation of those who thought of opposing the government may be gauged from the fact that Procopius says at the beginning of his violently critical *Secret History* that he could only have published his work during Justinian's lifetime on pain of death. In the trials of the 580s (Chapter 3), no less a person than the patriarch of Antioch was summoned to Constantinople and charged with paganism. His close friend, Anatolius, the provincial governor, was suspected of involvement with pagan cult in Edessa, and the affair developed to include suicide, murder and an icon concealing an image of Apollo. The trials eventually took place in Constantinople to the accompaniment of popular rioting against the leniency of the Emperor Tiberius and the patriarch Eutychius, after which Anatolius, the former governor, was thrown to the beasts in the Hippodrome, then impaled and finally his body was torn apart by wolves (Evagrius, *HE* V.18; cf. John of Ephesus, *HE* III.27–35, V.37).[50] The reign of Justinian had also seen a hardening of Byzantine attitudes towards Jews and Samaritans, especially after major Samaritan revolts in AD 529 and 555; in the latter the proconsul of Palestine was killed. Predictably, during the affair in AD 579 the hunt was extended to include Jews, Samaritans and Montanists.

How genuine these charges were is hard to establish. But though paganism certainly offered a convenient handle for a political or personal attack, the sources generally suggest that in the east until a late date many people of all ranks did retain a good many beliefs and practices of pagan origin along with their Christianity. By no means every temple had been converted into a church when John of Ephesus, the future church historian, was sent in AD 542 on his evangelizing mission to western Asia Minor.[51] It seems that in the west, with its different history, paganism was less persistent except in the countryside, which underlines its connection in the east with the as yet unbroken tradition of classical education and culture. But even in the countryside, western bishops like Caesarius of Arles in the early sixth century placed a very high priority on evangelization, which suggests that the battle was by no means won.[52]

Gauging the end of ancient paganism is not an easy matter, when so many of our sources are Christian. However, the concern of preachers and government alike for the eradication of pagan practice is a striking feature of the period, from John Chrysostom in Constantinople at the turn of the fourth and fifth centuries to the acts of the late seventh-century Council in Trullo which are still concerned with the subject. One persistent theme which recurs in so many different kinds of Christian texts that it must correspond to real life is the tendency to believe in fate and especially in astrology; we may guess that in fact large numbers of the population, then as now, simultaneously harboured sets of quite contradictory beliefs, as indeed is indicated in the stories of cures by healing saints and by the many surviving amulets from this period.[53] Though Cyril Mango is right to emphasize that the Byzantine thought-world owed more to 'a construct of the Christian and Jewish apologists built up in the first five or six centuries A.D.' than to any real conception of classical culture,[54] nevertheless he probably underestimates the persistence of pagan ideas and practice, though these are of course not necessarily to be identified with 'classical' ideas. It is no easier to assess the actual contribution of Christianization to the evolution of classical antiquity into a medieval world,[55] or, in particular, to decide whether Christianization was the reason for or the result of other changes in the social fabric.

PRIVATE LIFE

We have already discussed the spread of ascetic practices, and the respect that was given to Christian holy men and women (Chapter 3). Even if we take the figures given for monks and ascetics in Egypt with a degree of scepticism, the number of men and women in the empire as a whole who had dedicated themselves to the religious life must have amounted to thousands by the fifth century, and some coenobitic monasteries were very large, holding over 200 monks.[56] Although the general principles of ascetic life were also shared by some pagans, notably Neoplatonists, they had no such monasteries, and belonged on the whole to élite groups in society; their numbers were therefore in comparison very limited. It is also difficult to know how widely the ideals of monastic and ascetic life were shared in society generally. One feature which is striking, however, is the interest in biography – lives of Christian and, in some cases pagan, individuals. Even if idealized and presented within the framework of literary and religious cliché, these works signalled an increase in the attention given to individuals, and early Christianity has been seen as indicative of a new emphasis in this direction.[57] The advance of Christianization also brought changes in attitudes to the dead. Whereas under Roman law there had been a strict prohibition on burial inside cities, many Christians were now buried in and around the great basilicas themselves, as we know from the many simple mosaic inscriptions which recorded them, while many monasteries, like that of Euthymius in the Judaean desert, incorporated the tomb of their founder and a charnel house for the monks themselves.

Social and religious change also had economic implications: after Constantine removed the existing legislation which laid down penalties for members of the upper class who did not marry, celibacy became a serious option even for the rich, when it could have profound and disturbing effects on inheritance and distribution of wealth. Jerome's successful efforts to promote an extreme ascetic ethos among the daughters of the Roman aristocracy in the late fourth century are well known, and caused natural resentment in the parts of their circle that were still pagan.[58] But perhaps the commonest form of renunciation for this class, however, came when a married couple who had produced one or two children to ensure the family inheritance, decided subsequently to abstain from sexual relations and sell their property for the benefit of the church. For Paulinus, who became bishop of Nola in Campania, and who took this step with his wife in the early fifth century, we have a good deal of detailed evidence in his own letters and other contemporary sources; but the most sensational case was undoubtedly that of the Younger Melania (so-called to distinguish her from her equally pious grandmother of the same name) and her husband

Pinianus, who sold their colossal estates *c.* AD 410, against the wishes of her father Valerius Publicola, when she was only 20 and he 24. Melania and Pinianus had properties literally all over the Roman world;

> when they acquired several islands, they gave them to holy men. Likewise, they purchased monasteries of monks and virgins and gave them as a gift to those who lived there, furnishing each place with a sufficient amount of gold. They presented their numerous and expensive silk clothes at the altars of churches and monasteries. They broke up their silver, of which they had a great deal, and made altars and ecclesiastical treasures from it, and many other offerings to God.
>
> (Clark, *Life of Melania*, 19)

It was not quite a matter of giving one's all directly to the poor;[59] all the same, the sheer scale of the renunciation is extraordinary. Melania, who is said to have made it clear that she did not wish to marry or have sexual relations, had been forced to give way and had given birth to two children; when both died in infancy her ascetic wishes finally prevailed. She owned estates in Spain, Africa, Mauretania, Britain, Numidia, Aquitaine and Gaul, several of them having hundreds of slaves, and her estate near Thagaste is said to been bigger than the town itself. In this way the literal adoption of asceticism at the top ranks of society caused a sharp break with existing social practice, and (even though much of the senatorial class still at this time remained pagan) a considerable disruption of family and inheritance. Though we lack the quantitative evidence, the growth of monasticism must also have had its effect on the structure of the family; it provided an acceptable alternative to marriage, and played a major role in the redistribution of wealth.[60]

How far individual renunciation really redistributed wealth towards the poorer classes is less easy to judge. Yet even after we have allowed for the undoubted and spectacular enrichment of the institutional church, the development of Christian almsgiving and social welfare is one of the major features of the period, and took the form not merely of alms distribution, but also of the building and maintenance of charitable establishments such as hospitals and old people's homes. Christian charity, which in some senses replaced classical euergetism (civic endowments) – though the latter still continued in some cases – had very different objects and mechanisms.[61]

As we know from modern society, changes in sexual practice are among the hardest things to judge with any accuracy. In the ancient world, from which we mostly lack personal sources such as private letters or diaries,[62] quite apart from any kind of statistics, the problem is doubly difficult. The goings-on in Merovingian royal circles, recorded, for example, by Gregory of Tours, make it clear that Christianity made little difference to the morals of that court at least, except perhaps when a bold bishop dared to intervene. As for society in general, it is hard to know whether the general approval given to asceticism really made an impact on the sexual lives of the majority. While many sermons exhorted Christians to sexual continence, it would be natural to assume that (like the many sermons addressed to the continuance of pagan or Jewish practices) there was in practice a gap between what was claimed by the preacher and the real situation. It would be dangerous, however, to conclude that they had no effect at all, and the large number of contemporary saints' lives testifies to the widespread approval for these attitudes, as well as themselves providing many individual examples.[63] This does not mean of course that existing sexual practice changed dramatically in all, or even in many cases. Only inscriptions can give much statistical information about family size in the ancient world (and even these are deceptive, for we rarely have a large enough statistical sample). On this basis a recent study concludes that there was no real difference between pagan and Christian families. It is interesting to find that among the better-off classes, which were able to afford funerary monuments, a family size comparable with the modern nuclear family seems to have been the norm. The church condemned contraception with a vehemence that suggests that it was seen as widely practised, but there were other means of reduction in family size, including the sale of infants and infanticide by exposure, a long-established practice in the ancient world.[64]

It would be a great mistake to romanticize marriage or family life in the late empire by introducing modernist assumptions – for most people, it remained both brutal and fundamentally asymmetrical, as can be seen from Augustine's discussion of the role of the father in the *City of God*, where what is emphasized above all is the power relation in which he stood towards the rest of the household, starting with his wife (*Civ. Dei* 19.16).[65] Life expectancy remained short, especially for women of child-bearing age, and infant mortality was high, while the methods available for limitation of families (not necessarily with the consent of the mother) were crude and painful. As for children, they are still the forgotten people in ancient sources, and it is not much easier to find evidence about their lives than it is in earlier periods. This does not mean that individuals did not care about the children, but it does mean that children themselves were still given a low priority in the written record, a fact which is significant in itself. The Gospel sayings about children (see Matt. 19.14) lagged far behind those about rich and poor in their actual social effect.

Yet even on a minimalist view the drain of individuals and resources from family control to the church in its various forms clearly did have a profound effect on society. Even if in an individual case a family did not send one of its members to the monastic life or change its sexual habits sufficiently sharply to reduce the level of procreation, it probably did, if it was rich enough, make gifts to the local church, and these themselves could be on a lavish scale. Perhaps more important than the practical results of these ideas in individual cases was the degree of moral and social control which the church now claimed over individual lives, and which began to show for example in restrictions on marriage within permitted degrees.[66] Christianization may not have changed the hearts of individuals as much as has often been thought, but there were important ways in which it did claim to control the outward pattern of their lives.

WOMEN[67]

Christianity did however have the effect of bringing women into the public sphere. They could travel to the Holy Land, found monasteries, learn Hebrew, choose not to marry or to become celibate, dedicate themselves to the religious life and form friendships with men outside their own family circle, all things which would scarcely have been possible before. In contrast, we might remember, nearly all Christian slaves and *coloni* remain among the great mass of unknown ancient people, whom nobody wrote about. When the alternative was probably a life of drudgery or boredom, asceticism offered at least the illusion of personal choice. No one will try to maintain that women's status or freedom dramatically improved – indeed, as they were also seen as the repository of sexual temptation, much of the theological literature of the period has a distinctly misogynistic tone;[68] but no attempt was made to deny women's equal access to holiness, and, in some circles, male–female friendships became possible in ways hard to imagine in pagan society.[69] It is a notable feature of late antique Christian literature that it begins to give attention to women in a way that would have been hard to imagine in the classical past. Gregory of Nyssa's *Life* of his sister Macrina is such a well-known saint's life from the late fourth century that one tends to forget how remarkable it actually is in having a woman for its subject.[70] Like the poor, women became a subject of attention. Inevitably, we know most about upper-class Christian ladies like Melania the Younger, Jerome's friend Paula and her daughters, or the deaconess Olympias, the friend of John Chrysostom. In view of Jerome's awkward temperament it is touching to see that Paula, Fabiola and Eustochium were buried alongside him at Bethlehem, for it had been foretold that

> the lady Paula, who looks after him, will die first and be set free at last from his meanness. [For] because of him no holy person will live in those parts. His bad temper would drive out even his own brother.
> (Palladius, *Lausiac History* 36.6–7, trans. Meyer; cited by P. Brown, *The Body and Society*, New York, 1987, 378)

Women such as these were indeed not typical, yet such lives would not have been possible at all in a previous age.[71] For most, it was more a matter of attitude than of real change in lifestyle, and even here the range of possibilities was defined in an extremely narrow way. Against the apparent broadening of opportunities ran the fact that precisely during this period the Virgin Mary emerged as a major figure of cult and worship. The direct reasons may have been Christological (Chapters 1 and 3), but the emergence of her cult carried powerful symbolic messages for women: whereas Eve represented woman's sinfulness and potential to corrupt, Mary stood for her purity, demonstrated by virginity and total obedience.[72] This development in the cult of the Virgin, especially around the time of the Council of Ephesus (AD 431), was preceded by an increasingly strident advocacy of virginity itself by many of the late fourth-century Fathers; this, too, while not confined to women, tended to be presented in terms of the woman's traditional image as seductress.[73] Since, as in most societies before and since, men still represented rationality, while women were defined in terms of their sexual identity, it is hardly surprising if the price of a degree of freedom for women was the denial of their sexuality. This was an ideal which was certainly also carried out in practice, as we

149

see from the legendary female saints like Mary of Egypt, who concealed their sex altogether and dressed as men, usually to be revealed as female only on their deathbeds.[74]

Close study of the large amount of legislation on marriage and other matters affecting women from Constantine to Justin II (AD 565–78) reveals both continuities and changes. Women are still seen as essentially dependent and in need of protection, their status is strictly subordinate to that of their husbands and their legal access is limited. The great bulk of Roman law affecting individuals was little changed by Christianization, and indeed much of it was re-enacted by the Christian emperors. But new legislation also concerned itself with the protection of public morality, and especially with the protection of chastity; it became much more difficult for a woman to initiate divorce, and obstacles were put in the way of remarriage; from Constantine onwards a succession of laws penalized women far more strictly than men for initiating unjustified divorce proceedings, until in AD 548 Justinian equalized the penalties. Even under the Christian emperors, however, marriage itself remained a civil and not a religious affair. On the other hand, the rights and obligations of mothers over their children were considerably strengthened, especially by Justinian, to whom the largest body of relevant legislation belongs, and all of whose innovations were actually in the direction of improving the legal position of women.[75] The actual role of Christianization in bringing about such change is, however, far from clear; the law was changing during this period, certainly, but the motivation for those changes is another matter. Perhaps the most striking feature remains simply the amount of attention given in imperial legislation to matters concerning women; this is important enough in itself.

Thus the ways in which women could enter the public sphere, though they existed for a few, were still strictly limited. The pagan intellectuals Hypatia and Athenaïs, the latter the daughter of an Athenian philosopher who became empress (as Eudocia) after she had been taken up by the Emperor Theodosius' pious sister Pulcheria (Chapter 1), were equally or even more exceptional. On the other hand, within the religious sphere, on a family basis or in the religious life, women gained more status than they had had before. In this sense – women being invariably assigned to the private sphere – it might be said that private life and private values became more valued and more important in this period. In some ways the constraints on women, which were great, actually intensified, but – and this was extraordinary enough given the social environment – even within the constraints of contemporary moral and religious teaching, the inner self was not exclusively defined as male.

In many ways this was a tumultuous period, when many existing social barriers were weakened, if not actually broken. One of the most marked features of the period is clearly the progress of Christianization, which involved social change and the development of an authoritarian ideology.[76] But the fragmentation of Roman society in the west, the advent of barbarian settlement and the subsequent development of barbarian kingdoms also disturbed existing norms, though whether they brought any greater freedom is a different matter. In the eastern empire the sixth century, and especially the reign of Justinian, marked an apogee in the history of early Byzantium, with a strong emperor, powerful ministers and centralized government. At the same time, however, urban violence reached unprecedented levels (see Chapter 7), and there was much questioning of the relations of centre and periphery. The ambitious policies of Justinian brought the empire, and Justinian's successors, into difficulties which are clearly perceptible in their relations with the strong neighbouring power of Sasanian Persia in the late sixth century. Justinian was a codifier of the law and himself a legislator of unparalleled energy. But he did not succeed in achieving long-term security or internal harmony for the empire. As the next two chapters will show, the evident prosperity of parts of the eastern empire in the sixth century was not enough to preserve it from other challenges.

7

Urban change and the end of antiquity

An enormous amount has been written in recent years about towns in late antiquity. There are several reasons for this. In the first place, the development of early Byzantine archaeology, which we have noted in many contexts already, is obviously a major factor. The effects are cumulative: there is simply more material available and more highly developed techniques for assessing it. This in turn is itself cumulative – the more sites that are well excavated, the more possible it becomes to arrive at reliable diagnoses of the data in an individual case. Second, unlike the medieval world, the civilization and high culture of classical antiquity, and thus also of the Roman empire, rested on a network of cities. The end of classical antiquity thus seems to imply the end of classical cities, and vice versa. Third, there is also a special factor so far as the eastern empire is concerned: Byzantinists have for the last generation or so been engaged in a controversy of their own about the extent to which cities in the eastern empire disappeared during the seventh century, and thus whether or not there was a more or less complete break or disconti- nuity between medieval Byzantium and its classical roots.[1] Finally, urbanism and urban history together constitute a major subject of interest in historical studies generally. These various motivations together have contributed to a huge outpouring of work on the subject in recent years, the results of which we must now try to assess.

TOWN AND COUNTRY – SURVEY ARCHAEOLOGY

While on the whole in the Roman empire the maintenance of culture, government and fiscality depended on cities, the proportion of the population that worked on the land was extremely high, and the proportion of overall revenues that derived from the land was even higher. Only a very few ancient cities were large by modern standards, and most were extremely small. The population of Constantinople at its height in the sixth century may have reached half a million; that of Rome, perhaps more than a million under Augustus, had declined considerably by the later Roman period and was further reduced during the Gothic wars of Justinian;[2] in the east, only Antioch and Alexandria came anywhere near these two. Thus the countryside accounted for by far the greatest mass of the population, and, through agricultural production, contributed the basis of most of the empire's wealth. Even if trade, or rather, production, was somewhat more important in the global economic equation than has sometimes been thought (Chapter 4), the land continued to provide the economic base; and cities on the whole, rather than being primary centres of production themselves, continued to depend on their rural hinterland for their economic well being.[3] Furthermore, in recent archaeological and economic studies increasing attention has in fact been given to country as well as city, partly under the influence of the relatively new technique of survey archaeology, in which excavation is not undertaken but all surface finds are picked up and recorded over a given geographical area.[4] A number of major surveys have been conducted in widely separated regions, which focus on a given area and include all surface remains, thus taking a broad chronological sweep which can allow insights into diachronic change not possible on the basis of other evidence. The evidence thus produced may of course be much more informative for one period than for another, and there are some basic methodological problems inherent in all such surveys; nevertheless, some have produced important evidence for late antiquity. Among recent such surveys are, for instance, for Italy, the South Etruria surveys,[5] for Spain, the Guadalcuivir survey, an aerial photography project for north-east France,[6] for North Africa, the UNESCO Libyan valleys survey and the important work of P. Leveau on Caesarea and its hinterland in modern Algeria[7] and for Greece the surveys in Boeotia, Melos and Methana.[8] In northern Syria the pioneering work of G. Tchalenko long dominated the field, together with his attribution of the prosperity observable in the substantial architecture of the large villages on the limestone massif to an olive monoculture.[9] More recently, French scholars working in Syria have produced an important preliminary study of the Hauran,[10] and a good deal of work has been done in modern Jordan and Israel, especially the Golan heights and the Negev, where settlement reached a peak in the late antique period.[11] Studies of this kind focusing on Palestine and Syria are particularly important in assessing population movement and for judging the state of these areas on the eve of the Arab conquests; they will be discussed in more detail in Chapter 8.

The veritable deluge of information from here and elsewhere (much more such work is currently going on or is still unpublished) opens up many exciting possibilities, but at the same time presents some major difficulties. It is tempting to use it at once in order to draw general pictures of what was happening in a wider province or area, and many such attempts have already been made.[12] But survey work can yield misleading results, for a variety of reasons, which include the simple ones of the actual difficulty of identification of some kinds of sherds and the possible intervention of pure chance in accounting for certain 'assemblages' (the technical term for the range of materials found). Recognition of these dangers is making some archaeologists more cautious in interpreting their finds, and adds to the difficulties which historians experience in using survey publications. It is obviously extremely difficult in any case to keep up with the latest situation in such a fast-moving field, and what is written on this basis runs the risk of running out of date very quickly. It is also difficult to gain access to all the publications, which tend to be very scattered and often in obscure journals or archaeological reports. But the impact of this work is very great, particularly in certain geographical areas, and the very fact that so much has been done and is still going on means that a history of the later Roman empire in the old style is simply inadequate for today. One of the major disadvantages of studying ancient history has always been the paucity of the available evidence, and especially the lack of documentary sources. 'Total' history in the sense in which the term was used by the French *Annales* school, that is, history which takes in all the long-term and underlying structures and considers every kind of evidence, material as well as textual, will never be possible for the ancient world by comparison with the early modern and modern periods; but the prospect has come much nearer than anyone would have expected.

LIMITATIONS AND STRENGTHS OF
ARCHAEOLOGICAL EVIDENCE

Though studies of individual towns in conjunction with their rural hinterland mark a valuable first step,[13] we are hindered by the fact that the sites for which an integrated treatment of texts and material evidence is possible remain relatively few. Where urban sites are concerned, all sorts of practical constraints dictate the course of archaeological work, especially the extent of subsequent settlement. Many major late antique cities will never be excavated simply because they have been the site of continuous settlement ever since the ancient period. On such a site, the traces of the late antique and medieval city may now be barely visible. For similar reasons, in many other cases only small parts can be excavated. This is the case with Constantinople itself.[14] Though excavations took place in the Great Palace area as early as the 1930s, the layout of the palace in its different phases has to be largely reconstructed from difficult textual evidence. Further excavation has taken place in and near the Hippodrome and on the site of the great church of St Polyeuktos built by Anicia Juliana in the early years of Justinian's reign, and the city walls have received attention too, but the fact that much work otherwise has concentrated on individual churches indicates another important factor operative in determining the nature of archaeological research, namely the motivation for selection of sites. This has often been dictated in our period by the intense interest shown in churches or in Byzantine mosaic decoration. Carthage, on the other hand, provides an example of an important late antique city where major excavation was prompted in the 1970s by the threat of development ('rescue archaeology') and undertaken on an international scale by UNESCO. During the Islamic period the centre of settlement moved to nearby Tunis, and ancient Carthage is now part of a residential suburb. Systematic excavation over a large area was therefore impossible, but teams from several different countries were assigned specific areas within the ancient urban complex. Their interests and priorities were not however identical, and some of the sites themselves yielded material rich in one particular period and less so in others. Taken together, their results have nevertheless been extremely important in a number of ways (Chapter 4). Even so there are still many gaps, and no complete picture of the late antique city can yet emerge. Indeed, one of the objects of the excavators was to determine the actual extent of settlement in particular parts of the city.

155

Thus in the nature of things archaeological evidence can supplement the historical record and add important new evidence otherwise unknown. A spectacular example of what can be shown by epigraphic evidence is provided by Aphrodisias in Caria (southwest Turkey), a city only sparsely attested in literary sources, but which has yielded an astonishing amount of evidence, chiefly from its abundant inscriptions, about urban development and city life in late antiquity.[15] Since it was a major centre of sculpture, drawing on famous marble quarries, it has also turned up a mass of splendid finished and half-finished late antique sculpture which is extremely important not only in the context of Aphrodisias itself but also for wider issues of iconography and style. Some of this evidence, like the literary evidence for the families of Paralius and Asclepiodotus already noted (Chapter 6), tells us much about the survival of pagan and classical culture in a provincial town; this is especially true of the striking series of sculptured heads of late antique philosophers only recently published.[16] Finally, many Greek inscriptions also survive from Aphrodisias, through which we can trace the efflorescence of Greek verse inscriptions and thus the availability of training for this specialized literary accomplishment in the fifth-century east.[17] These are only some of the results of the important excavations conducted at Aphrodisias over a thirty-year period to date. In particular, the inscriptions of Aphrodisias give us a virtually unbroken record of urban history from its acquisition of the status of free and federate city during the Triumviral period to its change of name in the early seventh century from Aphrodisias (city of Aphrodite) to Stauropolis (city of the Cross) and its survival as a shadow of its former self through the eighth and ninth centuries, when sources are almost absent, to undergo some rebuilding like other Byzantine sites in the tenth and eleventh centuries. As we have seen, though Aphrodisias is an important centre for our knowledge of late paganism, here too a temple was converted into a church, perhaps in the fifth century.[18]

Aphrodisias provides an example of an individual site with an extraordinarily rich and spectacular amount of archaeological remains, including sculptural and epigraphic material of breathtaking quality and importance.[19] A good many of the later inscriptions are undatable, largely because their conventional language and style remained so constant over the period. Even so, it is possible here, as it rarely is elsewhere, to piece together a real, if incomplete, view of changing patterns in city life in the late antique period. As we shall see, some other sites offer this possibility too, each in its own way, among them Ephesus in Asia Minor and Apamea in Syria.[20] But even apparently clear archaeological evidence can be difficult to interpret. There may for instance be no external dating indicators, such as coins or inscriptions, and the stratigraphy and pottery dating may be unreliable. In particular, archaeological evidence can only tell us *what* happened, not why it happened. It is very tempting, in the absence of specific indications, to link certain sorts of archaeological evidence to historical factors or events known from other sources. We have a particular instance of this in our period in that many of the late Roman fortifications in the Balkans cannot be dated from the material evidence alone. Since Procopius' *Buildings* tells us about Justinian's massive building programme in those areas, it is therefore always tempting to suppose a given site to be Justinianic; yet closer study of the *Buildings* reveals that Procopius often exaggerates or misrepresents the nature and extent of Justinian's building programme. Some recent studies have suggested that many of these structures may in fact have been built by Anastasius and only refurbished by Justinian, if that.[21] But Procopius' statements vary in credibility, and some are confirmed by other evidence, so that we cannot simply take the easy way out and be uniformly sceptical. A further illustration of the range of problems encountered is provided by the plentiful evidence for earthquakes in the late antique and early Byzantine period, for it can be fatally easy to attribute damage to material remains to a convenient earthquake. However, this may fail to take into account the fact that unless the literary sources give precise details there is usually no way of knowing the scale of the earthquake, which may well have been a mere tremor. In any case, as archaeologists are well aware, such a connection is not fact and can only remain on the level of hypothesis.[22] Finally, even when major earthquakes are known to have taken place, they have in most historical periods proved a stimulus to rebuilding, often on a large scale, as indeed can be seen in the case of Antioch in our period.

THE 'DECLINE OF CITIES' AND THE END OF CLASSICAL ANTIQUITY

With this growth in archaeological investigation, the problem of late antique or early Byzantine cities, which was formerly posed in theoretical and ideological terms,[23] can be rephrased in terms of 'urban change'. In simple terms, if we put together the evidence from archaeological investigation of sites very widely scattered round the Mediterranean, a general picture seems to emerge of contraction, and of characteristic shifts in urban topography. There is plenty of evidence from widely different regions to suggest that significant urban change was already taking place before the end of the sixth century.[24] But the picture is not uniform, and much of the evidence is still emerging. There is unlikely to be a single or simple cause, even if in individual cases particular local factors may be plausibly adduced. Rather, we are in the presence of deep-seated social and economic change, which seems to have been taking place all round the Mediterranean by the end of this period. The rest of this chapter will investigate the process in more detail.

THE NATURE OF LATE ANTIQUE TOWNS

Here it will for once be useful to use the term 'late antique' in a particular sense, to denote the towns of late antiquity before this process of change had taken serious hold. The model is still the typical provincial city of the Principate, with its Roman architecture, its public buildings, baths, theatre, temples, forum, broad colonnaded streets and perhaps also its circus or amphitheatre – Aphrodisias in its heyday provides a good example.[25] These are cities planned for public life and well equipped for the leisure of their well-to-do citizens, the members of the curial class, who were also the city's benefactors.[26] With the coming of the fourth century the upkeep of the cities had become more difficult and building had slowed down, but the arrangement of public space remained much as it had been. Indeed, such cities seemed the embodiment of culture. Procopius describes in panegyrical terms the founding of a new city at the spot where Belisarius' expedition landed in North Africa, and where, he claims, a miraculous spring had gushed forth to give them water just when they needed it; with the building of a town wall and all the accoutrements of a city, the rural population of the headland henceforth adopted civilized manners and lived like men of culture: 'the rural people have cast aside their ploughshares and live like city-dwellers, exchanging their rural lifestyle for civilization' (*Buildings* VI.6.15, cf. *Vandal Wars* I.15.31ff.). Elsewhere Procopius lists among the standard attributes of a city, stoas, a bath, an aqueduct and lodgings for magistrates (*Buildings* V.2.1–5, Helenopolis in Bithynia).[27] This view was already archaic when

Procopius wrote. It was an urban style which had required public and private investment, both to build and to maintain its public buildings. It also implied a life of cultured leisure, if only for the richer citizens, with a range of public activity, in the forum, at the baths, at the circus, while in the Roman period its temples characteristically looking out over the forum implied the survival of paganism.

THE CHANGING CITY

Justinian built such a city at his own birthplace in Illyricum, named Justiniana Prima and generally identified with Caricin Grad (50 km south of Nish) – or so Procopius claims, for his account is even vaguer than it is for the new city on the African coast, simply listing some of the standard elements noted above (*Buildings* IV.1.19–27). But urban life in the Balkans had been sharply interrupted by the Hun and Ostrogothic invasions, and Anastasius' and Justinian's programmes of restoration and fortification were mainly palliative.[28] Despite Procopius' claims, it seems that there was little real urban life in these settlements in the sixth century, and building and signs of culture begin to dry up together. This is the picture at Stobi in the former Yugoslavia and at Nicopolis and Philippopolis in Bulgaria.[29] Things were also difficult in Greece, where late sources suggest that in the late sixth century some cities, including ancient Sparta, Argos and Corinth, were abandoned by their inhabitants in favour of safer places. Archaeological and other evidence does not always confirm this over-simplified picture, but it does seem that the pattern of urban settlement was changing significantly during the later sixth and seventh centuries. At Corinth, the remaining population retreated to the fortified height of Acrocorinth, which became typical of Byzantine settlements in Greece. This impression of a search for places of refuge is reinforced in many sites in the former Yugoslavia and the Balkans, where inhabited centres contracted and regrouped around a defensible acropolis, or were abandoned in favour of such positions elsewhere. The early Byzantine walls at Sparta, as elsewhere, enclosed only the ancient acropolis and not the civic centre; it was presumably hoped that they would provide a place of refuge for the population in time of attack.[30] This then is one sort of urban change which can be seen in a variety of places, and for which the obvious explanation is that it was prompted by danger of raids or invasion. The late *Chronicle of*

Monemvasia connects the move of population in Greece explicitly with the Slav invasions of the 580s, but the extent of Slav invasion is highly contentious and exact dates difficult to establish.[31] According to this source the population of Lakedaimon, ancient Sparta, settled at Monemvasia, a rocky crag on the east coast of the Peloponnese, very hard of access; but the actual date of the foundation of Monemvasia is extremely obscure, and Lakedaimon remained inhabited in the Byzantine period. The general phenomenon of population movement, if it happened in this way, was probably more gradual, and a number of different factors may have been operative in bringing it about, including possibly a shift in economic activity.[32] Athens itself was not occupied by the Slavs, but it suffered invasion by Slavs and Avars in about AD 582, which shows clearly in the coin evidence, and which caused considerable destruction by fire. Although it was used as a base against the Slavs by the Emperor Constans II in AD 662–3, new building, if any, was 'shoddy', involving subdivision into smaller rooms and the use of former fine buildings as sites for olive-presses. Similar phenomena are also encountered frequently in North Africa, and at the village of Olympos in Attica, for instance, such reuse involved a former baptistery.[33]

The last two features, subdivision and 'encroachment' on the sites of former grand buildings, can be seen in different forms in many other regions. Typically, the grand houses, maintained in many areas into the sixth century or even later, are divided into smaller rooms for multiple dwelling, often with mudbrick floors over or instead of the splendid mosaics which are so characteristic of the fine houses. This can be vividly seen at Carthage, where a large peristyle house (built round a courtyard in classical style) in the 'Michigan sector' was subdivided into much poorer accommodation by the seventh century, and where the same smaller divisions appear on the Canadian and British sites. At Apamea, peristyle houses were restored after the capture of the city by the Persians in AD 573, and apparently maintained until the Arab conquest.[34] But elsewhere 'encroachment', either by poorer dwellings or, commonly, by small traders and artisans, frequently occurs over existing public spaces, such as the late antique forum or, as at Anemurium in southern Turkey, on the site of the palaestra.[35] In the latter case this change of use had started early, after the disruption to the city caused by Persian invasion in the third century, and the artisanal activity in the area apparently flourished; but by the late sixth and seventh centur-

Plate 10 An olive-press astride a former main street, Sbeitla, Tunisia, probably seventh-century.

ies the other civic amenities such as baths and aqueducts were no longer functioning. A particularly striking example of 'encroachment' is found at Sbeitla in modern Tunisia, where an olive-press, perhaps seventh-century, sits right on top of the former main street.

The presence of burials within central areas of the town, and even on the sites of earlier fine housing or public buildings is another common feature at Carthage and other North African sites in this period, indicating a major shift in attitudes towards urban space. It is tempting to think in terms of economic necessity, 'squatting' and, where there is some textual evidence to support the idea, as at Carthage, of an influx of refugees from invasion in other areas. Local factors will also have been important, for instance at Luni near La Spezia on the west coast of Italy, where the decline of the marble trade from nearby Carrara must have affected the town, and where, though it survived into the seventh century, a clear decline in material wealth can be seen from at least the sixth century. Local conditions differed: some of the major cities of Asia Minor, Ephesus and Sardis, for example, which had enjoyed a period of prosperity and expansion in late antiquity, seem to have maintained late antique civic life until the Persian invasions of the early seventh century.[36] But the phenomena of encroachment and change of use are themselves so widespread, even if the pace varies in different places, that it seems clear that a widespread process of urban change was going on, and that this must be connected not only with particular causes such as the plague (see pp. 111, 164) or invasion, but also with overall administrative and economic factors, above all the relation of provincial cities to the central administrative organization. Antioch in Syria, for instance, the second city of the eastern empire, was hard hit by plague, earthquake and Persian invasion in the mid-sixth century, followed by the deportation of many of its citizens to Persia, not to mention the seventh-century invasions and the Arab conquest. Some of the phenomena at Antioch can be paralleled in other eastern cities, such as Laodicea and Damascus, where perhaps the most characteristic feature is the encroachment over the colonnaded streets of late antiquity by little shops or artisanal buildings, which one is tempted to read as the prototype of the medieval souk.[37] Clearly in this part of the empire the question arises of what this 'medieval' development owed to the Islamic conquest. The eastern provinces will be discussed further in Chapter 8; so far as this phenomenon is concerned, however, it is increasingly clear that it was part of a wider process already going on over a much bigger geographical area, despite influential local variants.

INTERPRETING URBAN CHANGE

As suggested above, archaeological evidence is often difficult to interpret and, in particular, difficult to link directly with historical events. But in some cases, as in the case of street building at Caesarea in Palestine, there was still considerable activity going on in the later sixth century, and Justinian's building programme undoubtedly included some spectacular achievements, such as the great Nea church at Jerusalem, shown on the sixth-century mosaic map of the city from Madaba in Jordan. In this case, excavation dramatically and unexpectedly confirmed the accuracy of Procopius' description (*Buildings* V.6.1).[38] Major building work also took place in a number of Near Eastern cities after the middle of the sixth century, among them Gerasa (Jerash) in Transjordan, and some magnificent floor mosaics from churches in the area date from the seventh and even the eighth centuries.[39]

The arguments are certainly not easy to balance. It is partly a question of what indicators one uses: Whittow, for instance, argues for the prosperity of Edessa (Urfa, south-east Turkey) in the sixth century from the large sums of gold paid to Chosroes I in AD 540 and 544 (Chapter 5), and the quantities of silver in the city when it was captured by the Persians in AD 609.[40] But a study of settlement patterns in the region provides a control, from which it appears that while settlement density reached an unprecedented peak from the fourth to the sixth centuries, from the seventh century there was a dramatic fall in occupation.[41] This should serve as a caution both against separating urban history from that of settlement in the same area, and against relying too much on one kind of evidence. Edessa did indeed continue as an urban centre through the Islamic period, until the Byzantine recovery in the tenth century, but the silver it possessed in the sixth century does not tell us very much about the general distribution of wealth or about urbanism as such; moreover, evidence suggestive of 'decline' may sometimes in fact indicate population movement for other reasons. Complex readjustments seem to have been taking place in many areas, which involved rural and urban sites and their mutual relationships. There are, moreover, serious gaps in our knowledge due both to the accident of excavation sites and to the lack of certain sorts of evidence. For reasons of local settlement, little may survive of a phase known to have been a prosperous city. Such is the case with the Roman settlement on the central tell at Pella (Fihl) in Jordan, which was largely destroyed by very extensive late Roman building.[42] Casual information from good textual sources such as the *Life of Symeon the Fool* (for Emesa/Homs, seventh century, but referring to the sixth century),[43] the *Miracles of St Demetrius* (early seventh century, Thessaloniki)[44] or the *Life and Miracles of Theodore Tiro* (eighth century, Euchaita, Helenopontus)[45] sometimes belies any general theory of urban decline. Even more important to remember is the fact that the picture is literally changing all the time as new evidence comes to light and theories have to be revised. Many excavations on major sites are still continuing, and the season's work can and does frequently overturn previous results – the important site of Pella is a case in point. Finally, a reliable ceramic typology for the Near East is only now beginning to be agreed. But it also seems likely that there was much more regional variation than previously supposed, in particular in the eastern provinces.

How far it is possible to generalize, even within these limitations, let alone across the Mediterranean, is obviously very questionable. Yet some general causes of change can be suggested. One of them is the plague which hit Constantinople and Asia Minor in the mid-sixth century and which continued to strike Syria in successive waves throughout the seventh century. The effects are certainly hard to quantify (see Chapter 5), but it is hard not to think that plague must have been a factor in undermining the generally thriving state of cities in the Near East in the early part of the sixth century. Since neither epigraphic nor papyrological sources offer clear evidence of the scale of mortality, and one can make only a general connection between urban and settlement decline and the factor of plague, it is dangerous to use the plague of AD 542 as a dating reference in the absence of other evidence. On the other hand, arguments which seek to downplay its effects in relation to individual sites must logically be equally suspect.[46] Historians vary sharply in the amount of weight that they are willing to attach to the sixth- and seventh-century plague. Yet the fact remains that this seems to have been the first appearance of bubonic plague in Europe; its impact must therefore have been far greater than that of the regular diseases which ravaged ancient cities as a matter of course. In just one example from the literary sources outside the three main descriptions of the epidemic, when the plague struck their monastery, the monks of the Judaean monastery of Chariton went *en masse* to the ancient holy man Cyriacus, who was living as a hermit at Sousakim, to ask for his help against the disease, and brought him to live in a cave nearby.[47] According to the literary sources, the sixth century also experienced a high incidence of earthquakes, which in some cases can be plausibly connected with the material record.[48] But this may be attributable to increased recording of earthquakes by Christian chroniclers interested in pointing out the signs of God's wrath rather than to a quantitative rise in their actual incidence. Other external factors can also be adduced for reduced prosperity in certain areas, such as the suggested withdrawal of military resources from south-east Palestine and Arabia in the early sixth century in favour of reliance on Arab allied tribes; withdrawal of garrisons would imply a lower level of economic demand in the region in the future, and poorer roads and communications.[49]

Finally, what was the role if any of Christianization in the move away from the civic life of classical antiquity, with its baths, temples and public entertainments? Again there is no simple solution. Bishops fulminated against the games and the theatre, and some objected to public baths on moral grounds. The great temples slowly and gradually went out of use – though not everywhere and not always without protest – and were often converted into churches. Even average-sized towns in the sixth century might contain far more and far larger churches than their population would seem to warrant, and these often went on being extended and altered after other forms of public building seem to have stopped, a feature which is strikingly exemplified by the large churches of Sbeitla in North Africa. The church and individual bishops gradually assumed more and more responsibility for social welfare in their communities, not only in the distribution of alms and maintenance of hospices but also by storing food and distributing it in the times of famine which were a regular feature of ancient urban life. Eutychius, the sixth-century patriarch of Constantinople, performed this service for the people of Amasea during his years of exile, and the early seventh-century patriarch of Alexandria known as John the Almsgiver acquired his epithet from his reputation for urban philanthropy. Other holy men and monks also performed similar roles: a story told about St Nicholas of Sion, near Myra in Lycia, tells how when the plague struck the metropolis of Myra in the sixth century, Nicholas was suspected of warning neighbouring farmers not to go to the city to sell their provisions for fear of infection. The governor and the city magistrates sent for the saint from his monastery, and Nicholas visited several settlements, where he slaughtered oxen and brought wine and bread with him to feed the people.[50] But while the fabric of life in both town and country had thus changed very significantly with Christianization, Christianity did not itself directly bring about urban change. Rather, by stimulating church building on the one hand and by influencing social practices on the other, it was one among a range of other factors which together converged to change and undermine the urban topography inherited from the High Empire.[51] However, the question can also be looked at in a more fundamental way, in terms of the economic role of the church, and in particular the shifting economic relation between the civic authorities and the church, which came to represent, let us say by the later sixth century, an actual shift of resources in favour of the church. As a result, the latter's agents, especially bishops, took on the role of providers and distributors of wealth which formerly lay with the civil authorities. Since the role of cities within the empire had always been closely identified with finance – exchange, monetary circulation, collection of taxes – this shift inevitably had profound consequences for their future.[52]

ECONOMY AND ADMINISTRATION OF EARLY BYZANTINE CITIES

Since the fourth century, the *curiales*, the better-off citizens on whom the government depended for the running of cities, had been complaining loudly about their increased burdens (Chapter 4). Both the chorus of complaint and the theme itself were of long standing, and those who, like the Emperor Julian, the rhetor Libanius or the historians Ammianus Marcellinus and, later, Procopius, saw themselves as champions of traditional values invariably also took up the cause of the cities whose future they perceived to be under threat. There were some grounds for their fears: government pressure on the curial class, who provided a convenient target for ways of increasing revenue or at least trying to ensure its collection, certainly increased as time went on. The city councils themselves faced financial difficulties, especially those with splendid buildings to keep up. Many found it difficult to keep their councils up to strength with enough *curiales* of adequate income.[53] But cities showed an obstinate tendency to survive, and 200 years after Constantine's legislation on decurions/*curiales* most were still in a reasonable state, while some were more densely populated and more prosperous than they had ever been (see Chapter 8). Both the rhetoric and the legal evidence can mislead, if taken too literally.

Yet the style of life which these cities had supported for so long did clearly begin to undergo a transformation towards the end of our period, and whether we are proponents of disruption or continuity, urban life was certainly drastically curtailed in the years immediately following. Deeper causes were at work besides the general pressures of invasion, insecurity, increased military expenditure by the central government, plague and so on. One such deeper cause has already been noted, namely the gradual shift of

Plate 11 The city of Scythopolis (Bet Shean), birthplace of the sixth-century monk and hagiographer Cyril of Scythopolis. Scythopolis remained a flourishing city throughout the seventh century and into the eighth.

resources away from the old-style city administration towards the church. Another relates to long-term changes in administration. The practical impact of both now needs to be explained.

First, the question of administration, which is related to the situation of the state itself, especially towards the end of the period, and which has economic implications too. The role of the imperial administration in city affairs had shown a tendency to increase even from the early empire, a trend which was naturally enhanced as revenues became harder to collect through the urban élites. Thus the fiscal needs of the state made the imposition of imperial tax officials in provincial cities a logical step, just as the unfortunate *curiales* themselves were bound by repeated legislation forbidding them to escape their responsibilities. By the sixth century the provincial governor had gained even more local authority at the expense of the city councillors, and despite attempts by the emperors to reverse the process, city councils had seriously declined. Their affairs were dealt with in practice by an official known as the 'father' of the city, who came to be chosen, significantly, not by the council but by a group on which the local landowners and *curiales* were joined by the bishop and clergy. Both John the Lydian and Evagrius, in the middle and late sixth century respectively, suggest that the councils (*curiae*) themselves no longer functioned. But surprisingly, those Roman cities which were still functioning in the west after the invasions and even after the formation of the barbarian kingdoms retained their earlier practices in the continued responsibility of *curiales* for tax collection.[54]

It is extremely difficult to assess the implication of these changes in individual cases. As Jones points out, the loss of city autonomy through the decline of councils does not necessarily mean a drop in population.[55] However, general population increase in the east, evidenced in the dense settlement of marginal land on the desert fringe, must have added to the problems of the towns, for a rise in the number of the poorer citizens will itself have brought conse-quent economic and other problems.[56] But there will have been countless individual reactions, as a result of which some *curiales* escaped into the imperial service or became senators (both of which statuses released them from their fiscal responsibilities), while others evaded the law by moving to villas in the countryside. Yet others went into the church as clergy, a process which the emperors had also tried to stop, while others, if only a few, turned to the ascetic life and renounced their property. One consequence may have been that their places were taken by the less well-off, so that the curial order overall became steadily poorer.[57] Maintenance of the curial order also depended on the continued availability of the traditional educational system. This too, as we have seen, came under attack from imperial legislation against pagans and heretics as teachers, and was no doubt undermined by the gradual process of Christianization. Taken together, these changes add up to an undermining of the traditional financial and human resources of cities and a significant change in the personnel who are taking decisions about how an individual city should be governed. If the resources are forthcoming from other directions, for instance from the bishop, the city may not be impoverished, but its fundamental nature is likely to change. The question of urban 'decline' is often posed in terms of the decline of the curial order; however, a better formulation of the issue would be to focus on the inevitable effects on urban attitudes and practice of these long-term changes in their administrative personnel. 'Decline' of cities does not follow universally from decline of the curial order, but if their government changes so significantly, cities will simply not be the same. In the eastern provinces, the seventh century saw in quick succession the severe effects of the Persian invasions, followed by the Arab conquests which deprived Byzantium of a high proportion of its territories. The same period also saw the beginning of a far more drastic and fundamental upheaval in the Byzantine administrative system generally, from which a new governing class eventually emerged, together with a military organization that was rurally based. These changes are well outside our present brief, but they do press home the lesson that whether or not there was 'continuity', the Byzantine city proper was likely to be very different from the late antique, and that the urban change of the late sixth century is best interpreted within this very long-term context.[58]

Like the 'flight of the *curiales*', the shift of resources towards the church was a process which took place on many different levels. Jones's stress on the place of clergy and monks among his celebrated 'idle mouths' who constituted a drain on the late Roman state now seems a rather crude and positivistic approach. Yet it also hints at a fundamental, if much more complicated, set of changes, among which the actual recruitment of individuals into the clergy and the monastic life (the 'idle mouths') represents only the tip of the iceberg. We must also note the increasing role played by bishops and clergy, including the *chorepiscopi* (rural bishops), in the affairs of cities and countryside alike, and in negotiations with the provincial governor; this is clearly visible already in the letters of Theodoret of Cyrrhus in northern Syria in the fifth century, where indeed villages rather than towns seem to have been the norm, while in early seventh-century Alexandria the patriarch John the Almsgiver was dealing with matters of trade and taxation alike. Then there is the question of the number and size of gifts and legacies made to churches, strikingly demonstrated in the rich silver treasures owned by small Syrian churches, which are not so much a sign of the prosperity of the region as of an economic situation in which the balance was being steadily tipped towards the church.[59] It is not a question of increased resource, but of redistribution of resource; in other words, the surplus, if any, is being spent in different ways. If this situation coincides, as seems to be the case in certain areas and in certain periods, with an actual diminution of resources, then we can realistically talk of decline. But, more fundamentally, cities begin to look different because the priorities of those who run them have changed.

We should not therefore be surprised if the rich epigraphic sources of the earlier period tail off in favour of Christian funerary inscriptions, which are by comparison disappointingly brief, or are replaced by hagiographic sources in the form of local saints' lives or miracle collections. While the latter material is often rightly viewed with suspicion by historians because of its obvious bias and its tendency to conventional exaggeration, it clearly reflects the changed point of view. Several cities in the crucial period are well provided with evidence of this sort, which shows not only that they continued as vital centres but, even more importantly, how their urban life was now articulated. One or two have already been mentioned, such as Thessaloniki in the early seventh century, known from the *Miracles of St. Demetrius*, composed by the archbishop of the city soon after AD 610; others include Seleucia in Cilicia, and late sixth-century Anastasioupolis in Galatia, known from the *Life* of Theodore of Sykeon.[60] Even having made all the necessary allowances for natural bias and rhetorical exaggeration, the picture that emerges from these and many comparable texts is of an urban life no less vital but quite different in kind and flavour from what we associate with the late antique city in the first part of the period, still with its municipal pride, its public spaces, its great buildings and its civic autonomy. Times had changed. A comparison has been made between cities at the end of our period and the decaying industrial towns of modern Britain.[61] As with all such comparisons, the differences are many, and this one perhaps suggests more change in the economic base than is actually warranted. But it also does well to highlight the fundamental change in mentality which had taken place.

URBAN VIOLENCE

These cities could be turbulent places. We have already encountered rioting in the context of religious division, especially in certain explosive urban centres such as Alexandria. When the word was given for the destruction or conversion of a temple, bishops often led the way in provoking the feelings of the crowd; the imperial authorities on the other hand are found trying to restrain such enthusiasm. In AD 400 the Emperor Arcadius wrote to the enthusiastic Bishop Porphyrius of Gaza, urging him to remember that the city was full of taxpayers as well as pagan statues.[62] Rioting in Constantinople was endemic in the fifth and sixth centuries, and in the most serious episode, the so-called Nika revolt of AD 532 (Chapter 5), the emperor himself was ready to flee, and the disturbance was put down only at the cost of great loss of life when imperial troops had been sent in under Belisarius. The immediate reasons for this episode had to do with the execution of some criminals who belonged to the circus factions, the Blues and Greens, but soon came to focus on Justinian's unpopular ministers, especially the praetorian prefect John the Cappadocian, whom the emperor hastily replaced. During the rioting much of the central area of the city was burned down, including Constantine's church of St Sophia, giving Justinian the opportunity to recover his prestige by extensive rebuilding. These are not, it should be noted, revolutionary uprisings, but short-lived explosions of violence against a highly unstable background. While religious and political issues were of course likely to be thrown up as soon as violence began, even if they had not actually triggered it off, sustained movements for religious or political reform are not in question in this period. Protests against this or that piece of imperial policy, especially if it had to do with taxation or an unpopular minister, were common in Constantinople, and similar manifestations elsewhere mimicked those of the capital, but urban violence in this period, though it was extremely common, did not turn into revolution.[63]

Nor, though Procopius liked to think that they were the work of 'rabble', were they generally speaking expressions of the feelings of the poor or the masses. Only once is a riot explicitly ascribed to the 'poor' (in AD 553, as a result of a debasement of the bronze coinage – again the emperor immediately gave way), and riots about bread or grain were relatively infrequent, thanks to the care which the authorities took to ensure the supply and keep the population quiet on this issue.[64] Apart from the prejudice shown by writers like Procopius, there is no reason to think that the better-off or middling parts of the urban population were any less given to rioting than the really poor; many episodes were sparked off by passionate enthusiasms for chariot-racing on the part of all classes, and especially by members of the 'factions' of Blues and Greens themselves, that is, the organized groups, effectively guilds, of charioteers, performers, musicians and supporters who staffed the public entertainments of late antique cities, and the wider constituency of their followers. Urban violence associated with the 'parties' became more and more frequent all over the east in the sixth century, reaching a peak with the demonstrations in many cities towards the end of the reign of the tyrant Phocas in the early seventh century (see Chapter 1). Historians have persistently supposed that this can only be explained on the assumption that the Blues and Greens were associated with particular religious or ideological standpoints, but the actual lack of evidence for such connections in any organized sense has been conclusively demonstrated by Alan Cameron (*Circus Factions*, Oxford, 1976), and the assumption rests on a misunderstanding of the dynamics of the ancient city. The Blues and Greens were not political parties, and they followed no consistent policy. Urban violence does however seem to have increased in level and frequency towards the end of the period, a phenomenon in which increased urban population must have played a major part.

But the explanation also lies at a more structural level, in the ceremony and the public theatre that are the hallmarks of urban life in late antiquity, and which had their roots very far back in the Principate. In the late antique period, not only did the emperor confront the people (and vice versa) in the Hippodrome at Constantinople; provincial governors also behaved similarly in their local setting. The great churches were the scene of similar manifestations; here too, large crowds often gathered in emotional circumstances, when passions could be easily inflamed. When rioting broke out, symbols of authority in the form of imperial or official statues, or the portraits of patriarchs and bishops, were frequently torn down or damaged. Oddly, the people, or rather, some among them, acquired a real opportunity to express their views on public occasions, which they often did by chanting acclamations of the authorities, mixed in with political messages. Chariot-racing, and the context of the hippodrome, offered an obvious physical setting, and many riots began in the circus, but theatres were also frequently the scene of such episodes. In both places a contributory factor was the highly structured festivals and performances in late antique Greek cities, in which each social and professional group had its own designated place, as was the case in the theatre at Aphrodisias.[65] A remarkable example of organized crowd control is provided by the theatre claque known at Antioch in the late fourth century, but surely not unique to Antioch: these were professional cheerleaders who could manipulate audiences to powerful effect; since local governors were also expected to attend the theatre, they were often at the claque's mercy.[66] On the other hand, enthusiasm for star performers, especially charioteers, was also a major factor: many contemporary epigrams celebrate famous charioteers, among them one of the most famous, Porphyrius, in whose honour as many as thirty-two are known. Two great statue bases survive, inscribed with these epigrams; they were erected, side by side with many other monuments, on the *spina* of the Hippodrome in Constantinople, round which the chariots raced.[67] To mark special feats, Porphyrius and his rivals might be commemorated in statues made of silver, gold, silver and bronze or gold and bronze, the gifts of their loyal fans, the Blues and Greens.[68] Unfortunately the statues themselves have not survived, but the peak of such commemoration, to judge from the surviving evidence, was reached under Justinian. The theatre at Aphrodisias remained in use in the sixth century, as is clear from the factional inscriptions, but early in the seventh century the stage building collapsed and was not repaired, and already a wall-painting of the archangel Michael shows that at least part of the building was being differently used.[69] Alan Cameron suggests that increasing financial difficulties are likely thereafter to have made the continued maintenance of chariot-racing difficult. Procopius typically complains that Justinian closed down theatres, hippodromes and circuses so as to save money (*Secret History*, 26.8–9).[70] But while this fits other indications, such as the fact that the circus at Carthage seems to have gone out of use during the sixth century, the true explanation is likely to have been more complex.

The early Byzantine city was thus a place of continual public confrontation, and the frequent mentions of rioting in our sources suggest that it was highly unstable. But perhaps we should put urban riots in the same historiographical category as earthquakes: they are commonly recorded, but we have no very accurate way of judging their intensity except where the information happens to be especially detailed. Late antique cities did not decline or collapse because of urban violence, and the riots were never fully revolutionary, even in the last years of Phocas. Rather, they were normally contained at an acceptable level, and Evelyne Patlagean has suggested that these public manifestations, ranging from the peaceful shouting of acclamations to full-fledged urban violence, in fact occupied a structural role in the overall consensus between government and governed, part of an uneasy but accepted balance whereby the authorities, on the one hand, supplied the people with both the essentials of life and the setting for the expression of opinion, and, on the other, came down with an iron grip when necessary, a collusion in the face of which the church sometimes took an independent role, but was more often a collaborator.[71]

A final factor which needs to be emphasized is the role played by the government in the food-supply of major cities, especially Rome and Constantinople (Chapter 4), which reinforced the dependency of the population on the authorities, while at the same time encouraging and maintaining numbers of citizens at a large and potentially dangerous level. The system was highly organized and left little scope for private contractors. The cost to the government of maintaining the *annona* was very great. In addition, it ensured that political rather than economic factors were dominant in the stability of the larger cities, and placed the government and the population of the capital in an artificial position of alternate confrontation and dependence, which could lead all too often to public disturbance. Furthermore, it rendered the capital highly vulnerable to any breakdown in supply. It was eventually external circumstances which brought about this breakdown, and with it a great reduction in the population at both Rome and Constantinople. At Rome, the *annona* was continued after AD 476 by the church, but not on the same scale as before, while at Constantinople, the fatal change came with the loss of Egypt, the main supplier of grain, to the Persians in the early seventh century, after which contraction was rapid. It is a useful corrective, when considering urban change in the period, to remember the artificially high level of public investment in certain aspects of urban life, whether through the *annona* or through building programmes, which should warn us in turn that urban prosperity is not in itself a good indicator of the general prosperity or otherwise of the empire.[72]

CONCLUSION

Late antique and early Byzantine towns constitute a vibrant and exciting field of research in present conditions, and generalizations run the risk of subsequent falsification. But there is enough evidence to show very clearly that by the late sixth century at the latest many, probably most, cities were experiencing fundamental changes. While far from being the whole explanation, one of the contributory factors was indeed the process of Christianization and the increasing impact of the church. Cities were not in a simple state of 'decline'. Nor were the old structures being broken down by movements from below. And there is certainly no sign that cities became more nearly like centres of production than they had been earlier in the ancient world.

A good deal of space has been devoted in this chapter to the fate of cities alone, despite the fact that scholars are now increasingly realizing the need for an overall view of town and country. The next chapter will therefore include some suggestions in that direction.

8

The eastern Mediterranean – settlement and change

The last chapter revealed the enormous amount of recent scholarship devoted to the fate of towns, and the efforts of scholars to discover whether, and why, there may have been a 'decline' in the sixth century. So far as the east is concerned, much of the motivation for this lively interest derives from hindsight – from the awareness that the Arab conquests were just round the corner, and (as with the west in AD 476) the knowledge that most of the eastern provinces were to be so quickly and easily lost to the eastern empire. In a striking number of cases, the inhabitants of the cities we have been discussing simply surrendered them to the invaders. Historians have always wanted to explain the speed and ease of the Arab conquests; it is natural to look for at least a partial answer in the state of the eastern provinces in the immediately preceding period.

To discuss the conquests themselves in any detail, or to review all the arguments that could be put as to the reasons for their success, would take us far beyond the scope of this book. But the situation of the eastern provinces before and at the time of the conquests is very relevant to the argument so far. Traditionally, an explanation for the easy capitulation of the east to the Arabs (Islamicization itself should be viewed as a separate issue) has been found in the fact that in this period the eastern provinces – Syria and Egypt, in particular – were the home of Monophysitism; it is assumed therefore that the population was hostile to and disaffected from the Byzantine government, and for that reason glad to shed its yoke. Yet Chalcedonianism was still strong in the east, especially in Palestine, and Nestorianism in Persia and Syria. Without going into further details at this point, the argument rests on a very simplistic view of the religious topography of the region; there were other good reasons for the success of the conquests, which were equally or, often, even more important. As is often the case, religious factors have to be put back into the general historical context and judged in that light.

SETTLEMENT AND POPULATION CHANGE

The question then is to what extent deep and long-term changes were already taking place in the demographic structure of the east, and in the relation of town to country, in the period before the seventh-century invasions. A first clue may be found in the progressive reliance of the government for its eastern defences on the Arab phylarchs, who based themselves not in cities, the traditional centres of Roman/Byzantine culture and the location of most of the army units in the later empire, but rather in desert encampments and even perhaps at the so-called 'desert palaces'. The Christian Ghassanids would congregate at the pilgrimage centre of St Sergius at Resafa or, it has been argued, at the shrine of John the Baptist at er-Ramthaniyye on the Golan Heights, while the pro-Sasanian Lakhmids had their base at al-Hira. Assessment of their contribution to the pattern of settlement in the early Islamic period is still in its infancy.[1] A different phenomenon is also emerging with increasing clarity, namely the high density of settlement in certain areas from the late fifth century into the sixth. This is true of certain parts of southern Palestine, the Golan and especially the Negev, which reached its highest density of settlement, and presumably of population, at this point (Chapter 7). For once we have the evidence of papyri, from Nessana in the south-west Negev, as well as archaeological evidence from urban centres such as Rehovot in the central Negev,[2] Oboda and Elusa, which also developed during this period, to set alongside the results of surveys. There is plentiful evidence of viticulture and olive-growing in this region, as well as material evidence of elaborate irrigation methods for agriculture in this dry region, such as dams, aqueducts, cisterns and the like. The comparison with modern techniques for cultivating arid regions such as the Negev is very striking, although this evidence requires careful analysis and conclusions can be premature. Interestingly, and indeed just as one might expect in view of the pattern of late antique urbanism outlined in the last chapter, the towns of this period in the Negev seem to have been more market and administrative centres for the surrounding countryside, which was thickly

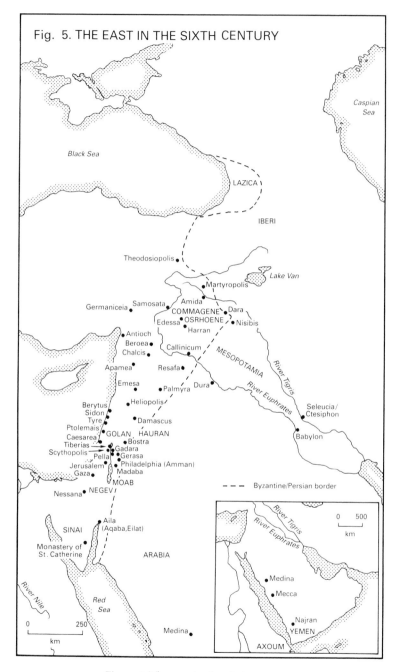

Fig. 5. THE EAST IN THE SIXTH CENTURY

Caspian Sea

Black Sea

LAZICA

IBERI

Theodosiopolis •

Lake Van

Martyropolis •

Germaniceia • Samosata • Amida Dara
COMMAGENE •
Edessa • OSRHOENE • Nisibis
Harran •

Antioch •
Beroea • Callinicum •
Chalcis •
MESOPOTAMIA
Apamea • Resafa •
Emesa • Dura •
Palmyra • *River Tigris*

Berytus • Heliopolis • *River Euphrates*
Sidon •
Tyre • Damascus • Seleucia/
Ptolemais • Ctesiphon
Caesarea • GOLAN HAURAN
Tiberias • Bostra • Babylon
Scythopolis • Gadara
Pella • Gerasa
Jerusalem • Philadelphia (Amman)
Gaza • Madaba
MOAB
– – – Byzantine/Persian border
Nessana • NEGEV

SINAI Aila
(Aqaba,Eilat)

Monastery of ARABIA
St. Catherine •

River Nile

Red Sea

Medina •

0   250
km

0   500
km

River Tigris
River Euphrates

Medina •

Mecca •

Najran •
YEMEN

AXOUM

Figure 5 The east in the sixth century.

178

Plate 12 Marginal land: Nessana as it is today. An important cache of sixth–seventh century papyri in Greek, Latin, Syriac and Arabic was found here in 1935 during excavation of one of the churches.

dotted with villages, than real urban centres on the late classical model.

A similar pattern of settlement density can be traced in other ways too. More generally, for instance, the large number of mosaic pavements surviving from churches, synagogues and other buildings from this period in Palestine demonstrate the level of investment in buildings, if not that of general prosperity. The prosperity of the large city of Scythopolis (Bet Shean) shows no sign of declining until the city was hit by a major earthquake, probably in AD 749; a bilingual balance from the city, inscribed in Greek and Arabic, seems to suggest that the local population had found a *modus vivendi* with the Arabs of the Umayyad period, while a Greek inscription of AD 662 from Hammat Gader, on the east coast of the Sea of Galilee, uses dating by both the regnal year of the caliph Mu'awiya and the era of the former Greek colony of Gadara.[3] While there is much regional variation, evidence of high settlement density also seems to be true of areas as far away as the region round Edessa in Mesopotamia (Chapter 7). Reliable stratigraphy from excavation, which would yield more reliable dating indicators, is admittedly often lacking, and surface finds may prove misleading. Yet population growth, development of towns and increased levels of cultivation and irrigation[4] have been noted in a variety of surveys. In contrast, there seems to have been a distinct falling away in many cases from the seventh century onwards, when, besides the effects of plague, the civil war under Phocas and the later invasions must also have taken their toll, together with a high degree of emigration to the west. All this precludes any straightforward equation of military investment with prosperity, and raises the question of how the demographic increase itself is to be explained.

Various reasons have been put forward, including the economic benefits of the pilgrim traffic. Another explanation looks to long-distance trade as a major factor in understanding the changes in the region over the period. The caravan trade had been of major importance in accounting for the prosperity of Palmyra in the early empire, as we know from ample documentary evidence, though the city suffered a decline when the rise of the Sasanian empire made free passage difficult. In the fifth century another Arab leader called in Greek Amorkesos (Imru' al-Qays), formerly subject to the Persians, gained control of the island of Jotabe, possibly in the Gulf of Aqaba:

[he] left Persia and travelled to that part of Arabia adjacent to Persia. Setting out from here he made forays and attacks not upon any Romans, but upon the Saracens whom he encountered. He seized one of the islands belonging to the Romans, which was named Jotabae and, ejecting the Roman tax collectors, held the island himself and amassed considerable wealth through collecting taxes. When he had seized other villages nearby, Amorkesos wished to become an ally of the Romans and phylarch of the Saracens under Roman rule on the borders of Arabia Petraea.

(Malchus, fr. 1, Blockley)

The enterprising Imru' al-Qays now sent his local bishop to put his case to the Emperor Leo, who was not only persuaded, but invited Imru' al-Qays to Constantinople, entertained him to dinner, presented him to the senate and made him a *patricius*, much to the disapproval of the historian who tells the story. When Imru' al-Qays left, Leo gave him gifts and public money from the treasury, and Imru' al-Qays in return presented the emperor with 'a very valuable icon of gold set with precious stones'. The story shows very well the role played by Christianization in Byzantine diplomacy, as well as the techniques used to control border territories and manage the Arab tribes. At the end of the fifth century, however, Jotabe was recaptured by the governor of Palestine.[5]

An interesting feature of this area is the extent of Jewish influence, notably in southern Arabia.[6] When in the early sixth century a Jewish king, Dhu Nuwas, persecuted Christians, including Byzantine merchants, expeditions were launched against him from Ethiopia (Axum), whose interests coincided with those of Constantinople. Byzantium itself was eager to maintain access to the southern trade route to the Far East; concern for trade with Ethiopia and Arabia thus played a major role in Byzantine diplomatic relations with Axum and South Yemen in the early sixth century. Though this has now been vigorously questioned, it has long been supposed that it was this caravan trade that gave Mecca its importance in the lifetime of Muhammad.[7] Finally, to take a further example from the north of the area, Sergiopolis (Resafa) near the Euphrates, the main Ghassanid centre, was not only a major religious site, the focus of pilgrimage to the shrine of St Sergius; it was also located on a major caravan route which made it the site of fairs and markets as well as religious gatherings. It is not surprising, then, that controlled passage of merchandise was a major feature of the treaty between Rome and Persia of AD 562; the third clause reads, 'Roman and Persian merchants of all kinds of goods, as well as similar tradesmen, shall conduct their business according to the established practice through the specified customs posts' (Menander, fr. 6, Blockley, *Menander the Guardsman*).

Trade was therefore certainly a factor which loomed large in government policy during the late fifth and sixth centuries. However, to suppose that the signs of prosperity and increased levels of settlement which can be observed in many parts of the region are all to be attributed to trade would carry further implications about changing modes and objects of production, about the beneficiaries of such trade, and about the degree of monetarization, all of which have yet to be explored. It is not at all obvious that this increased settlement implies economic growth in the modern sense, and it seems doubtful whether the caravan trade alone could account for the increase. We are far from being able to demonstrate that there was any real transformation of the economic system; instead, the fact that the eastern provinces enjoyed relative peace during the fifth century must have been a major contributory factor, and may even account for the apparent economic growth.

LOCAL CULTURES AND HELLENISM

While a great deal of work has been and is being conducted by archaeologists in these areas, in relation both to the military sites and to settlement patterns in general, the results are thus as yet far from clear. But there is also another dimension to the problem, namely the question of the interplay of cultures, not only the interpenetration of Arab and Byzantine, but also that of the Greek and Semitic elements in the culture of the region generally.

Something has been said already of Hellenism and local cultures in the east (Chapter 6), and we must now return to the question in more detail. A particular danger lies in the fact that the use in our period of two main languages, Greek and Aramaic, together with the recognition that Greek is the language of the administration and of high culture, tends to lead to the assumption of a major divide between the two along an élite/popular axis; this is sometimes accompanied by the further assumption that Greek hardly existed at all east of the Euphrates. In fact, Greek philosophy had been read at Edessa long before the fourth century, and Greek learning also penetrated to the famous schools at Nisibis and Seleucia-Ctesiphon and, later, Gundeshapur. A further difficulty arises from the flowering of both Christian and secular literature in Syriac (the Aramaic dialect of Edessa and its environs) which took place in our period.[8] So striking is this literature, and the social and cultural background which it assumes, that it has often tended to lead to an idealization of Syriac Christianity and Syriac spirituality in contrast to mainstream Greek culture. Probably the most famous exponent of this culture was St Ephrem ('Ephrem Syrus'), who moved from Nisibis to Edessa, when the former was ceded to the Persians in AD 363. Ephrem's highly metaphorical and imaginative poetry indeed strikes the classical reader as very unfamiliar, though the Greek influences on it may be greater than commonly supposed.[9] In any case, Ephrem was quickly translated into Greek, and a large body of material also exists in Greek under his name, which was later much cited in the Greek monastic literature. Contemporaries may not therefore have felt the distinction with the same force as we do. After Ephrem, Syriac came to be used as a major literary language for secular and ecclesiastical works of various kinds, including church history, chronicles, saints' lives, homilies and theological treatises. The growth of institutionalized Christianity promoted literacy among monks and clergy, led to the establishment of monastic centres and a growth in the production of Christian texts. Yet again, following earlier precedents, a great deal of translation took place, and many works circulated in several versions, Greek, Syriac, and sometimes Armenian, Georgian or, later, Arabic as well, the latter three usually in translations made from the Syriac.

Syriac was therefore far from being the language of popular literature. On the other hand, the culture of an important bishop like Theodoret, bishop of Cyrrhus in northern Syria in the fifth century, a major figure in church controversies and a voluminous writer, was chiefly Greek; he wrote in Greek and owed his culture to the traditions of Greek rhetorical education, writing letters to officials and churchmen in rhetorical Greek, and many other Greek works, including a refutation of heresies and a set of *Lives* of Syrian ascetics, even though many of his flock knew only Syriac. The culture of the Syrian city of Antioch, the second city in the eastern empire, was also essentially Greek; it was the earliest home of Christianity outside Judaea and the centre of one of the two major Greek schools of theology and biblical interpretation. We know that at Jerusalem the liturgy was conducted in Aramaic as well as

Greek when the pilgrim Egeria went there in AD 384. Yet even at Edessa, the very home of the great Syriac literary tradition in late antiquity, Greek was in use till late in the Islamic period. A linguistic map of Syria, Mesopotamia and Palestine might show that Mesopotamia, taken as a whole, was the least Hellenized (that is, the least Greek-speaking) and Palestine the most. But while there is a tendency among scholars to associate Syriac with Monophysitism and Greek with Chalcedonianism, that is, imperial orthodoxy, this was by no means always the case in practice.

The process of acculturation, encompassing the notions of 'Hellenism' and of Syriac or 'Semitic' culture, is extremely difficult to trace in this period. Many earlier accounts unfortunately approach it chiefly from the theological and literary angles, and it is only now beginning to be treated in a full historical perspective, using the entire range of available evidence.[10] One of the main problems certainly lies with the terminology: 'Syriac' denotes a language, not a culture. Moreover, the literature which we associate with the term 'Syriac' did, it is true, originate in a region considerably removed, and in certain ways very different, from the Hellenized coastal cities such as Caesarea, or indeed from much of Palestine.[11] The term 'Syrian', on the other hand, is, misleadingly, used in several different ways – to denote the geographical area of modern Syria or that of the Roman province of Syria or in a broader geographical sense ('Greater Syria') or finally, even more misleadingly, ethnically, that is, to denote the population of the area. Yet those who spoke Greek were not necessarily any less Syrian or 'Semitic' than those who used Aramaic. Once that is admitted, however, the very notion of Syriac culture as a separate entity is called into question. At the very least, the concept needs a much closer degree of geographical precision. Funerary inscriptions from the Golan and from modern Jordan, for example, indicate that Greek was still in widespread use by individuals up to the seventh century, and many churches, including the fine churches at Jerash (Gerasa) in the so-called Decapolis, whose other cities included Philadelphia (modern Amman), were decorated with fine mosaic inscriptions in Greek verse as late as the middle of the eighth century and after. A mosaic map with inscription in Greek from Umm er-Rasas, east of the Dead Sea and some 56 km south of Amman, seems to date from as late as AD 785, and further construction, again with an inscription in Greek, in the same church is dated to AD 756.

Three points have to be kept in mind to avoid being misled when considering these issues: first, while the administration and institutions of the empire placed an overlay of Greek on local conditions, this had already been the case for centuries, since the foundations of Alexander the Great and the Seleucid empire. Any real notion of Greek as the language of outsiders in our period is therefore largely inappropriate. Second, the spectacular development of Syriac literature in late antiquity is a phenomenon which must be taken fully into consideration. Third, however, it tends to be overlooked that Semitic culture had already been represented by Arabs, and later by a form of Arabic, in these regions since the Nabataean period (ended AD 106).[12] The linguistic and cultural pattern was extremely complex. For instance, an Arab dynasty ruled Edessa itself, and its affiliations can be clearly seen in the city's reliefs and mosaics. Yet the same city has produced a third-century mosaic of Orpheus complete with Syriac inscription. At Palmyra, with a bilingual culture in Greek and Palmyrene, the temple of Bel proclaims its Semitic roots, though like the cella of Ba'al Shamin, it was converted into a church. In north-eastern Arabia, on the other hand, Aramaic appears from the second century BC onwards, and Nestorian Christianity was well established there in late antiquity, with Syriac as its liturgical language;[13] there were also many Nestorians in south-eastern Arabia (Oman) when the area was under Sasanian rule before the Arab conquests.[14] Again, while Syriac was the written language of the Persian Nestorian church, Arabic was the spoken vernacular of the Christians in Arabia, and Pahlari was also used.[15] The culture of the Near East in late antiquity was a fascinating mosaic which can only be interpreted by reference to local differentiation. The great difficulty remains of matching modern notions of 'Arab', 'Syrian', 'Semitic' and other such terms, which are still entangled in a mesh of confusion and even prejudice, with the actual situation in our period.

What might perhaps be observed in late antiquity is a heightened awareness of and readiness to proclaim local traditions, with a consequent increase in their visibility. The disturbance at the centre of power in the third century has often been seen in terms of such a rise to prominence of local cultures. But the spread of Christianity clearly also acted as something of a catalyst so far as Syria was concerned. Syrian holy men and women in the fifth century offered outstanding and sometimes extraordinary examples of asceticism, and Syriac literature took its impulse from Christianity. Stylite saints, beginning with Symeon the Elder, with his pillar at Qalat

Siman near Antioch, originated in Syria, and large numbers of Syriac-speaking monks made their way to Constantinople to take part in the theological debates organized by Justinian at the beginning of his reign. Yet the Christianization of Syria had progressed very slowly in its early stages and was still incomplete in the sixth century.[16] Again, there is no simple description which can do justice to the whole picture; one should simply emphasize again the complexities evident in these regions before the Arab conquests, if only to suggest that the latter were not a simple affair of military victory, nor even, given the previous extent of cultural interpenetration, and particularly the role of the Ghassanids and other pre-Islamic Arab groups, altogether surprising.

THE PERSIAN AND ARAB INVASIONS

Some dates and a general outline of events are an essential preliminary. First, the Sasanians. Justinian's peace of AD 562 did not in fact produce a lasting settlement between Byzantium and Persia, and new campaigns were conducted by his successors, Justin II (565–78), Tiberius (578–82) and Maurice (582–602), whose decision to help restore the Persian king Chosroes II from exile (AD 591) led to Rome's gaining the substantial concessions of the border cities of Martyropolis and Dara.[17] But after Maurice's fall to the usurper Phocas and his execution (AD 602), Chosroes invaded Byzantine territory in force, taking Antioch and then Jerusalem (AD 614), from which the Persians carried off the True Cross to Ctesiphon. According to Christian sources, the Persians sacked the city with great slaughter and deported many of its inhabitants; the fall of Jerusalem was followed by that of Alexandria (AD 617), and Persian armies also stormed through Asia Minor, sacking Ephesus and Sardis and reaching Chalcedon, to lay joint siege to Constantinople with the Avars in AD 626. The Emperor Heraclius made an extraordinary counter-attack, having left Constantinople to its own defence in AD 622, and taking the war into the heart of Persian territory, where his victory ensured the fall of the Sasanian dynasty to the Arabs soon afterwards, he restored the Cross to Jerusalem in AD 630.[18] Since the last two decades of the sixth century, the empire had also had to contend with assaults from the Avars and Slavs in the Balkans, and it was in this context, in a situation of insufficient pay or supplies, that the soldiers raised Phocas as emperor in AD 602. As for Heraclius' victories, they were commemorated by a great procession in Constantinople and celebrated in the bombastic poetry of George of Pisidia,[19] but swiftly cancelled out, in one of the greatest ironies in history, by the advance of Arab armies on Syria. The Arab advance was spectacular: three battles, at Ajnadayn, between Jerusalem and Gaza, Fihl (Pella) and the river Yarmuk, took place between AD 634 and 637; Damascus fell after a long siege, Jerusalem was surrendered by the patriarch Sophronius in AD 638 and Alexandria fell in AD 642. The unfortunate Heraclius saw his armies defeated at the Yarmuk; bidding a famous farewell to Syria, as reported in the Syriac and Arabic sources, he returned to Constantinople, where he died in AD 641.[20]

REASONS FOR THEIR SUCCESS

It is obvious even from this very cursory outline that the eastern empire was experiencing a variety of serious difficulties even before the appearance of new Arab armies in Syria. The usurpation of Phocas indicates that it was difficult to keep up military pay and supplies after decades of campaigning, and Avar and Slav raids in the Balkans and Greece had already had serious effects on those areas (Chapter 7). The capital only just managed to survive the siege of AD 626 and the events leading up to it,[21] and the financial difficulties which Heraclius experienced are very evident in the emergency measures which he took, such as striking silver coin from church treasures. Byzantine recruitment for the Persian campaign represented a huge and unrepeatable effort. Moreover, Heraclius had himself only very recently, in AD 609–10, marched overland in a dramatic expedition from Carthage to Constantinople and put down Phocas, in a context of severe urban disturbances in the eastern provinces.[22] Finally, it is increasingly clear from archaeological evidence as well as literary sources that the Persian invasions of Asia Minor, Syria, Palestine and Egypt caused serious and widespread destruction, besides inspiring a stream of refugees to leave the east, first for North Africa and then for Sicily and south Italy, where they established a substantial and enduring Greek-speaking presence. Indeed, the acts of the 'Lateran Synod' held in Rome in AD 649, dominated by a group of eastern monks under the leadership of one of the greatest of Greek orthodox theologians, St Maximus Confessor, were written in Greek with an eye to influencing opinion in Constantinople. The degree of Byzantine restoration after the recovery of the Persian-occupied territory is very uncertain, and is likely to have been slight, for little time elapsed before the next invasion and Heraclius' resources were already over-extended.

In such circumstances the success of the Arab advance presents less of a surprise. Muhammad himself died in AD 632 at Medina, and was succeeded by Abu Bakr. The Byzantines were slow to realize that the invaders were other than 'Saracen' raiders with whom they had been familiar since the fourth century, and emphasize their 'barbarian' ferocity. It is only later that Byzantine writers begin to show awareness of the religious content of Muhammad's teaching. The chronicler Theophanes (died AD 817) reports a hostile account:

> Muhammad taught those who hearkened to him that he who killed an enemy or was killed by an enemy entered paradise. He said paradise was a place of carnal eating, drinking and intercourse with women: there were rivers of wine, honey and milk, and the women there were not like those here, but of another sort, and intercourse was longlasting and its pleasure enduring. He said many other prodigal and foolish things. Also his followers were to have sympathy for one another and help those treated unjustly.
>
> (Theoph., de Boor, 334; Turtledove, 35)

But while there was as yet little understanding, and a strong emphasis on the sufferings of the local populations, especially in the Syriac sources, archaeological and other evidence suggests that the 'conquests' themselves did not after all represent a major break in continuity in the eastern Mediterranean provinces, especially as the Islamic rulers at first simply took over the main framework of the Byzantine administration and continued to employ Greek-speaking officials to run it. The more important change was to come later, with the transfer of government further east to Baghdad in the mid-eighth century.

The reasons for the Muslim advance from Arabia towards Palestine and Syria are still debated. It would seem however that a major advance was already taking place further south while Heraclius was occupied with the celebration of his victory over the Persians. Despite a defeat at Mu'ta in AD 629, largely at the hands of other Arab tribes, an Arab army took Tabuk in northern Hejaz, whereupon three important Byzantine centres in eastern Palestina Tertia, Udruh and Aila (Aqaba), both legionary fortresses, as well as

Jarba, simply surrendered, giving the Muslims access to southern Palestine. The chronicler Theophanes claims that they were aided by desert tribes who had been refused their usual payment from the Byzantines: 'the oppressed Arabs went to their fellow-tribesmen and showed them the route to the land of Gaza, which is the mouth of the desert for Mt Sinai and is very rich' (Turtledove, 36).[23] Again, the chronology of these events is very hard to establish, even if there is more to Theophanes' version than just anecdote, but when the Muslims did reach the Negev and Gaza it seems clear that these areas were quite undefended, for they met relatively little resistance. Whatever the reasons, the infrastructure of defence which might have stopped the Muslims as they moved from Arabia into Palestine and Syria was simply not there.

All this would be enough to explain a great deal, even if there were no religious factors to invoke. But there were other religious groups besides Christians. The Christian sources blame the Jews of Palestine for aiding the Persian invaders, and claim that when the Persians left they put the Jews in charge of Jerusalem on their behalf. Seeing the Christian Byzantines defeated, the Jews not surprisingly entertained Messianic hopes of the restoration of the Temple. Byzantine reactions to this were naturally extremely hostile, and after the defeat of the Persians Heraclius issued a decree ordering the compulsory conversion of all Jews (AD 632). From the reign of Justinian, Jews in the Byzantine empire had been subjected to increasingly severe sanctions and prohibitions; now Byzantine hostility intensified and they were again blamed for collaboration, this time with the Muslims. It would be unwise to trust the Christian sources, which are extremely biased, but the Jewish presence does seem to have been an important factor in pre-Islamic Mesopotamia, Syria and Palestine, and one can see dim reflections in the hostile Christian sources of the fact that an important Jewish school of rabbinics still existed at Tiberias, and perhaps played a significant role in these years. Indeed, Islam itself owed much to Judaism, respecting the Jewish Scriptures and claiming to represent the inheritance of Abraham. In the event, Heraclius' policy could be put into effect only to a very limited extent, and under Islam the lot of the Jews of Palestine probably slightly improved.[24] As for the Christian population, the ordinations of Monophysite clergy in Greater Syria under Justinian had certainly had the effect both of creating a divided church and of giving the Monophysites an established position. But to imagine that the east was uniformly

Monophysite is a mistake, even in strongly Monophysite areas; the patriarchate of Antioch, for instance, passed several times between Chalcedonian and Monophysite control and there were both Monophysite and orthodox communities in Edessa when Heraclius stayed there during his campaign. Palestine itself was largely Chalcedonian, and its hierarchy of bishops opposed both Monophysitism and the new compromise known as Monothelitism (the doctrine that Christ had one will), which Heraclius now evolved in yet another desperate attempt at unity. The Palestinian hierarchy was headed by Sophronius, who became patriarch of Jerusalem in AD 634, only to surrender it to the Muslims in AD 638, and the irony to modern eyes is that even during the very period of the Arab conquest the church was much more concerned to rally support against the new imperial doctrine of Monothelitism than it was about the military dangers which were upon it.[25]

Not only did Heraclius' initiative fail to bring about unity, it imported yet another division, splitting even the Chalcedonian hierarchy, who on the usual view should have been the emperor's supporters. Clearly religious division between Christian groups must have weakened resistance to the invaders in terms of lowered confidence and disunity, but it does not follow that Monophysites would actually have preferred Arab to Byzantine rule, as is often assumed. The real factors were military, political and economic, and lie in the weakened Byzantine presence in the eastern provinces before, rather than simply during, the Persian and Arab conquests. Then, too, the cities of the east had been divided, as we see from the vivid accounts of factional violence in the last days of Phocas given by the Coptic historian, John of Nikiu (whose work we have in an Ethiopic translation). Blues and Greens, Christians and Jews, Chalcedonians and Monophysites had all played their parts. A curious work known as the *Doctrina Jacobi nuper baptizati* ('The teachings of James the newly baptized'), dating from the late 630s and supposedly written by a Jew baptized in accordance with imperial policy in order to convince his fellow Jews, gives many details of James' youth when he took part in these factional disturbances himself:

> [in the reign of Phocas], when the Greens, at the command of Kroukis, burned the Mese [in Constantinople] and had a bad time [cf. *Chron. Pasch.*, 695–6 Bonn], I roughed up the Christians and fought them as incendiaries and Manichaeans.

And when Bonosus at Antioch punished the Greens and slaughtered them [AD 609], I went to Antioch . . . and, being a Blue and on the emperor's side, I beat up the Christians as Greens and called them traitors.

(*Doctrina Jacobi* I.40)[26]

A straightforward appeal to Monophysitism is thus by no means enough to explain the conquests. We must now turn to questions of defence, or at least military investment in the area. It will be seen that these too are inseparable from the broader questions of settlement, demography and population.

THE EASTERN FRONTIER

The subject of frontiers and defence in the later Roman empire, and the eastern frontier in particular, has become extremely controversial in recent years. Much of this attention has been focused around two propositions championed in E. N. Luttwak's influential book, *The Grand Strategy of the Roman Empire* (Baltimore, Maryland, 1976) (incidentally the work of a modern strategist, not an ancient historian). They are, first, that the empire had a 'grand strategy', that is, that military installations were the result of rational planning at top level, and second, that the late empire, from Diocletian onwards, practised a planned policy of 'defence-in-depth', according to which a system of frontier defence was backed up by mobile field armies stationed further back in Roman territory. Although both these propositions have been widely accepted, and feature without question in many later studies, they have more recently been strongly challenged, to the extent that, for the east at least, a new orthodoxy has been developing.[27] The issue is partly methodological: whereas Luttwak and others took late Roman imperial pronouncements too much at their face value, we have seen that there was not only a gap between alleged motivation and actual practice, but also between actual practice and stated aims. It is even more of a mistake to assume that the imperial government of the later period was able to carry through all the elaborate schemes claimed for it for example by Procopius. Recent study of the material remains of military installations in the east also prompts a revision of Luttwak's thesis, and a different view of the purpose of Roman military investment there.

The build-up of Roman forces in the east had begun much earlier;

indeed, the history of Roman involvement in the territories bordering the Sasanian empire is conspicuously more dynamic than on the
other borders of the Roman empire. According to Fergus Millar,
Trajan's Parthian war of AD 106 marked 'the beginning of an
obsession which was to take a whole series of Roman emperors on
campaign into Mesopotamia, and sometimes down as far as Seleucia
and Ctesiphon on the Tigris'.[28] Under Septimius Severus in the
early third century, two extra legions were created for service in the
east, and five cities in the new province of Mesopotamia – Edessa,
Carrhae, Resaina, Nisibis and Singara – were given the status of
Roman colonies; eight legions were now stationed in the zone
which stretched south from here to Arabia. From now on Rome
was faced with the strong military regime created by the Sasanians
on its eastern borders; from the third to the early seventh centuries
the two powers confronted each other. Highly damaging incursions
took place in the fourth century under Shapur I and in the sixth and
early seventh under Chosroes I and Chosroes II, and Rome was
obliged to make an expensive peace in AD 363 after the ill-fated
Persian expedition of the Emperor Julian which ceded to Persia the
important border city of Nisibis; this had previously had been
established under a treaty made by Diocletian as the single point of
market exchange between the two empires. We have seen the cost to
Byzantium in military and financial terms of the wars of the sixth
and seventh centuries. It is natural to think therefore that the
essential purpose of the Roman military installations was defensive,
both against the Sasanians and against the assumed threat from
nomad tribes, but recent scholars have pointed out that for most of
the period neither of the two empires seriously thought of trying to
defeat the other or occupy territory on a large scale, and argued that
the Roman defence system was in fact much concerned with prestige, internal security and the policing of the border areas. Contemporary authors sometimes suggest grandiose defensive schemes,
as Zosimus does for Diocletian, or claim total success in securing
the border, as Procopius does for Justinian. But both writers share
with most of their contemporaries a black-and-white picture of
civilization under threat from outside, and especially from the
nomadic menace – a view in which they were joined until recently
by modern scholars; in contrast, current research presents a very
different conception of the relation between 'nomadic' and settled
groups.[29]

Much of the argument turns on the interpretation of the purpose of the archaeological remains on the ground, which is notoriously difficult. Nevertheless, Isaac is not the only scholar to have argued that the military roads which are so conspicuous in this area, especially the *strata Diocletiana*, a road from north-east Arabia and Damascus to Palmyra and the Euphrates, and the earlier *via nova Traiana*, from Bostra to the Red Sea, were meant not as lines of defence, but rather as lines of communication. The concept of 'defence-in-depth' frequently encountered in the scholarly literature, like that of an 'inner' and an 'outer' *limes*, imposes an inappropriately modernizing idea on the evidence.[30] Even the identification of the many apparently defensive and fortified structures found in this region can be uncertain, and many individual sites remain controversial; some sites may have changed in use considerably over a period of several centuries, with necessary alterations done from time to time. Legionary fortresses such as Udruh and Lejjun seem to have housed much smaller units (1,000–1,500) than had been the case in the early empire; this is consonant with the changed late Roman army and also with the smaller provinces into which the east was now divided. The legions were now only a part, perhaps a small part, of the total force, and warfare between Rome and Persia was beginning to be more often a matter of sieges of fortified towns, where the troops were mainly stationed; indeed, the forts or fortlets were not necessarily the bases of regular troops at all. The position of the supposed peasant militia known as the *limitanei* is also difficult to establish with certainty; while they are often blamed in later sources and by modern scholars for their alleged poor performance, they are not in fact attested until at least the late fourth century, and were then simply the regular soldiers of the border zone. It would not of course necessarily follow even if they were to some extent a peasant militia, as opposed to being regular soldiers, that they were necessarily worse soldiers than the latter when it came to action.[31]

In the Sasanians, the Byzantines faced a rival power which was for once not only their equal in military capacity, but also at times capable of ruthless and aggressive campaigns against Roman territory.[32] We have seen already the helplessness of the eastern cities when faced with the armies of Chosroes I, as well as the financial cost of peace to the Byzantine empire (Chapter 5). Despite the great peace treaty of AD 562, Justinian's successors were still engaged with the problem of war with Persia, where the reforms of Chosroes I led to the strengthening of the military aristocracy. Ironically,

Chosroes II, who had suffered a coup at home and owed his throne to the Emperor Maurice, and who had showed an attachment to the Christian shrine of St Sergius at Sergiopolis (Resafa) by promising a jewelled cross if the saint could give him victory (Theophylact V. 1.8),[33] proved just as ruthless an enemy as Chosroes I had been. While conquest as such was out of the question on the Byzantine side, the Persian invasions of the early seventh century departed from previous precedent. The Persians not only delivered near-fatal blows to many Roman cities in Asia Minor, and stimulated flight among the Christian populations, especially the monks and clergy, of Palestine and Egypt, but also actually occupied and ruled the Byzantine east – if only through proxies – for a period of some fifteen or so years. Even though the nature of their rule remains extremely obscure,[34] there can be no doubt that this episode, together with the cumulative effects of previous decades of warfare between Byzantium and Persia, must have played a large role in explaining the ease of the Islamic conquests.

On the Byzantine side, despite the large amount of material evidence for the system of defence, interpretation of the system as a whole, and indeed the very question of whether there actually was an overall system, are still very far from being finally established. Many fortifications without actual garrisons may have functioned mainly as deterrents, for use only on an ad hoc basis. The standard view of a rigid defensive scheme can no longer be seriously sustained. But many other factors also came into play, and we can see that the question of defences apart, the history of this region in the period was very far from static. The decline of the Nabataean kingdom, with its capital at Petra in Jordan, the creation of the province of Arabia in AD 106, the brief independence, defeat and collapse of Palmyra in the late third century, had all brought profound economic and cultural consequences for the region in general. The adoption of Christianity by Constantine had brought substantial investment in Jerusalem and other holy sites by emperors and members of the imperial family and by wealthy individuals such as Jerome's friend Paula and as a result of the booming pilgrim traffic from the fourth century onwards. In terms of security and military affairs, however, a conspicuous element which was to become more and more important as time went on was provided, as we have already noted, by Rome's dealings with the semi-nomadic Arab tribes of the region who, from the fourth century onwards, were increasingly used by both empires as military allies. The

penetration of these regions by Arabs was not simply a phenomenon that began with what are generally known as the Arab conquests in the seventh century; indeed, perhaps the most spectacular
demonstration of 'the partial acculturation of Arab tribes and rulers
living along the edge of the areas of Graeco-Roman settlement' is
provided by the famous inscription of AD 328 from Namara in
southern Syria, written in Arabic in Nabataean characters and
commemorating the Lakhmid king Imru' al-Qays, 'king of all the
Arabs'.[35]

Both the Romans and the Persians relied more and more on Arab
('Saracen') federate allies, and by the early sixth century each power
had a well-established client following led by powerful tribal
groups, the Persians relying on the Lakhmids, whose base was at al-
Hira, and the Romans on the Ghassanids, Monophysite Christians
centred on Resafa, between Sura and Palmyra. These 'phylarchates'
not only assisted regular Roman forces, fighting alongside them as
al-Harith the Ghassanid and his troops did at the battle of
Callinicum in AD 531, but even came to replace them and were
entrusted with military missions on their behalf. Conservative
Byzantine authors such as Procopius were readily inclined to suspect them of treachery, as he does in the case of al-Harith at
Callinicum: '[Arethas and the Saracens] in this way broke ranks and
separated themselves, so that they gained the reputation of having
betrayed the Roman cause to the Persians' (BP I.18.36).[36] A little
before this, Procopius had written that 'Arethas was extremely
unfortunate in every inroad and every conflict, or else he turned
traitor as quickly as he could. For as yet we know nothing certain
about him' (BP I.17.48). The fact was, however, that the phylarchs
played an increasingly central role in the security of the border
lands, and were paid to do so by their patrons. Indeed, when the
Muslims moved north from Arabia in the early seventh century,
these federates were suspected of having helped them because their
regular subsidies from the Byzantines had dried up. In depending
on such tribal groupings at the expense of regular military investment the imperial government was in a sense reviving its centuries-
old policy of clientage, and following policies similar in practice to
those employed a century earlier in the west. They were of course
policies which could all too easily rebound to the government's
disadvantage. Nor were they consistently applied: while Justinian
gave al-Harith the titles of phylarch, patrician and king precisely
in order to counterbalance the Lakhmids under al-Mundhir

(Procopius, *BP* I.17.45–8), his successor Justin II cut off subsidies and turned against the victorious Mundhir the son of al-Harith the Ghassanid, leaving Dara and Apamea undefended. Though Mundhir was subsequently brought back to allied status, Byzantine suspicion prevailed again and he was exiled to Sicily by the Emperor Tiberius in AD 580 (John of Ephesus, *HE* VI.3–4, III.40–42; Evagrius, *HE* V. 6–9, 20).[37]

We have already seen the sparsity of Byzantine forces in the east at the time of the invasion of Chosroes I in the early 540s. Clearly this must be connected with Justinian's problems of manpower and finance during his wars in the west, but the reliance on Arab federates had begun much earlier, and its effects intensified in the later sixth century. *Limitanei* were not being paid, the records seem to have been in a state of chaos, and to judge from the absence of sixth-century finds on many sites it seems that legionary forces were actually withdrawn from south-east Palestine, seriously weakening the possibility of resistance to the Muslims in the seventh century. This, combined with the serious effects of the seventh-century Persian invasion, would go far towards explaining the surrender of Udruh and Aila and the opening of the easy route to the north which was to have such fateful consequences. Finally, the great difficulties experienced by Heraclius in recruiting and supplying an adequate army against the Persians suggest that Byzantine military weakness was indeed a reality by the early seventh century.

The study of the eastern provinces in the late antique and early Islamic periods is currently going through a period of tremendous growth, as a result of which many old ideas are likely to be discarded before new interpretations are reliably established. Though the differences between east and west are great, the eastern provinces in the seventh century shared with the fifth-century west both external threats and the dangers of internal fragmentation. Significant changes in urban and rural settlement, Christianization, the interpenetration of Greek with local cultures and the impact of the military and fiscal needs of the Byzantine state are all very evident well before the last great Persian invasion of the early seventh century and the arrival in Syria of the followers of Muhammad.[38] The story of the origins and expansion of Islam itself fall outside the compass of this book. Yet when the Muslims left Arabia and encountered Roman troops in Palestine and Syria, they found the Roman Near East already in a ferment of change.

Conclusion

The Roman empire did not come to an end through revolutionary change. There was no uprising or revolutionary impulse that brought about collapse, and in so far as class struggle existed (and there were certainly massive inequalities) it was for the most part passive and inert. Though a vigorous case has been put for an unwillingness on the part of the lower classes to continue fighting the government's battles by the early seventh century in the east, and at a much earlier date in the west, the actual reasons for the eventual loss of both western and eastern provinces were more numerous and more complex. It is more fruitful in the context of current research to look for changes in the balance of centre and periphery and at the shifting relations of local cultures. Consideration of the *longue durée* is more helpful than the appeal to immediate causal factors. The extraordinary tenacity of the late Roman state can too easily be forgotten in the search for explanations of its supposed decline and fall. Thus, while Justinian's wars may have fatally overstretched the state economy, he was nevertheless able to sustain a massive war effort over a very long period and on several fronts, to establish a new and substantial Byzantine administrative and military system in the newly reconquered provinces of North Africa and Italy, and to carry through an empire-wide building programme which was still impressive even if only partly his own. That his successors experienced difficulties in maintaining his example was hardly surprising.

The empire was vulnerable to external developments as well as to its own internal problems. Not merely was it faced by the 'barbarian invasions' in the west (which, as we saw, were deflected from the east only with some difficulty) and the Persian invasions, followed by the Arab conquests, in the east: changes in central Asia led in the

197

fifth century to danger from the Huns, fortunately dissolved after the death of Attila, and later to the appearance of the Hephthalites, who threatened Constantinople at the end of the reign of Justinian. By this time the empire was already attempting to use the Avars to control other groups such as the Slavs in the Danubian regions. Corippus approvingly describes their haughty reception by Justin II at the beginning of his reign (*Iust.* III.151ff.), but Justin's high-handedness to these and other potential enemies proved disastrous; large payments to the Avars by his successor Tiberius II (AD 578–82) did not prevent them from becoming a major threat, or from besieging Constantinople in AD 626.[1] Needless to say, contemporaries had only a vague idea of the ethnic origins of the Avars and the Turks,[2] whose prominence in the late sixth century was followed in turn by the emergence, by the end of the seventh, of two other Turkic peoples, the Bulgars and the Khazars. Faced with these movements, the empire had few options, and oscillated between trying to make alliances, backed up with payment of subsidies, and, when necessary, fighting. This was indeed the normal state of affairs, varying only in degree; war, not peace, was the norm, and when peace did prevail for a time it had usually been bought at a high cost.

Seen against this background, the 'decline' explanation appears outmoded. It is premised on the idea that it is reasonable to expect cultures and societies to be able to maintain themselves indefinitely in the same state. Phrases such as 'the end of classical antiquity' and the like assume an entity, 'classical antiquity', which is not itself liable to change. But societies do not exist in a vacuum. The world itself is in a constant state of change. In the same way, myriads of small and large changes happened both within the vast territories of the empire and outside its borders: it is these changes taken together which have misleadingly been labelled 'decline'. But it is not the historian's place either to sit in moral judgement on his subject or to impose inappropriate classical norms.

A different mode of explanation can be derived from some recent work in anthropology, according to which complex societies tend of themselves to become ever-more complex until finally they reach the point of collapse.[3] This at first sight avoids the difficulty of confusing explanations of change with actual descriptions of it. But it is not clear whether it really succeeds, or how appropriate a theory it is when applied to the Roman empire. Indeed, despite the ever-more convoluted rhetoric employed in law and administration, the later Roman empire had in some ways become a less complex society than before. Despite the valiant attempts of the central government to import more and more checks and controls, its effort was cancelled out in practice by the stubborn tendency of the population simply to go on in its own way. A further danger in such generalizing explanations is that they may fail to take into account the actual historical variables – for while it may be useful to see the Roman empire in comparison with other imperial systems, it was also a society *sui generis*, held together by a unique balance of factors which historians are still in the process of trying to understand. We must not lose sight of the particularity of late antiquity in the zeal to explain away the fall of the Roman empire.

In view of the unfavourable view which many classicists and ancient historians have traditionally taken of Byzantium, the present flow of research on the eastern provinces in late antiquity seems somewhat paradoxical, until we realize that it is very largely concerned with the same new undertaking of acculturation and cultural change that lies behind comparable work on the west. The field is led by archaeology; under the influence of theoretical considerations, archaeologists are giving more and more attention to studying the interaction of cultural systems and especially the process of acculturation. Ethnoarchaeology and the study of subcultures leads them to take a longer and a broader view, and to turn less readily to literary sources for 'corroboration' of detailed hypotheses. This approach has been developed with particular reference to earlier periods, and even to prehistory. But late antiquity – a period of cultural change and acculturation on a grand scale – also offers tremendous scope in this direction. The effect of taking it up will be to change the agenda for historians too.

One question is how far the influence of the state actually penetrated. Despite the political shifts, when seen from the longer perspective it is arguable that neither the establishment of the barbarian kingdoms in the west nor the Arab conquests brought the degree of change in the underlying social and economic structures of Europe that can be seen from the eleventh century onwards. In the west, one can detect a difference between the agricultural methods and crops more suitable to the heavy northern soil and colder climate of northern Germany and France and the wine- and oil-based economy of the Mediterranean; yet the same northern provinces, with the same ecology, had also been part of the Roman empire. In the east, both archaeologists and historians are agreed that the seventh-century Arab conquests in Palestine and Syria brought little real break in continuity. Before the end of the millennium, neither east nor west made the economic and cultural advances which were to produce the Renaissance and early modern Europe.[4] Much too much emphasis is still placed on the 'collapse' of the Roman empire and the 'transformation' of the classical world, and too little on the long-term continuities.

The search for the causes, in the traditional sense, of this 'transformation' also tends to obscure the particularity of individual experience in late antiquity, the range and variety of which in fact gives the period its undoubted imaginative appeal to modern eyes. A time of rapid change, when local structures were often more meaningful than the Roman state, when people could choose from a variety of allegiances, when differing cultural and mental systems jostled for pre-eminence, is, after all, something that we can all recognize, and with some of whose problems we might identify in our own post-modern world. As is clear from our own problems of nomenclature when dealing with this period, neither the 'medieval' nor the 'Byzantine' mentalities were yet fully established, and the Islamic world-view was still well in the future.[5] The term 'imagined communities' has been used to mark a certain stage in the development of the modern sense of national identity.[6] While it would be very misleading to import into it the concept of nationalism in anything like the modern sense, in our period, too, new ways of constructing social identity were coming into being all round the Mediterranean, without as yet any certainty as to which ones would survive. We, at 1,400 or 1,500 years' remove, have the advantage of knowing the outcome. But history is about change, and those who are living in the middle of it are the last to recognize it for what it really is.

Notes

1 CONSTANTINOPLE AND THE EASTERN EMPIRE IN THE FIFTH CENTURY

1 Foundation and subsequent history of Constantinople: C. Mango, *Le développement urbain de Constantinople (IVe–VIIe siècle)*, Paris, 1985; G. Dagron, *Naissance d'une capitale: Constantinople et ses institutions de 330 à 451*, Paris, 1974; R. Krautheimer, *Three Christian Capitals*, Berkeley and Los Angeles, Calif.,1983, 41–67 (but attributing too much to Constantine himself).

2 Neither survives; for their construction, see C. Mango, 'Constantine's mausoleum and the translation of relics', *Byzantinische Zeitschrift* 83 (1990), 51–61.

3 See in general P. Chuvin, *A Chronicle of the Last Pagans,* Cambridge, Mass., 1991 (English translation of the fuller French edition), and below, Chapter 3.

4 Below, Chapter 8.

5 The most straightforward introduction to the late Roman administrative system remains that of Jones, *LRE*, I, chs 13 and 16.

6 The best guides are Peter Heather and John Matthews, *The Goths in the Fourth Century*, Translated Texts for Historians 11, Liverpool, 1991 (a very interesting collection of sources in translation, including the main accounts of Ulfila and selections from the Bible in Gothic); and Peter Heather, *Goths and Romans, 332–489*, Oxford, 1991.

7 See J. H. W. G. Liebeschuetz, *Barbarians and Bishops. Army, Church and State in the Age of Arcadius and Chrysostom*, part II, Oxford, 1990; Alan Cameron and Jacqueline Long, with Lee Sherry, *Barbarians and Politics at the Court of Arcadius*, Berkeley and Los Angeles, Calif., 1993.

8 See Alan Cameron, *Claudian*, Oxford, 1970.

9 See Heather, *Goths and Romans*, 193–224; Liebeschuetz, *Barbarians and Bishops*, 55–85; H. Wolfram, *History of the Goths*, Berkeley and Los Angeles, Calif., 1988, 150–61. Knowledge of these complicated events depends a good deal on the tendentious Latin poems of Claudian and the highly political, but allegorical and obscure *De Regno* by Synesius in Greek, both very difficult sources to use.

10 Augustine's meditations on this theme are contained in his great work, the *City of God*, finished only some years later; Orosius' *History against the Pagans* answered the same questions in far simpler terms and was to become a textbook for the medieval west. Note that at this period, and in this book, the terms 'orthodox' and 'catholic' mean roughly the same, i.e., 'not heretic', though the term 'catholic' is more usually applied to the west; it is not of course yet used in the sense of 'Roman Catholic', nor is 'orthodox' to be understood as having the same connotations as 'eastern orthodox' would today.

11 See K. Holum, *Theodosian Empresses. Women and Imperial Dominion in Late Antiquity*, Berkeley and Los Angeles, Calif., 1982; Alan Cameron, 'The empress and the poet', *Yale Classical Studies* 27 (1981), 272ff.; E. D. Hunt, *Holy Land Pilgrimage in the Later Roman Empire AD 312–460*, Oxford, 1982, 220–48.

12 See Liebeschuetz, *Barbarians and Bishops*, part III; on the complex sources, see 199–202; also id., 'Friends and enemies of John Chrysostom', in A. Moffatt (ed.), *Maistor*, Canberra, 1984, 85–111; Elizabeth A. Clark, *Jerome, Chrysostom and Friends*, New York, 1979 (translated sources). Brief narrative in S. G. Hall, *Doctrine and Practice in the Early Church*, London, 1991, 187–90.

13 Below, Chapter 8 and see T. E. Gregory, *Vox Populi. Popular Opinion and Violence in the Religious Controversies of the Fifth Century AD*, Columbus, Ohio, 1979.

14 See Chapter 5, and for eastern bishops, R. Lizzi, *Il potere episcopale nell'Oriente Romano*, Rome, 1987; western: Peter Brown, *The Cult of the Saints*, London, 1981.

15 For the antecedents, with an emphasis on church councils, see Judith Herrin, *The Formation of Christendom*, Oxford, 1987.

16 Hall, *Doctrine and Practice*, 234 (see chs 20 and 21 for the Councils of AD 431 and 451); sources: Stevenson, *Creeds*, 271–344.

17 Hall, *Doctrine and Practice*, ch. 19.

18 See W. H. C. Frend, *A History of the Monophysite Movement*, Cambridge, 1972.

19 See J. Nelson, 'Symbols in context: rulers' inauguration rituals in Byzantium and the west in the early middle ages', in D. Baker (ed.), *The Orthodox Churches and the West*, Studies in Church History 13, Oxford, 1976, 97–118.

20 *Chronicon Paschale*, trans. Whitby and Whitby, 114; Theophanes, *Chron.*, 181–6 de Boor.

21 Races and Blues and Greens: Alan Cameron, *Circus Factions*, Oxford, 1976; with C. M. Roueché, *Performers and Partisans at Aphrodisias*, London, 1992, and for similar phenomena, and acclamations, in religious contexts, see Gregory, *Vox Populi*.

22 Below, Chapter 2; see C. Wickham, *Early Medieval Italy*, London, 1981, 19ff.; B. Croke, 'AD 476: the manufacture of a turning point', *Chiron* 13 (1983), 81–119.

23 Galla Placidia had formerly been captured in the Visigothic sack of Rome and married to Athaulf (AD 414).

24 The sources for all these events are very scattered, the Greek histories of

Priscus, Candidus and Malchus surviving only in fragments (see Blockley, I).

2 THE EMPIRE, THE BARBARIANS AND THE LATE ROMAN ARMY

1 For a conspectus of 'explanations' of this event, some of them curious, see D. Kagan, *The End of the Roman Empire. Decline or Transformation?*, 2nd edn, Lexington, Mass., 1978; A. M. Rollins, *The Fall of Rome: a Reference Guide*, Jefferson, 1983. See J. A. Tainter, *The Collapse of Complex Societies*, Cambridge, 1988, 128–52, with earlier references; this discussion provides a very good introduction to the problem, but is not sufficiently critical of secondary literature, and gives too little attention to the contrast between east and west; see further, Conclusion and Select critical bibliography.
2 See Jones, *LRE*, ch. 8.
3 For eastern reactions to the fall of Rome see W. E. Kaegi Jr, *Byzantium and the Decline of Rome*, Princeton, NJ, 1968.
4 Jones, *LRE* ch. 6, and see Chapter 1 above.
5 W. Goffart, *Barbarians and Romans, AD 418–584. The Techniques of Accommodation*, Princeton, NJ, 1980, ch. 1, provides a critical introduction to the topic of the barbarian invasions and a useful counter to the often exaggerated claims based on national interest which have been made in the modern literature; and for a critical overview see Ian Wood, 'The barbarian invasions and the first settlements', *CAH* XIII, forthcoming.
6 Huns: O. J. Maenchen-Helfen, *The World of the Huns*, Berkeley and Los Angeles, Calif., 1973; C. D. Gordon, *The Age of Attila. Fifth-Century Byzantium and the Barbarians*, Ann Arbor, Michigan, 1960 (translated sources); Goths: P. Heather, *Goths and Romans 332–489*, Oxford, 1991, ch. 4 (the best discussion); H. Wolfram, *History of the Goths*, Berkeley and Los Angeles, Calif., 1988, 117ff.; Huns crossing the Danube (AD 394–5): ibid., 139.
7 Heather, *Goths and Romans*, 135–6.
8 See T. S. Burns, 'The battle of Adrianople: a reconsideration', *Historia* 22 (1973), 336–445. Similarly, Zosimus ends his *New History* with the disaster of the sack of Rome by Alaric in AD 410.
9 Heather, *Goths and Romans*, ch. 5.
10 R. Collins, *Early Medieval Europe 300–1000*, London, 1991, ch. 6, describes these events in more detail and with source references.
11 See Chapter 4.
12 See I. Wood, 'The end of Roman Britain: continental evidence and parallels', in M. Lapidge and D. Dumville (eds), *Gildas: New Approaches*, Woodbridge, 1984; id., 'The fall of the western empire and the end of Roman Britain', *Britannia* 18 (1987), 251–62; R. Hodges, 'The Anglo-Saxon migrations', in L. M. Smith (ed.), *The Making of Britain I: The Dark Ages*, Basingstoke, 1984; S. Esmonde Cleary, *The Ending of Roman Britain*, London, 1989; more generally, P. H. Salway, *Roman Britain*, Oxford, 1981.

13 Jones, *LRE*, I, 183–7.
14 See P. S. Barnwell, *Emperors, Prefects and Kings. The Roman West, 395–565*, London, 1992; J. M. Wallace-Hadrill, *The Barbarian West 400–1000*, rev. edn, Oxford, 1985; id., *Early Germanic Kingship in England and on the Continent*, Oxford, 1971; P. H. Sawyer and I. N. Wood (eds), *Early Medieval Kingship*, Leeds, 1977; Edward James, *The Origins of France. From Clovis to the Capetians, 500–1000*, London, 1982; R. Latouche, *Caesar to Charlemagne*, London, 1968, gives many source extracts in translation.
15 See Chapter 5; the classic work on Vandal Africa is still C. Courtois, *Les Vandales et l'Afrique*, Paris, 1953; however, a new picture is emerging of Vandal trade with the rest of the Mediterranean, for which see Chapter 4. For Greek and Latin after the Byzantine reconquest, see Averil Cameron, 'Byzantine Africa. The literary evidence', in J. Humphreys (ed.), *University of Michigan. Excavations at Carthage VII*, Ann Arbor, Michigan, 1982, 29–62.
16 Trans. Penguin Classics; for the division of the kingdom between Clovis' four sons after his death see I. Wood, 'Kings, kingdoms and consent', in Sawyer and Wood (eds), *Early Medieval Kingship*, 6–29; the Byzantine historian Agathias includes a laudatory history of the Merovingian dynasty in his *Histories*, written early in the 570s (see Averil Cameron, *Agathias*, Oxford, 1970, 120–1). In general, see E. James, *The Franks*, Oxford, 1988.
17 See Chapter 5. E. A. Thompson, *Romans and Barbarians, The Decline of the Western Empire*, Madison, Wisconsin, 1982, contains some important articles on the Gothic wars, for which see Chapter 6; in general on the Ostrogoths, see T. Burns, *A History of the Ostrogoths*, Bloomington, Indiana, 1984; Wolfram, *History of the Goths*, 247–362.
18 For the social and economic changes in the late sixth century see especially T. S. Brown, *Gentlemen and Officers. Imperial Administration and Aristocratic Power in Byzantine Italy AD 554–800*, Rome, 1984; brief description in C. Wickham, *Early Medieval Italy*, London, 1981, 74–9.
19 Gregory's own writings, especially his letters, are a basic source; see J. Richards, *Consul of God. The Life and Times of Gregory the Great*, London, 1980; C. Straw, *Gregory the Great. Perfection in Imperfection*, Berkeley and Los Angeles, Calif., 1988; another is the early medieval record of the popes, *Liber Pontificalis* (trans. R. Davis, *The Book of the Pontiffs*, Liverpool, 1989, 1992).
20 Thus Wickham, *Early Medieval Italy*, 15, says, 'The holocaust in Italy came in the great age of wars, 535–93: the shifts of balance under the German rulers, first Odoacer (476–93) and then the Ostrogothic kings (490–553) were trivial by contrast.' For Theodoric's regime and the Gothic wars see further, 21–7.
21 After 1,000 years, consuls then ceased to be appointed except when the office was taken by Byzantine emperors themselves: see Alan Cameron and Diane Schauer, 'The last consul. Basilius and his diptych', *JRS* 72 (1982), 126–45.
22 Below, Chapter 5; see also J. Moorhead, 'Italian loyalties in Justinian's

Gothic War', *Byzantion* 53 (1983), 575–96; id., 'Culture and power among the Ostrogoths', *Klio* 68 (1986), 112–22.

23 See Cameron, *Procopius*, 192–202, with further bibliography; for Cassiodorus, J. J. O'Donnell, *Cassiodorus*, Berkeley and Los Angeles, Calif., 1982; R. Macpherson, *Rome in Involution. Cassiodorus' Variae in their Literary and Historical Setting*, Poznán, 1989; a selection from the *Variae* is translated with notes by S. Barnish, Translated Texts for Historians 12, Liverpool, 1992.

24 See Burns, *History of the Ostrogoths*, 101f.; J. F. Matthews, 'Anicius Manlius Severinus Boethius', in Margaret Gibson (ed.), *Boethius*, Oxford, 1981, 15–43; see also Henry Chadwick, *Boethius*, Oxford, 1981.

25 Trans. Penguin. For the poems see G. O'Daly, *The Poetry of Boethius*, Chapel Hill, NC, 1991.

26 For the Visigoths at Toulouse see Wolfram, *History of the Goths*, 172–242, and on the aftermath of Vouillé, 243–6.

27 See Roger Collins, *Early Medieval Spain. Unity in Diversity, 400–1000*, London, 1983 (32–41 on the present period); understanding Visigotic involvement in Spain in the fifth century depends very much on the *Chronicle* of Hydatius: Thompson, *Romans and Barbarians*, 137–60, 188–207; in general see also Edward James (ed.), *Visigothic Spain. New Approaches*, Oxford, 1980; P. D. King, *Law and Society in the Visigothic Kingdom*, Cambridge, 1972.

28 The bibliography is vast, but see the works mentioned above; J. Le Goff, *Medieval Civilization 400–1500*, Eng. trans., Oxford, 1988, makes available in English the distinctive approach of the French *Annales* school. Volume I of the revised *Cambridge Medieval History* (forthcoming) will provide an up-to-date guide; by contrast, the new *Cambridge Ancient History*, vol. XIV (also forthcoming) treats the same period from the perspective adopted here.

29 See Chapters 4 and 7.

30 For Venantius see George, *Venantius Fortunatus*. Ian Wood, 'Administration, law and culture in Merovingian Gaul', in Rosamund McKitterick (ed.), *The Uses of Literacy in Early Medieval Europe*, Cambridge, 1990, 63–81, explores the various cultural permutations. For the church's role in public building see Bryan Ward-Perkins, *From Classical Antiquity to the Middle Ages. Urban Public Building in Northern and Central Italy, 300–850*, Oxford, 1984.

31 See King, *Law and Society in the Visigothic Kingdom*, introduction.

32 See R. MacMullen, 'Barbarian enclaves in the northern Roman empire', *Antiquité Classique* 32 (1963), 552–61; for Gallia Belgica, between the Rhine and the Seine and extending south to the Jura, see E. M. Wightman, *Gallia Belgica*, London, 1985, 250–6, 308–11; ead., *Roman Trier and the Treveri*, London, 1970, 250–4; E. James, 'Cemeteries and the problems of Frankish settlement in Gaul', in P. Sawyer (ed.), *Names, Words and Graves: Early Medieval Settlement*, Leeds, 1979, 55ff.; H. W. Bohme, *Germanische Grabfunde des 4. und 5. Jahrhunderts zwischen unterer Elbe und Loire*, Munich, 1974; M. Rouche, *L'Aquitaine des Wisigoths aux Arabes (418–781)*, Paris, 1977;

R. Christlein, *Die Alamannen*, Stuttgart, 1978. K. Randsborg, *The First Millennium AD in Europe and the Mediterranean*, Cambridge, 1991, ch. 4, esp. 65–81, sets changes in settlement in a broader European perspective, with bibliography.

33 See M. Todd 'The Germanic peoples', *CAH* XIII (forthcoming) for an excellent survey.

34 J. Percival, *The Roman Villa*, London, 1976.

35 Heather, *Goths and Romans*, emphasizes this weakness in the literary sources, e.g., p. 141.

36 For this see C. Wickham, 'The other transition: from the ancient world to feudalism', *Past and Present* 103 (1984), 3–36.

37 See R. C. Blockley, 'Subsidies and diplomacy: Rome and Persia in late antiquity', *Phoenix* 39 (1985), 62–74; E. Chrysos, 'Byzantine diplomacy, AD 300–800: means and ends', in J. Shepard and S. Franklin (eds), *Byzantine Diplomacy*, Aldershot, 1992, 25–39; J. Durliat, 'Le salaire de la paix sociale dans les royaumes barbares (Ve–VIe siècles)', in H. Wolfram and A. Schwarcz (eds), *Anerkennung und Integration: zu den wirtschaftlichen Grundlagen der Völkerwanderungszeit (400–600)*, Vienna, 1988, 21–72.

38 Barbarian federates: J. H. W. G. Liebeschuetz, *Barbarians and Bishops. Army, Church and State in the Age of Arcadius and Chrysostom*, Oxford, 1990, 32–47. A similar relation existed between the eastern government and the Arab phylarchs in the sixth century (Chapter 8).

39 Heather, *Goths and Romans*, 194–224 is the latest (and excellent) discussion; see also Liebeschuetz, *Barbarians and Bishops*, 55–76, with 76–85 on the role of Alaric in the formation of a Gothic identity.

40 See Jones, *LRE*, I, 249–53.

41 Against, S. J. B. Barnish, 'Taxation, land, and barbarian settlement', *Papers of the British School at Rome* 54 (1986), 170–95.

42 See Heather, *Goths and Romans*, 221–2, and T. S. Burns, 'The settlement of 418', in J. Drinkwater and H. Elton (eds), *Fifth-Century Gaul. A Crisis of Identity?*, Cambridge, 1992.

43 See A. Ferrill, *The Fall of the Roman Empire. The Military Explanation*, London, 1986, which (though simplistic) gives a general overview and attempts an explanation.

44 See MacMullen, *Corruption*, 175.

45 MacMullen, *Corruption*, 145; his appendix C, 209–17, lists the evidence for all periods; see also his *Soldier and Civilian in the Later Roman Empire*, Cambridge, Mass., 1963.

46 See B. Isaac, 'The meaning of the terms "limes" and "limitanei" in ancient sources', *JRS* 78 (1988), 125–47. But MacMullen is no doubt right to argue that soldiers in frontier posts had often also farmed land in practice from a much earlier date – part of the 'confounding of roles' (*Corruption*, 175–6).

47 Useful on the deficiencies of the eastern army in Italy in the sixth century: Thompson, *Romans and Barbarians*, ch. 5. M. Hendy, *Studies in the Byzantine Monetary Economy, c. AD 300–1450*, Cambridge, 1985, 164–8, computes the cost of Justinian's army in North Africa; this is a dangerous procedure, however, because it depends on the figures

given in ancient sources, which can be notoriously unreliable.

48 See the full discussion in Liebeschuetz, *Barbarians and Bishops*, 32–47; and cf. the list of known barbarians in the Roman army in the fourth century given in MacMullen, *Corruption*, 201–4.

49 See in particular de Ste Croix, *Class Struggle*, 509–18; Ferrill, *The Fall of the Roman Empire*, passim.

50 Again, a drop in manpower in the late empire is easy to postulate but hard to establish. Jones, *LRE*, II, 1040–5 cautiously concludes that while there is likely to have been a drop in population, it was not on sufficient a scale as to provide a major explanation for decline; there is in fact evidence for population increase in the east: E. Patlagean, *Pauvreté économique et pauvreté sociale à Byzance, IVe–VIIe siècles*, Paris, 1977, 232–5, 426–9, and see below, Chapter 8.

51 The actual number of barbarians entering the empire is extremely difficult to establish, for lack of reliable information in the sources; it was obviously large *in toto*, but individual bands were often quite small. Again, the figures given in literary sources vary wildly and are often unreliable; however, one that is commonly quoted and which may provide a reasonable guide is the total of 80,000 for the Vandals when they entered Africa, given by Victor of Vita I.1.2, and by Procopius, *BV* I.5.18. This seems to include men, women, children, old people and slaves, and implies a fighting force certainly no greater than a quarter of the total (for this and the evidence generally on barbarian numbers, on which modern scholars vary no less than the ancient sources, see MacMullen, *Corruption*, 191 and n. 68).

52 The classic statement is that of the French historian A. Piganiol, at the end of his book, *L'Empire chrétien (325–395)*, 2nd edn, Paris, 1972, 'the empire did not die a natural death, it was assassinated'.

53 Jones, *LRE*, II, 1,042 seems to accept a figure of over 600,000; see also 679–80. On the *Notitia* see J. H. Ward, 'The Notitia Dignitatum', *Latomus* 33 (1974), 397–434; J. C. Mann, 'What was the *Notitia Dignitatum* for?', in R. Goodburn and P. Bartholomew (eds), *Aspects of the Notitia Dignitatum*, Oxford, BAR, 1976, 1–8.

54 For the Gothic wars, see Thompson, *Romans and Barbarians*, 77–91; earlier: MacMullen, *Corruption*, 191–2.

55 MacMullen, *Corruption*, 41, 174; further discussion in id., 'How big was the Roman army?', *Klio* 62 (1980), 451–60; C. R. Whittaker, 'Inflation and the economy in the fourth century AD', in C. E. King (ed.), *Imperial Revenue, Expenditure and Monetary Policy in the Fourth Century AD*, Oxford, 1980, 1–22; R. Duncan-Jones, 'Pay and numbers in Diocletian's army', *Chiron* 8 (1978), 541–60 (rev. in id., *Structure and Scale in the Roman Economy*, Cambridge, 1990, 105–17).

56 Diocletian and the late Roman frontier system: E. Luttwak, *The Grand Strategy of the Roman Empire*, Baltimore, Maryland, 1976; Ferrill, *The Fall of the Roman Empire*; against, B. Isaac, *The Limits of Empire*, Oxford, 1990; for the east see the spectacular photographs published by David Kennedy and Derrick Riley, *Rome's Desert Frontier from the Air*, London, 1990; P. Freeman and D. Kennedy (eds), *The Defence of the Roman Empire in the East*, I–II, Oxford, BAR, 1986; D. H. French

and C. S. Lightfoot (eds), *The Eastern Frontier of the Roman Empire*, I–II, Oxford, BAR, 1989, and see below, Chapter 8.

57 Progressive Roman retreats and the insuperable problems of frontier defence: MacMullen, *Corruption*, 177–91.

58 For this see J. Drinkwater, *Roman Gaul*, London, 1983; id., *The Gallic Empire*, Stuttgart, 1988.

59 See Wightman, *Gallia Belgica*, 300–5 ('The loosening of control'); cf. 301: 'the power of the frontier people was becoming more and more evident, the distinction between Romans and barbarians more blurred'.

60 Trans. E. Fitzgerald (1930), II, 477.

61 On demilitarization see Liebeschuetz, *Barbarians and Bishops*, 16–21; MacMullen, *Corruption*, 177.

3 CHURCH AND SOCIETY

1 Jones, *LRE*, I, 167–9.

2 The period from the fourth to the seventh centuries is often defined as an 'age of spirituality': see K. Weitzmann (ed.), *The Age of Spirituality*, New York, 1979; the transition to Byzantine art tends to be seen in similar terms, see E. Kitzinger, *Byzantine Art in the Making*, Cambridge, Mass., 1977.

3 cf. de Ste Croix, *Class Struggle*.

4 Not least by Peter Brown (see bibliography, p. 238); and see *The Making of Late Antiquity*, Cambridge, Mass., 1978; 'Late antiquity', in P. Ariès and G. Duby (eds), *History of Private Life*, I, Eng. trans., Cambridge, Mass., 1987, 235–313. For a recent emphasis on 'spirituality' see Susan Ashbrook Harvey, *Asceticism and Society in Crisis. John of Ephesus and the Lives of the Eastern Saints*, Berkeley and Los Angeles, Calif., 1990.

5 For the social and political force of the world-view developed by early Christianity see M. Mann, *The Sources of Social Power*, I, Cambridge, 1986; for the importance of communication (preaching, writing, visual representation) in propagating this world-view see Averil Cameron, *Christianity and the Rhetoric of Empire*, Berkeley and Los Angeles, Calif., 1991.

6 Described by Procopius, *Buildings* I.1.22ff. and in a long poem by Paul the Silentiary written in honour of its rededication in 563; see R. Krautheimer, *Early Christian and Byzantine Architecture*, rev. edn, Harmondsworth, 1975, 215–40, especially 237 on the antecedents of St Sophia; translations: Mango, *Art*, 72–102.

7 For this church, and for the hymn in Syriac which celebrated it as symbolizing heaven see Kathleen McVey, 'The domed church as microcosm: literary roots of an architectural symbol', *Dumbarton Oaks Papers* 37 (1983), 91–121.

8 See R. M. Harrison, *A Temple for Byzantium*, London, 1989; poem: *Anth. Pal.* I.10. See Gregory of Tours, *De gloria martyrum* 102; part of the *Narratio de S. Sophia* is translated in Mango, *Art*, 96ff.

9 See Marlia Mundell Mango, *Silver from Early Byzantium. The Kaper*

Koraon and Related Treasures, Baltimore, Maryland, 1986, 98, and see the introduction.

10 See R. Milburn, *Early Christian Art*, Berkeley and Los Angeles, Calif., 1988, 126–9.

11 Ambrose: R. A. Markus, *The End of Ancient Christianity*, Cambridge, 1990, 143–9; Chrysostom (whose fortunes as bishop of Constantinople provide a very good example of the power network of secular authorities, monks, congregation, rival bishops and lesser clergy, within which a prominent churchman now operated): J. H. W. G. Liebeschuetz, *Barbarians and Bishops. Army, Church and State in the Age of Arcadius and Chrysostom*, Oxford, 1990, 166–227; K. Holum, *Theodosian Empresses. Women and Imperial Dominion in Late Antiquity*, Berkeley, Calif., 1982.

12 The classic work on Augustine is Peter Brown's biography, *Augustine of Hippo*, London, 1967; for a short introduction to Augustine's thought see Henry Chadwick, *Augustine*, Oxford, 1986. The key work on Christian education is the *De doctrina christiana*, and see also the *De catechizandis rudibus*.

13 For an introduction see F. M. Young, *From Nicaea to Chalcedon*, London, 1983, 265–89.

14 See R. Van Dam, *Leadership and Community in Late Antique Gaul*, Berkeley and Los Angeles, Calif., 1985, 167, and in general on all these issues in the fifth-century west.

15 For the patronage of western bishops in this period, and their exploitation of relics for reasons of local prestige, see Peter Brown, *The Cult of the Saints*, London, 1981; Van Dam, *Leadership and Community*, 177–300. There is a great deal of evidence for fifth- and sixth-century Gaul, where Caesarius of Arles (AD 502–42) later exercised a more provincial but essentially similar role: see C. E. Stancliffe, *St. Martin and his Hagiographer*, Oxford, 1983; W. Klingshirn, 'Charity and power: Caesarius of Arles and the ransoming of captives in sub-Roman Gaul', *JRS* 75 (1985), 183–203.

16 P. Chuvin, *A Chronicle of the Last Pagans*, Eng. trans., Cambridge, Mass., 1990, gives a lively account of Christian measures against pagans and pagan reactions to them, especially in urban intellectual circles; see also G. Fowden, 'Bishops and temples in the eastern Roman empire, AD 320–435', *JThS* n.s. 29 (1978), 53–78; R. P. C. Hanson, 'The transformation of pagan temples into churches in the early Christian centuries', *Journal of Semitic Studies* 23 (1978), 257–67; W. E. Kaegi Jr, 'The fifth-century twilight of Byzantine [sic] paganism', *Classica et Mediaevalia* 27 (1966), 243–75; R. Van Dam, 'From paganism to Christianity in late antique Gaza', *Viator* 16 (1985); F. Trombley, 'Paganism in the Greek world at the end of antiquity: the case of rural Anatolia and Greece', *Harvard Theol. Rev.* 78 (1985), 327–52. Hypatia: J. Rist, 'Hypatia', *Phoenix* 19 (1965), 214–25. Alan Cameron, 'The empress and the poet', *Yale Classical Studies* 27 (1982), 217–89, emphasizes the intolerance, but also the complications, of the involvement in religious matters of the imperial family in the east in the early fifth century.

17 See Holum, *Theodosian Empresses*, 147–74.

18 Generally: see J. Meyendorff, *Imperial Unity and Christian Divisions*, Crestwood, NY, 1989; J. N. Kelly, *Early Christian Doctrines*, 5th edn, London, 1977. J. Herrin, *The Formation of Christendom*, Oxford, 1987, 91–127, contains a good discussion of the Fifth Council of AD 553–4, which marked an important stage in the breach between west and east.

19 For more detail, see W. H. C. Frend, *A History of the Monophysite Movement*, Cambridge, 1972; the ordinations: Susan Ashbrook Harvey, 'Remembering pain: Syriac historiography and the separation of the churches', *Byzantion* 58 (1988), 295–308.

20 See Jones, *LRE*, II, ch. 22 ('The church').

21 See G. D. Hunt, *Holy Land Pilgrimage in the Later Roman Empire AD 312–460*, Oxford, 1972, ch. 7.

22 See Holum, *Theodosian Empresses*; Alan Cameron, 'The empress and the poet'. Eudocia's verse inscription on the baths at Hammat Gader on the east coast of the Sea of Galilee: J. Green and Y. Tsafrir, 'Greek inscriptions from Hammat Gader: a poem by the Empress Eudocia and two building inscriptions', *Israel Exploration Journal* 32 (1982), 77–91; Hunt, *Holy Land Pilgrimage*, ch. 10.

23 See Ashbrook Harvey, *Asceticism and Society in Crisis*, 80–7; Cameron, *Procopius*, 76–81.

24 As in Ariès and Duby (eds), *History of Private Life*, I (see especially the chapter by Peter Brown).

25 The number is obviously exaggerated. Furthermore, John was a Monophysite and therefore an odd choice; see Chuvin, *Last Pagans*, 143–4. Missionary activity in this period, of which there was a great deal, was more typically directed at barbarians living on the edges of imperial territory and thus had a notably political motivation.

26 On this see F. R. Trombley, *Hellenic Religion and Christianization, c. 370–529*, 2 vols, Leiden, 1993; cf. T. E. Gregory, 'The survival of paganism in Christian Greece: a critical survey', *AJP* 107 (1986), 229–42; and see G. W. Bowersock, *Hellenism in Late Antiquity*, Cambridge, 1990.

27 Personal advantage: see R. MacMullen, *Christianizing the Roman Empire AD 100–400*, New Haven, Conn., 1984; imperial measures against pagans: P. Lemerle, *Byzantine Humanism*, Eng. trans., Canberra, 1986, 73–9.

28 See Chuvin, *Last Pagans*, 144–8; Bowersock, *Hellenism in Late Antiquity*, 35–40; and see Chapter 6.

29 For a brief introduction, S. G. Hall, *Doctrine and Practice in the Early Church*, London, 1991, ch. 17. The fifth and sixth centuries were the great period of the establishment of monastic foundations in the west; the great Benedict of Nursia was a contemporary of Cassidorus, while between his arrival in Gaul from Ireland, *c.* AD 575, and his death in AD 615, Columba was to found the great centres of Luxeuil, Fontaine and Bobbio.

30 For women religious in this period see Susanna Elm, *Virgins of God*, Oxford 1993.

31 The classic introduction is still D. J. Chitty, *The Desert a City*, Oxford, 1966; for the coenobitic organization instituted by Pachomius see

P. Rousseau, *Pachomius*, Berkeley and Los Angeles, Calif., 1985. Y. Hirschfeld, *The Judaean Desert Monasteries in the Byzantine Period*, New Haven, Conn., 1992, based on both archaeological and literary evidence, gives a fascinating picture of life in the many monasteries of the Judaean desert in the fifth and sixth centuries.

32 Trans. G. Clark, Translated Texts for Historians 8, Liverpool, 1989. Pythagoras: D. J. O'Meara, *Pythagoras Revived. Mathematics and Philosophy in Late Antiquity*, Oxford, 1989.

33 For a comparison in terms of written lives, see A. Meredith, 'Asceticism – Christian and Greek', *Journal of Theological Studies* n.s. 27 (1976), 313–22; and see the wide range of extracts in the sourcebook, V. Wimbush (ed.), *Ascetic Behavior in Greco-Roman Antiquity*, Minneapolis, Minnesota, 1990.

34 See especially Peter Brown, *The Body and Society. Men, Women and Sexual Renunciation in Early Christianity*, New York, 1988; Aline Rousselle, *Porneia: On Desire and the Body in Antiquity*, Eng. trans., Oxford, 1988.

35 For stylites see S. Ashbrook Harvey, 'The sense of a stylite: perspectives on Simeon the Elder', *Vigiliae christianae* 42 (1988), 376–94.

36 P. Brown, 'The rise and function of the holy man in late antiquity', *JRS* 61 (1971), 80–101, represented with additions in his *Society and the Holy in Late Antiquity*, Berkeley and Los Angeles, Calif., 1982, 103–52.

37 For some reactions to Brown's article and for other perspectives, see the contributions in S. Hackel (ed.), *The Byzantine Saint*, London, 1981; Julia Seiber, *Early Byzantine Urban Saints*, Oxford, 1977; L. M. Whitby, 'Maro the Dendrite: an anti-social holy man', in Michael Whitby, Philip Hardie and Mary Whitby (eds), *Homo Viator. Classical Studies for John Bramble*, Bristol, 1987, 309–17; Ashbrook Harvey, *Asceticism and Society in Crisis*.

38 The textual transmission of the early monastic literature is somewhat complex, but many of the stories of the Egyptian desert fathers are conveniently contained in Benedicta Ward, *The Sayings of the Desert Fathers*, London, 1975; and Russell, *Lives of the Desert Fathers*.

39 See A. Vööbus, *A History of Asceticism in the Syrian Orient*, 2 vols, Louvain, 1958–60; S. Brock, 'Early Syrian asceticism', *Numen* 20 (1973), 1–19 (reprinted in his *Syriac Perspectives on Late Antiquity*, London, 1984); Susan Ashbrook Harvey, 'Women in early Syrian Christianity', in Averil Cameron and Amélie Kuhrt (eds), *Images of Women in Antiquity*, London, 1983, (rev. edn, 1993), 288–98.

40 For the growth of icon worship see E. Kitzinger, 'The cult of images in the period before Iconoclasm', *Dumbarton Oaks Papers* 8 (1954), 85–150; texts in Mango, *Art*.

41 Public use of icons: Averil Cameron, 'Images of authority; élites and icons in late sixth-century Byzantium', *Past and Present* 84 (1979), 3–35 (reprinted in her *Change and Continuity in Sixth-Century Byzantium*. London, 1981); women and icons: Judith Herrin, 'Women and faith in icons in early Christianity', in R. Samuel and G. Stedman Jones (eds), *Culture, Ideology and Politics*, London, 1982, 56–83; with ead., *Formation of Christendom*, 307–10.

42 On both matters see Robin Cormack, *Writing in Gold*, London, 1985.
43 The wide variety can be seen in the comprehensive illustrations in Weitzmann, *Age of Spirituality*, the very valuable catalogue of a major exhibition held at the Metropolitan Museum of Art, New York, in 1978.
44 For this argument see Alan Cameron, 'The Latin revival of the fourth century', in W. Treadgold (ed.), *Renaissances before the Renaissance*, Stanford, 1984, 42–58, 182–4.
45 G. Vikan, *Byzantine Pilgrimage Art*, Washington DC, 1982, gives a very good introduction, with many examples. For pilgrimage itself see Hunt, *Holy Land Pilgrimage*; and the wider-ranging treatment by P. Maraval, *Lieux saints et pèlerinages d'Orient*, Paris, 1985; pilgrimage in Gaul: Van Dam, *Leadership and Community*, e.g., 249ff.
46 See D. J. Constantelos, *Byzantine Philanthropy and Social Welfare*, New Brunswick, NT, 1968.
47 For the example of Italy see B. Ward-Perkins, *From Classical Antiquity to the Middle Ages. Urban Public Building in Northern and Central Italy AD 300–850*, Oxford, 1984, part II, 'The rise of Christian patronage', esp. 51–84, 149–52.
48 See J. Herrin, 'Ideals of charity, realities of welfare. The philanthropic activity of the Byzantine church', in R. Morris (ed.), *Church and People in Byzantium*, Birmingham, 1990, 151–64; see also Chapter 6.
49 See the translation and commentary of the important Clark, *Life of Melania*.
50 Care taken for the giver's own family: J. Harries, '"Treasure in heaven": property and inheritance among the senators of late Rome', in E. Craik (ed.), *Marriage and Property*, Aberdeen, 1984, 54–70.
51 See the basic discussion by Peter Brown, 'Aspects of the Christianization of the Roman aristocracy', *JRS* 51 (1961), 1–11 (reprinted in his collection *Religion and Society in the Age of St. Augustine*, London, 1972, 161–72).
52 The problem is discussed in detail by Evelyne Patlagean, *Pauvreté économique et pauvreté sociale à Byzance, IVe–VIIe siècles*, Paris, 1977, 113–55, and cf. 181–96.
53 Trans. R. Davis, Liverpool, 1989.

4 LATE ROMAN SOCIAL STRUCTURES AND THE LATE ROMAN ECONOMY

1 See for instance Peter Garnsey and Richard Saller, *The Roman Empire. Economy, Society and Culture*, London, 1987; and Peter Garnsey, *Famine and Food Supply in the Graeco-Roman World*, Cambridge, 1988, ch. 15.
2 Among them A. H. M. Jones; see especially his articles on the colonate and on taxation in P. Brunt (ed.), *The Roman Economy*, Oxford, 1974; M. I. Rostovtzeff, *SEHRE*, ch. 12. cf., e.g., C. G. Starr, *The Roman Empire, 27 BC to AD 476*, Oxford, 1982, 164–5: 'politically the structure of the Later Roman Empire is one of the grimmest of all ancient times'; 'to modern man, the corrupt, brutal regimentation of the Later Empire appears as a horrible example of the victory of the state over the

individual'. Peter Brown's review discussion of Jones, *LRE*, in his *Religion and Society in the Age of St. Augustine*, London, 1972, 46–73, is still worth reading.

3 For example, A. H. M. Jones, 'Over-taxation and the decline of the Roman Empire', in Brunt (ed.), *The Roman Economy*, 82–9.

4 Alföldy, *Social History*, ch. 7.

5 *The Ancient Economy*, Berkeley and Los Angeles, Calif., 1973, 2nd rev. edn, London, 1985.

6 For a useful introduction to the issues and for further reading see Kevin Greene, *The Archaeology of the Roman Economy*, London, 1986, 45–66.

7 For a good general introduction to the Roman economy in the early empire, emphasizing its structural features, see Garnsey and Saller, *The Roman Empire*.

8 cf. Peter Brown, 'Eastern and western Christendom in late antiquity: a parting of the ways', in id., *Society and the Holy in the Late Antiquity*, Berkeley and Los Angeles, Calif., 1982, 166–95.

9 This is essentially the view of K. Randsborg, *The First Millennium AD in Europe and the Mediterranean. An Archaeological Essay*, Cambridge, 1991.

10 cf. Finley, *The Ancient Economy*; the main thesis of de Ste Croix, *Class Struggle*, is premised on the view that the numbers of slaves had declined in the late empire. For some of the problems, see R. MacMullen, 'Late Roman slavery', *Historia* 36 (1987), 359–82; C. R. Whittaker, 'Circe's pigs: from slavery to serfdom in the later Roman world', *Slavery and Abolition* 8 (1987), 87–122.

11 See A. H. M. Jones, 'The caste system in the Roman empire', in Brunt (ed.), *The Roman Economy*, 396–418; id., 'The Roman colonate', in ibid., 293–307; de Ste Croix, *Class Struggle*.

12 J. Gascou, 'Les grands domaines, la cité et l'état en Egypte byzantine', *Travaux et Mémoires* 9 (1985), 1–90, questions the older view of self-sufficient large estates in late Roman Egypt; see also Alan Bowman, *Egypt after the Pharaohs, 322 BC–AD 642*, Berkeley and Los Angeles, Calif., 1986.

13 This is naturally a very simplified account; for the theoretical issues see especially J.-M. Carrié, 'Le "colonat" du Bas-Empire: un mythe histor-iographique?', *Opus* 1 (1982), 351–70; id., 'Un roman des origines: les généalogies du "colonat du Bas-Empire"', *Opus* 2 (1983), 205–51; with A. Marcone, *Il colonato tardoantico nella storiografia moderna*, Como, 1988. See in general, Alföldy, *Social History*, 202ff. (but overstated).

14 See R. MacMullen, 'Judicial savagery in the Roman empire', *Chiron* 16 (1986), 147–66.

15 For a Marxist view which overstates its case in relation to the late empire, see P. Anderson, *Passages from Antiquity to Feudalism*, London, 1974; see C. Wickham, 'The other transition: from the ancient world to feudalism', *Past and Present* 103 (1984), 3–36.

16 As is done by modern historians who wish to stress the gloomy aspects of the late empire in order to explain its 'decline'; cf., e.g., Alföldy, *Social History*, 203–10. The same approach goes hand in hand with an

emphasis on social unrest (cf. ibid., 210–20).

17 See C. R. Whittaker, 'Late Roman trade and traders', in P. Garnsey, K. Hopkins and C. R. Whittaker (eds), *Trade in the Ancient Economy*, London, 1983, 170–3.

18 Whittaker, 'Late Roman trade and traders', 176–7. On the other hand, the large estates of late Roman Egypt, such as that of the Apiones at Oxhyrhynchus, were not self-sufficient; they hired local craftsmen and bought necessities such as mats and ropes from local monasteries.

19 On the senate, see Jones, *LRE*, II, ch. 15; M. T. W. Arnheim, *The Senatorial Aristocracy in the Later Roman Empire*, Oxford, 1972 (far too schematized); stratification: T. D. Barnes, 'Who were the nobility of the Roman empire?', *Phoenix* 28 (1974), 444–9. The senate was still important in sixth-century Constantinople: see H.-G. Beck, *Senat und Volk von Konstantinopel*, Sitz. bayer. Akad. der Wiss., Munich, 1966.

20 See Cameron, *Procopius*, chs 4 and 13.

21 Peter Brown, 'Aspects of the Christianization of the Roman aristocracy', *JRS* 51 (1961), 1–11, is still basic.

22 The government's dilemma is well brought out by F. Millar, 'Empire and city, Augustus to Julian: obligations, excuses and status', *JRS* 73 (1983), 76–96.

23 *LRE*, I, 748; see 740–57.

24 Jones, *LRE*, I, 391–6; and more generally MacMullen, *Corruption*, 148–67.

25 See A. Wallace-Hadrill (ed.), *Patronage in Ancient Society*, London, 1989, in particular Peter Garnsey and Greg Woolf, 'Patronage of the rural poor', at 162–6; R. P. Saller, *Personal Patronage under the Early Empire*, Cambridge, 1982.

26 Garnsey and Woolf, 'Patronage of the rural poor', 167; see also Alföldy, *Social History*, 215–16 (though too highly-coloured).

27 Much of volume III of Giardina (ed.) (*Le merci, gli insediamenti*), is devoted to these questions; cf. the review by C. Wickham, 'Marx, Sherlock Holmes and late Roman commerce', *JRS* 78 (1988), 183–93. See also the important collection, C. Morrisson and J. Lefort (eds), *Hommes et richesses dans l'empire byzantin I, IVe–VIIe siècle*, Paris, 1989.

28 Also recognized by contemporaries: see M. Hendy, *Studies in the Byzantine Monetary Economy c. AD 300–1450*, Cambridge, 1985, 158.

29 See C. Howgego, 'The supply and use of money in the Roman world, 200 BC–AD 300', *JRS* 82 (1992), 64–94.

30 See Garnsey, Hopkins and Whittaker (eds), *Trade in the Ancient Economy*, xiv–xxi; the argument is set out more fully in Hopkins's article, 'Taxes and trade in the Roman Empire', *JRS* 70 (1980), 101–25.

31 For mining see J. Edmondson, 'Mining in the later Roman empire and beyond: continuity and disruption', *JRS* 79 (1989), 84–102.

32 Jones, *LRE*, II, 1045, 'the basic economic weakness of the empire was that too few producers supported too many idle mouths'. Jones believed however that the late Roman army had doubled in size since the Principate (ibid., 1046).

33 See S. Thomas Parker, *Romans and Saracens. A History of the Arabian

Frontier, Winona Lake, 1986, 83–4, 112, 149; and Chapter 8 below; for barbarians, see Chapter 2; and cf. J. L. Teall, 'Barbarians in the armies of Justinian', *Speculum* 40 (1965), 294–322.

34 See Parker, *Romans and Saracens*, 143; and Chapter 8.

35 Hendy, *Studies in the Byzantine Monetary Economy*, contains a wealth of information not easily available elsewhere on the late Roman financial system, though the arrangement of the book makes it difficult to use and obscures understanding of diachronic change.

36 Jones, *LRE*, I, 468–9 (and in general on finance, 411–69; see also J. Durliat, *Les finances publiques de Dioclétien aux carolingiens (284–889)*, Sigmeringen, 1990).

37 See R. C. Blockley, 'Subsidies and diplomacy: Rome and Persia in late antiquity', *Phoenix* 39 (1985), 62–74.

38 Jones, *LRE*, I, 691–705; at Rome there were also free distributions of pork and of oil, the former causing some awkward problems of supply.

39 See Peter Garnsey, 'Grain for Rome', in Garnsey, Hopkins and Whittaker (eds), *Trade in the Ancient Economy*, 118–30; with his *Famine and Food Supply*, ch. 15 (up to AD 250); J. Durliat, *De la ville antique à la ville byzantine*, Rome, 1990; B. Sirks, *Food for Rome. The Legal Structure of the Transportation and Processing of Supplies for the Imperial Distributions in Rome and Constantinople*, Amsterdam, 1991.

40 See Jones, *LRE*, I, 438–48; Hendy, *Studies in the Byzantine Monetary Economy*, 475–92, and in general on these very difficult questions.

41 The issue is well discussed by Wickham, 'Marx, Sherlock Holmes and late Roman commerce', 190–3, who provides a good introduction to the fundamental Italian work by A. Carandini and others (especially C. Panella, 'Le merci: produzioni, itinerari e destini', in Giardina (ed.), III, 431–59; see also Carandini, in ibid., 3–19, for a more theoretical exposition; and C. Panella, 'Gli scambi nel Mediterraneo Occidentale dal IV al VII secolo dal punto di vista di alcune "merci"', in Morrisson and Lefort (eds), *Hommes et richesses dans l'empire byzantin I*, 129–41, who provides a very clear picture of the evidence). The typology of late Roman pottery, established only since the publication of John Hayes, *Late Roman Pottery*, London, 1972, depends on a number of important recent excavations, among which that by the British team at Carthage, like that of the Italians, is central: see M. G. Fulford and D. S. Peacock, in H. Hurst and S. Roskams (eds), *Excavations at Carthage: the British Mission*, I, part ii, Sheffield, 1984.

42 For the prosperity of North Africa in the pre-Vandal period and for the increasing scale of senatorial holdings there see C. Lepelley, *Les cités de l'Afrique romaine au Bas-Empire*, I–II, Paris, 1979, 1987; id., 'Peuplement et richesses de l'Afrique romaine tardive', in Morrisson and Lefort (eds), *Hommes et richesses dans l'empire byzantin I*, 17–30; Whittaker, 'Trade and the aristocracy in the Roman empire'.

43 For the North African economy during the Vandal conquest see M. Fulford, 'Carthage – overseas trade and political economy, AD 400–700', *Reading Medieval Studies* 6 (1980), 68–70.

5 JUSTINIAN AND RECONQUEST

1 See Cameron, *Procopius*. For the numbering of the books of Procopius' *Wars* (here referred to as *BP* I–II, *BV* I–II, *BG* I–IV) see Select critical bibliography, p. 242. The *Wars* were completed in AD 553–4; it is argued in Cameron, *Procopius*, that the *Buildings* probably dates from AD 554 and the *Secret History* from AD 551, but these works are dated by some scholars to the end of the decade.

2 The relations between these works, and the contradictions between them, are fully discussed in Cameron, *Procopius*.

3 See Maas, *John Lydus*.

4 Tony Honoré, *Tribonian*, London, 1978, ch. 1. For other accounts of Justinian's reign see R. Browning, *Justinian and Theodora*, London, 1971, rev. edn, 1987; J. W. Barker, *Justinian and the Later Roman Empire*, Madison, Wisconsin, 1966; the fullest is still E. Stein, *Histoire du Bas-Empire*, II, rev. J.-R. Palanque, Paris, 1949, repr. Amsterdam, 1968. Bury, *LRE*, I–II, is still worth reading as a straightforward narrative, heavily paraphrasing Procopius.

5 Honoré, *Tribonian*, ch. 1, gives the best introduction to Justinian's legal work. Besides these works there are the *Institutes*, a kind of compendium of Roman law for law students. All are in Latin, being concerned with existing and earlier Roman law, but Justinian's own new legislation (*Novellae*, *Novels*), of which a series of important laws belong to the 530s, were issued sometimes in Latin but more often in Greek.

6 For discussion of the former view, see Cameron, *Procopius*, ch. 2; the latter view is expressed in E. Kitzinger, *Byzantine Art in the Making*, Cambridge, Mass., 1977.

7 There were many displaced Monophysite monks and clergy living in Constantinople: see Susan Ashbrook Harvey, *Asceticism and Society in Crisis. John of Ephesus and the Lives of the Eastern Saints*, Berkeley and Los Angeles, Calif., 1990, 86ff. Not only were they protected by the Empress Theodora, who lodged them in part of the imperial palace, but were also allegedly visited by the emperor for the purpose of theological discussions.

8 Cf. the very hostile account of his reign in Evagrius Scholasticus' *Ecclesiastical History*, written in Constantinople in the 590s (see Pauline Allen, *Evagrius Scholasticus the Church Historian*, Louvain, 1981).

9 See Cameron, *Procopius*, ch. 14.

10 See Cameron, *Procopius*, ch. 10, 'Procopius and Africa'.

11 For the background see J. Moorhead, 'Culture and power among the Ostrogoths', *Klio* 68 (1986), 112–22 at 117–20. Amalasuntha was pro-Roman and wanted her son to be brought up like a Roman prince, which annoyed the Goths (Proc., *BG* I.2.1–22, 4.4); her knowledge of Greek and Latin: Cassiodorus, *Var.* 11.1.6; and see S. Barnish, *Cassiodorus: Variae*, Liverpool, 1992, introduction.

12 See the differing accounts in Proc., *BP* I.24; *Secret History* 12.12; *Buildings* I.20f. The rioting was put down by imperial troops under Belisarius himself, at a cost of many lives (30,000: John Malalas, *Chron.*, 476; 50,000: John the Lydian, *De Mag.* III.70).

13 See M. Maas, 'Roman history and Christian ideology in Justinian's reform legislation', *Dumbarton Oaks Papers* 40 (1986), 17–31.

14 Procopius tries to put the campaigns in the best possible light in the *Wars* (*BP* I.13f.), but his account has to be compared with those given, for example, by John Malalas, *Chronicle*, trans. Jeffreys, 269ff., and the church historian Zacharias Rhetor, *HE* IX. 4f.; see Cameron, *Procopius*, 157–9. He gives the 'true' version (i.e., one hostile instead of favourable to Belisarius) of later episodes in the Persian wars himself in the *Secret History*, 2f. The 'Eternal Peace' of AD 533: Stein, *Histoire du Bas-Empire*, II, 294–6.

15 Stein, *Histoire du Bas-Empire*, II, 486ff.; for Italy see below pp. 113ff.

16 See Cameron, *Procopius*, 159ff., esp. 163–4.

17 See Cameron, *Procopius*, 164–5; for the events, G. Downey, *A History of Antioch in Syria*, Princeton, NJ, 1961, 533–46.

18 See Pauline Allen, 'The "Justinianic" plague', *Byzantion* 48 (1979), 5–20; J. Durliat, 'La peste du VIe siècle. Pour un nouvel examen des sources byzantines', in C. Morrisson and J. Lefort (eds), *Hommes et richesses dans l'empire byzantin I, IVe–VIIe siècle*, Paris, 1989, 107–20, plays down its effects; J. Biraben, 'La peste du VIe siècle dans l'empire byzantin', in ibid., 121–5. See further below Chapter 7.

19 For whom see Sebastian Brock, 'Christians in the Sasanid empire: a case of divided loyalties', *Studies in Church History* 18 (1982), 1–19, reprinted in id., *Syriac Perspectives on Late Antiquity*, London, 1984.

20 For the numbers and the military difficulties during the Gothic wars, see the interesting discussion by E. A. Thompson, 'The Byzantine conquest of Italy: military problems', in id., *Romans and Barbarians. The Decline of the Western Empire*, Madison, Wisconsin, 1982, 77–91. For the costs of Justinian's wars see M. Hendy, *Studies in the Byzantine Monetary Economy c. AD 300–1450*, Cambridge, 1985, 164–71.

21 See Cameron, *Procopius*, 195–7.

22 For all this see Stein, *Histoire du Bas-Empire*, II, 564–604.

23 Agathias' *Histories*, trans. J. Frendo, Berlin, 1975; see Averil Cameron, *Agathias*, Oxford, 1970; Procopius: Cameron, *Procopius*, 54–5, 189–90. Procopius' disillusionment shows clearly in *BG* III–IV.

24 For discussion of the ceremony, see M. McCormick, *Eternal Victory*, Cambridge, 1986, 125–9; generally, Averil Cameron, 'Gelimer's laughter: the case of Byzantine Africa', in F. M. Clover and R. S. Humphreys (eds), *Tradition and Innovation in Late Antiquity*, Madison, Wisconsin, 1989, 171–90; also my 'Byzantine Africa: the literary evidence', in *University of Michigan Excavations at Carthage VII*, Ann Arbor, Michigan, 1982, 29–62. For John Troglita's campaigns and the period after Procopius' narrative ends, we have the *Iohannis*, an eight-book Latin epic poem by the African poet Corippus.

25 For Justinian's defences in Africa: D. Pringle, *The Defence of Byzantine Africa*, 2 vols, Oxford, BAR, 1981; cf. also J. Durliat, *Les dédicaces d'ouvrages de défense dans l'Afrique byzantine*, Rome, 1981.

26 Edited, with translation and commentary, by Averil Cameron, *In laudem Iustini minoris*, London, 1976; see *Pan. Anast.* 36f., I.18f. with notes.

27 Hendy, *Studies in the Byzantine Monetary Economy*, 166–7. This is one of the rare instances where we have some official figures, though such computations can be extremely misleading. The size of the army itself is unknown, but Belisarius' original force amounted to 15,000 according to Procopius (above, p. 108).

28 For Africa see Proc., *Buildings* VI; with Cameron, *Procopius*, ch. 10, esp. 177f. One of the main sources for North Africa under the Vandals is the Latin account by a local bishop, Victor of Vita, of the alleged sufferings of the Catholic church and population at the hands of the Arian Vandals; see the translation by J. Moorhead, Translated Texts for Historians 10, Liverpool, 1992.

29 *BV* II.8.25.

30 For the latter, see C. Lepelley, *Les cités de l'Afrique romaine au Bas-Empire*, I–II, Paris, 1979, 187.

31 For a critical view, see Cameron, *Procopius*, ch. 6, with B. Croke and J. Crow, 'Procopius on Dara', *JRS* 73 (1983), 143–59, and the correctives of L. M. Whitby, 'Procopius' description of Martyropolis' (*De Aedificiis* 3.2.10–14)', *Byzantinoslavica* 45 (1984), 177–82; id., 'Procopius and the development of Roman defences in upper Mesopotamia', in P. Freeman and D. Kennedy (eds), *The Defence of the Roman and Byzantine East*, Oxford, BAR, 1986, 717–35; id., 'Procopius's description of Dara (*Buildings* 2.1–3)', in ibid., 737–83. For Justinian's building in Greece, see Timothy E. Gregory, 'Fortification and urban design in early Byzantine Greece', in R. L. Hohlfelder (ed.), *City, Town and Countryside in the Early Byzantine Era*, New York, 1982, 43–64; and for Illyricum, Frank E. Wozniak, 'The Justinianic fortification of Interior Illyricum', in ibid., 199–209. Italy is omitted altogether from the *Buildings*, perhaps because having been a theatre of war from AD 535–4 it had little to record; the *Buildings* itself may belong to AD 554 or alternatively to AD 559–60.

32 So for the works on the Persian frontier and the Black Sea coast, where the status of Lazica was a matter for contention between Byzantium and Persia (see p. 112, and see B. Isaac, *The Limits of Empire*, Oxford, 1990); James Howard-Johnston, 'Procopius, Roman defences north of the Taurus and the new fortress of Citharizon', in D. H. French and C. S. Lightfoot (eds), *The Eastern Frontier of the Roman Empire*, 2 vols, Oxford, BAR, 1989, 203–29 at 217.

33 Howard-Johnston, 'Procopius'.

34 See Cameron, *Procopius*, 96–8; P. Mayerson, 'Procopius or Eutychius on the construction of the monastery at Mount Sinai: which is the more reliable source?', *Bull. Am. Schools. Oriental Research* 230 (1978), 33–8.

35 See Chapter 8.

36 For Italy see E. A. Thompson, 'The Byzantine conquest of Italy: public opinion', in id., *Romans and Barbarians*, 92–109; J. Moorhead, 'Italian loyalties during Justinian's Gothic war', *Byzantion* 53 (1983), 575–96.

37 For the change in atmosphere see Roger Scott, 'Malalas, the Secret History and Justinian's propaganda', *Dumbarton Oaks Papers* 39 (1985), 99–109.

38 See Cameron, *Procopius*, 69–71.

39 For Italy in this period see C. Wickham, *Early Medieval Italy*, London, 1981, especially 'The Lombard kingdom', 28–47; and for the exarchate, see T. S. Brown, *Gentlemen and Officers. Imperial Administration and Aristocratic Power in Byzantine Italy AD 554–800*, Rome, 1984.

40 See Roger Collins, *Early Medieval Spain*, London, 1983, 38 (with very full bibliographies); see also E. A. Thompson, *The Goths in Spain*, Oxford, 1969. The objective seems to have been the protection of Byzantine Africa in case of intervention from Spain by the Visigoths.

41 Brown, *Gentlemen and Officers*, chs 1 and 2 provides an excellent discussion of the evidence.

42 Wickham, *Early Medieval Italy*, 26.

43 For the divisive effects of the Fifth Council see J. Herrin, *The Formation of Christendom*, Oxford, 1987, 119–27; and for the Lateran Synod, ibid., 250–5. For the African bishops, see Cameron, 'Byzantine Africa'.

44 See Brown, *Gentlemen and Officers*, 34–7. Unfortunately we have very little comparable evidence for the church in Africa, and for similar reasons the effects of reconquest on North African society also remain extremely obscure.

45 For these developments see W. H. C. Frend, *A History of the Monophysite Movement*, Cambridge, 1972; E. Honigmann, *Evêques et évêchés d'Asie antérieure au VIe siècle*, Louvain, 1951; Susan Ashbrook Harvey, 'Remembering pain: Syriac historiography and the separation of the churches', *Byzantion* 58 (1988), 296–308; and cf. also her *Asceticism and Society in Crisis*.

46 It is therefore a question whether or not Procopius actually counts Justinian's reign from AD 518, as argued by the great editor of Procopius, J. Haury: see R. Scott, 'Justinian's coinage, the Easter reforms and the date of the Secret History', *Byzantine and Modern Greek Studies* 11 (1987) 215–21; Cameron, *Procopius*, 9; Bury, *LRE*, II, 422–3.

47 The economic and demographic effects of the plague are emphasized by C. Mango, *Byzantium. The Empire of New Rome*, London, 1980, 68–9. The population of Constantinople was at its peak before the plague struck in AD 542; Mango suggests that it had reduced to 40,000 in id., *Le développement urbain de Constantinople (IVe–VIIe siècle)*, Paris, 1985, 54.

48 Such criticisms show themselves most sharply in the *Secret History*, but they also permeate the *Wars*: see Cameron, *Procopius*, 62ff., and see esp. ch. 13. The fall of John the Cappadocian (see p. 121) came in AD 541; another minister whom Procopius accuses of corruption was Peter Barsymes, who became praetorian prefect early in AD 543 and thus had major financial responsibility for provincial taxation and army supply and maintenance (see Stein, *Histoire du Bas-Empire*, II, 761–9).

49 The *Life* of Eutychius, written by the deacon Eustratius, and the Syriac *Church History* of John of Ephesus, are the main sources: see Averil Cameron, 'Eustratius's Life of the Patriarch Eutychius and the Fifth Ecumenical Council', in J. Chrysostomides, (ed.), *Kathegetria. Essays Presented to Joan Hussey for her 80th Birthday*, Camberley, 1988, 225–47; ead., 'The Life of the Patriarch Eutychius: models of the past in

the late sixth century', in G. Clarke (ed.), *Reading the Past in Late Antiquity*, Rushcutters Bay, 1990, 205–23. J. Meyendorff, *Imperial Unity and Christian Divisions: the Church 450–680 AD*, Crestwood, NY, 1989, provides a good introduction to the theological disputes of this period.

50 See Cameron, *Procopius*, chs 2 and 14.

51 See respectively G. Downey, 'Justinian's view of Christianity and the Greek classics', *Anglican Theological Review* 40 (1958), 13–22; with id.,'Julian and Justinian and the unity of faith and culture', *Church History* 28 (1959), 339–49; and id., *Constantinople in the Age of Justinian*, Norman, Oklahoma, 1960; W. Ullmann, *Principles of Government and Politics in the Middle Ages*, 2nd edn, London, 1966; P. Lemerle, *Byzantine Humanism*, Eng. trans., Sydney, 1986, 73–9; Honoré, *Tribonian*, ch. 1.

52 For the Barberini and Archangel ivories, see K. Weitzmann (ed.), *The Age of Spirituality*, New York, 1979, nos 28 and 481; for the Ravenna mosaics, A. Grabar, *Byzantium. From the Death of Theodosius to the Rise of Islam*, London, 1966, 156–7 (with colour illustrations); for the Sinai icons, J. Trilling, 'Sinai icons: another look', *Byzantion* 53 (1983), 300–11; for St Sophia, Chapter 1 above; and C. Mango, *Byzantine Architecture*, New York, 1976, 107–23 (with black and white illustrations).

53 See Averil and Alan Cameron, 'The *Cycle* of Agathias', *Journal of Hellenic Studies* 86 (1966), 6–25.

54 For the poem, see R. Macrides and P. Magdalino, 'The architecture of *ekphrasis*: construction and context of Paul the Silentiary's Ekphrasis of Hagia Sophia', *Byzantine and Modern Greek Studies* 12 (1988), 47–82.

55 Romanos: E. Catafygiotu Topping, 'Romanos, on the entry into Jerusalem: a *basilikos logos*', *Byzantion* 47 (1977), 65–91; Malalas: see Elizabeth Jeffreys, with Brian Croke and Roger Scott, *Studies in John Malalas*, Sydney, 1990.

56 Cassiodorus: Chapter 2; Cameron, *Procopius*, 196–200.

57 See also Chapter 6; and Averil Cameron, *Christianity and the Rhetoric of Empire*, Berkeley and Los Angeles, Calif., 1991, ch. 6.

6 CULTURE AND MENTALITY

1 Above, introduction; this aspect is emphasized, for example, in the introduction to Sebastian P. Brock and Susan Ashbrook Harvey, *Holy Women of the Syrian Orient*, Berkeley and Los Angeles, Calif., 1987; and in Peter Brown's work, for example, *The Making of Late Antiquity*, Cambridge, Mass., 1978, which poses the question of how and why this enhanced spirituality may have developed in the fourth century. The same view is suggested by the titles of other works, for example, Brown's collection of essays, *Society and the Holy in Late Antiquity*, Berkeley and Los Angeles, Calif., 1982; and K. Weitzmann (ed.), *The Age of Spirituality*, New York, 1979.

2 See *The Making of Late Antiquity*, 21; and also Brown's *Persuasion and*

Power in Late Antiquity, Madison, Wisconsin, 1992. The discourse is cast wholly in the masculine gender; the words 'man' or 'men' themselves appear no less than nine times in the course of four small pages. P. Brown, 'Late antiquity', in P. Ariès and G. Duby (eds), *History of Private Life* I, Eng. trans., Cambridge, Mass., 1987, 235–311 at 248, allows for a move towards more companionate upper-class marriage in the second century, but still within a world of 'unquestioning class loyalty with which the powerful *man* both lovingly embraced and firmly controlled *his* city'. For arguments against the 'companionate marriage' argument (for which see P. Veyne, 'La famille, l'amour sous le Haut-Empire romain', *Annales ESC* 33 (1978), 35–63), see, for example, Richard P. Saller and Brent D. Shaw, 'Tombstones and Roman family relationships in the Principate: civilians, soldiers and slaves', *JRS* 74 (1984), 124–56 at 134–7; and further discussion in Kate Cooper, 'Insinuations of womanly influence: an aspect of the Christianization of the Roman aristocracy', *JRS* 82 (1992), 113–27.

3 See Averil Cameron, 'Redrawing the map: early Christian territory after Foucault', *JRS* 56 (1986), 266–71.

4 For this see Cameron, *Procopius*, 227ff.

5 See the classic article by Alan Cameron, 'Wandering poets: a literary movement in Byzantine Egypt', *Historia* 14 (1965), 470–509; for Eudocia, id., 'The empress and the poet: paganism and politics at the court of Theodosius II', *Yale Classical Studies* 27 (1982), 217–89. Nonnus of Panopolis is the most important of the fifth-century poets: author of a voluminous *Dionysiaca* and of a poetic paraphrase of St John's Gospel, he set a pattern of poetic style and diction which others followed extremely closely. For Dioscorus, against the Greek and Coptic background of Middle Egypt in the late sixth century: L. B. MacCoull, *Dioscorus of Aphrodito. His Work and his World*, Berkeley and Los Angeles, Calif., 1988.

6 See Blockley, 1981, 1983 (Eunapius, Olympiodorus, Priscus, Malchus). Most of their works have not survived entire, but we have more of Zosimus' *New History* (trans. Ridley); and see W. Goffart, 'Zosimus: the first historian of Rome's fall', *American Historical Review* 76 (1971), 412–21. Procopius, Agathias and Theophylact Simocatta (see Chapter 8) continued this tradition even into the seventh century.

7 See Glenn F. Chesnut, *The First Christian Histories*, Paris, 1977; Pauline Allen, *Evagrius Scholasticus the Church Historian*, Louvain, 1981.

8 See Alan Cameron, 'The date and identity of Macrobius', *JRS* 56 (1966), 25–38; for a bibliographical guide to late Latin secular literature see R. Browning, 'The later Principate', *Cambridge History of Classical Literature II*, Cambridge, 1982, chs 35–42, Epilogue (also published separately, 1983).

9 See Averil Cameron, 'Byzantine Africa: the literary evidence', in *University of Michigan Excavations at Carthage VII*, Ann Arbor, Michigan, 1982, 30–1; Luxorius: M. Rosenblum, *Luxorius. A Latin Poet among the Vandals*, New York, 1961.

10 For an introduction see G. Downey, *Gaza in the Early Sixth Century*,

Norman, Oklahoma, 1963; Carol A. M. Glucker, *The City of Gaza in the Roman and Byzantine Periods*, Oxford, BAR, 1987, with P. Chuvin, *A Chronicle of the Last Pagans*, Eng. trans., Cambridge, Mass., 1990, 115–17.

11 The source is his *Life of Severus*, which we have in Syriac from a Greek original; see Chuvin, *Chronicle of the Last Pagans*, 105–6.
12 There is inscriptional evidence for these families: see C. M. Rouaché, *Aphrodisias in Late Antiquity*, London, 1989, 85–7.
13 Chuvin, *Chronicle of the Last Pagans*, provides a first introduction to the subject and the bibliography. Among recent work that of Richard Sorabji is especially important (see his *Time, Creation and the Continuum: Theories in Antiquity and the Early Middle Ages*, London, 1983, and the papers edited by him in *Philoponus and the Rejection of Aristotelian Science*, London, 1987, and *Aristotle Transformed. The Ancient Commentators and their Influence*, London, 1990). See also A. H. Armstrong (ed.), *History of Later Greek and Early Medieval Philosophy*, Cambridge, 1970.
14 Brown, 'Late antiquity', 249–51.
15 Elaborate fourth-century mosaics of Socrates with six sages, Odysseus' return, Kallos (the personification of Beauty) and Cassiopeia at Apamea were subsequently built over when the cathedral was constructed; see J. Ch. Balty, *Mosaïques antiques de Syrie*, Brussels, 1977, 78–80, 88–9; *Guide d'Apamée*, Brussels, 1981, 115ff. These and the New Paphos mosaics are discussed, and the New Paphos mosaics illustrated, in G. W. Bowersock, *Hellenism in Late Antiquity*, Cambridge, 1990, ch. 4.
16 Trans. K. S. Guthrie, New York and Chicago, Ill., 1925, repr. 1977; see G. Fowden, 'The pagan holy man in late antique society', *JHS* 102 (1982), 33–59; and for the archaeological evidence for philosophical teaching at Athens, see Alison Frantz, *The Athenian Agora XXIV. Late Antiquity A.D. 267–700*, Princeton, NJ, 1988, especially 56–8, 82–92.
17 See the introduction by Saffrey, 250–65.
18 For this see the essays in H. J. Blumenthal and R. A. Markus (eds), *Neoplatonism and Early Christian Thought*, London, 1981. The thought of Boethius (*Consolation of Philosophy*) is also deeply imbued with Neoplatonic ideas (see Chapter 2).
19 See also Chuvin, *Chronicle of the Last Pagans*, 102–5.
20 Malalas, *Chronicle*, trans. Jeffreys, 264.
21 The Athenian Academy: Alan Cameron , 'The last days of the Academy at Athens', *Proc. Cambridge Philological Society* 195 (1) (1969), 7–29; but see H. J. Blumenthal, '529 and after: what happened to the Academy?', *Byzantion* 48 (1978), 369–85. Frantz, *Athenian Agora XXIV*, 82–92, also discusses Justinian's edict. Simplicius at Harran: I. Hadot, 'The life and work of Simplicius in Greek and Arabic sources', in Sorabji (ed.), *Aristotle Transformed*, 275–303, following M. Tardieu, 'Sabiens coraniques et <Sabiens> de Harran', *Journal asiatique* 274 (1986), 1–44; see Chuvin, *Chronicle of the Last Pagans*, 135–41.
22 See Henry Chadwick, 'Philoponus, the Christian theologian', in Sorabji (ed.), *Philoponus*, 41–56; see also Sorabji, 'John Philoponus', in ibid., 1–40.

23 See Robert Browning, *Medieval and Modern Greek*, 2nd edn, London, 1983.

24 P. Lemerle, *Byzantine Humanism*, Eng. trans., Canberra, 1986, 81–120; C. Mango, *Byzantium. The Empire of New Rome*, London, 1980, ch. 6.

25 See A. Momigliano, 'Pagan and Christian historiography in the fourth century AD', in his *The Conflict between Paganism and Christianity in the Fourth Century*, Oxford, 1983, 79–99. The social context of the system is discussed in detail by R. Kaster, *Guardians of Language. The Grammarian and Society in Late Antiquity*, Berkeley and Los Angeles, Calif., 1988.

26 See Blockley, II, part I, chs 2 and 3.

27 Chuvin, *Chronicle of the Last Pagans*, 93–4, based on Alan Cameron, 'Wandering poets' and 'The empress and the poet'. For the opportunities of social mobility offered by literary skill, see also K. Hopkins, 'Social mobility in the later Roman empire: the evidence of Ausonius', *CQ* 11 (1961), 239–49; id., 'Elite mobility in the Roman empire', in M. I. Finley (ed.), *Studies in Ancient Society*, London, 1974, 103–20.

28 For the case of history, well illustrated by Procopius, see Cameron, *Procopius*, especially ch. 1; and for the tradition of direct imitation of classical models, which could lead to real artificiality and affectation, see Averil and Alan Cameron, 'Christianity and tradition in the historiography of the later Roman empire', *Class. Quart.* 14 (1964), 316–28.

29 And thus have much in common with contemporary lives of pagan holy men: see Averil Cameron, *Christianity and the Rhetoric of Empire*, Berkeley and Los Angeles, Calif., 1991, esp. ch. 3, and on pagan holy men in general, see Fowden, 'The pagan holy man'.

30 See especially Elizabeth Jeffreys, 'Malalas' world-view', and Roger Scott, 'Malalas and his contemporaries', in E. Jeffreys, B. Croke and R. Scott (eds), *Studies in John Malalas*, Sydney, 1990, 55–86.

31 Many works of Augustine are also rich in social observation, not just of the upper classes: see Brent Shaw, 'The family in late antiquity: the evidence of Augustine', *Past and Present* 115 (1987), 3–51, esp. 5–6.

32 On Christianity and classical culture see also, for example, M. L. W. Laistner, *Christianity and Classical Culture in the Later Roman Empire*, Ithaca, NY, 1951; W. Jaeger, *Early Christianity and Greek Paideia*, Cambridge, Mass., 1961; G. A. Kennedy, *Classical Rhetoric and its Christian and Secular Tradition from Ancient to Modern Times*, London, 1980.

33 See R. Mathison, 'Epistolography, literary circles and family ties in late Roman Gaul', *TAPA* 111 (1981), 95–109.

34 See Averil Cameron, *Christianity and the Rhetoric of Empire*, *passim*, e.g., 200ff. on the sixth century.

35 Peter Brown, *The World of Late Antiquity*, Berkeley and Los Angeles, Calif., 1991, 181.

36 As in E. Kitzinger, 'The cult of images in the period before Iconoclasm', *Dumbarton Oaks Papers* 8 (1954), 85–150; see also J. Herrin, *The Formation of Christendom*, Oxford, 1987, 307f.

37 Brown, *World of Late Antiquity*. For a very useful collection of evidence about images in this period see Mango, *Art*; and for the late

sixth century, Averil Cameron, 'Images of authority: elites and icons in late sixth-century Byzantium', *Past and Present* 84 (1979), 3–25.

38 See L. Cracco Ruggini, 'The ecclesiastical histories and the pagan historiography: providence and miracles', *Athenaeum* n.s. 55 (1977), 107–26; ead., 'Il miracolo nella cultura del tardo impero: concetto e funzione', in *Hagiographie, Cultures et Sociétés, IVe–XIIe siècles*, Paris, 1981, 161–204; Averil Cameron, *Christianity and the Rhetoric of Empire*, ch. 6.

39 See Sebastian P. Brock, 'Greek into Syriac and Syriac into Greek', in his *Syriac Perspectives on Late Antiquity*, London, 1984, II; and id., 'From antagonism to assimilation: Syriac attitudes to Greek learning', in ibid., V.

40 For this process in the fourth century see P. Walker, *Holy City, Holy Places*, Oxford, 1990.

41 See H. L. Strack and G. Stemberger, *Introduction to the Talmud and Midrash*, Eng. trans., Edinburgh, 1990.

42 See R. L. Wilken, *John Chrysostom and the Jews*, Berkeley and Los Angeles, Calif., 1983; ch. 2 provides a useful introduction to the position of the Jews in late antiquity.

43 See Jones, *LRE*, II, 944–50.

44 In general, see Lee I. Levine, *Ancient Synagogues Revealed*, Jerusalem, 1981, with 90ff. on Rehob.

45 There is a problem with the term 'paganism', in that it does not denote an entity in itself, but only marks out what is not Christian; hence some scholars prefer the term 'polytheist'. But this is problematic too: some pagans were essentially monotheists, while some may feel that Christianity itself was less monotheist than this term would imply.

46 See Bowersock, *Hellenism in Late Antiquity*.

47 Against the cruder notions of a 'pagan reaction', in late fourth-century Rome, see Alan Cameron, 'Paganism and literature in fourth-century Rome', *Christianisme et formes littéraires de l'antiquité tardive*, Entretiens Hardt 23, Geneva, 1976, 1–40; id., 'The Latin revival of the fourth century', in W. Treadgold (ed.), *Renaissances before the Renaissance*, Stanford, 1984, 42–58.

48 The main source is the *Life of Isidore* by the Athenian Neoplatonist Damascius (forthcoming translation by P. Athanassiadi, Translated Texts for Historians, Liverpool).

49 Legislation against pagans: *CJ* I, 5, 18.4; 11, 10 ('the sacrilegious foolishness of the Hellenes'); see T. Honoré, *Tribonian*, London, 1978, 14–16; E. Stein, rev. J.-R. Palanque, *Histoire du Bas-Empire*, II, Paris and Amsterdam, 1949, repr., 1968, 370–3. The patrician Phocas, the *quaestor sacri palatii* Thomas and the ex-prefect Asclepiodotus were all put on trial; Asclepiodotus committed suicide, and so did Phocas when he was tried again on the same charge in AD 546.

50 See Chuvin, *Chronicle of the Last Pagans*, 144–8; Bowersock, *Hellenism in Late Antiquity*, 35ff.

51 Chuvin, *Chronicle of the Last Pagans*, 143–4; see Chapter 3.

52 On Caesarius see W. Klingshirn, 'Charity and power: Caesarius of Arles and the ransoming of captives in sub-Roman Gaul', *JRS* 75 (1985), 183–203; R. A. Markus, *The End of Ancient Christianity*,

Cambridge, 1990, 202–11, emphasizing that what Caesarius called 'pagan' was often simply a matter of custom. Evangelization in northern Italy at the beginning of our period: Rita Lizzi, 'Ambrose's contemporaries and the Christianization of northern Italy', *JRS* 80 (1990), 156–73.

53 See G. Vikan, 'Art, medicine and magic in early Byzantium', *Dumbarton Oaks Papers* 38 (1984), 65–86; H. Magoulias, 'The lives of Byzantine saints as sources of data for the history of magic in the sixth and seventh centuries A.D.: sorcery, relics and icons', *Byzantion* 37 (1967), 227–69; and Averil Cameron, 'Providence and freewill in late antiquity', in Leo Howe and Alan Wain (eds), *Predicting the Future*, Cambridge, 1993, 118–43.

54 'Discontinuity with the classical past in Byzantium', in Margaret Mullett and Roger Scott (eds), *Byzantium and the Classical Tradition*, Birmingham, 1981, 57.

55 Markus, *The End of Ancient Christianity*, 224–5, suggests instead that the process of change from ancient to medieval (which he sets in the late sixth century) was a kind of closing in of horizons, an 'epistemological excision', a 'drainage of secularity' (p. 226), in contrast with the broader horizons of the Christian world of late antiquity. For the drawing in of horizons in the east see also my *Christianity and the Rhetoric of Empire*, ch. 6.

56 See the study of the Judaean monasteries by Y. Hirschfeld, *The Judaean Desert Monasteries in the Byzantine Period*, New Haven, Conn., 1992 (note that the term 'Byzantine' refers to what we call here the late antique period).

57 There seems to be no recent general guide to saints' lives and other biographies in late antiquity, but see Averil Cameron, *Christianity and the Rhetoric of Empire*, esp. ch. 3. Patricia Cox, *Biography in Late Antiquity*, Berkeley and Los Angeles, Calif., 1983, is more limited than its title suggests; for the west, see Alison Goddard Elliott, *Roads to Paradise*, Hanover and London, 1987; and for a lively introduction to some rather exotic eastern material see Benedicta Ward, *Harlots of the Desert*, Oxford, 1987.

58 See J. N. D. Kelly, *Jerome*, London, 1975; P. Brown, *The Body and Society. Men, Women and Sexual Renunciation in Early Christianity*, New York, 1988, 366–86.

59 See R. Lizzi, 'Una società esortata all'ascetismo: misure legislative, motivazioni economiche', *Studi Storici* 30 (1989), 129–53.

60 Over-schematized but rightly stressed by J. Goody, *The Development of the Family and Marriage in Europe*, Cambridge, 1983; see also D. I. Kertzer and R. P. Saller (eds), *The Family in Italy from Antiquity to the Present*, New Haven, Conn., 1991.

61 It could be either an individual or a group matter: for the former, see F. E. Consolino, 'Sante o patrone? Le aristocratizia tardoantiche e il potere della carità', *Studi Storici* 4 (1989), 969–91. The church itself, through the initiative of bishops, took over some of the role of private benefactors in the sphere of public building: see B. Ward-Perkins, *From Classical Antiquity to the Middle Ages. Urban Public Building in Northern and Central Italy AD 300–850*, Oxford, 1984.

62 Most of the many surviving letters tell us nothing directly on the subject, and are semi-public and literary in character. The best source of actual private letters is the papyri, which often preserve fragments of letters written to each other by ordinary people, though these too can sometimes be difficult to interpret.

63 The problem of the evidence is discussed by E. Patlagean, *Pauvreté économique et pauvreté sociale à Byzance, IVe–VIIe siècles*, Paris, 1977, 145–55.

64 Brent D. Shaw, 'Latin funerary epigraphy and family life in the later Roman empire', *Historia* 33 (1984), 457–97; id., 'The family in late antiquity'; contraception: Shaw, 'The family in late antiquity', 44–7, and see K. Hopkins, 'Contraception in the Roman empire', *Comparative Studies in Society and History* 8 (1965), 124–51; infanticide and sale of infants: Shaw, 'Family in late antiquity', 43f.

65 See Shaw, 'Family in late antiquity', 10f. and esp. 28–38. Modern historians differ about the choice of celibacy made by Melania and other contemporary women, some arguing that it provided a degree of liberation, others that it was unnatural and distorted; the attitudes expressed here speak, though cautiously, for the former view.

66 Shaw, 'Family in late antiquity', 39; and see B. Shaw and R. P. Saller, 'Close-kin marriage in Roman society', *Man*, n.s. 19 (1984), 432–44.

67 For a detailed treatment see Gillian Clark, *Women in Late Antiquity*, Oxford, 1993.

68 See R. Rosemary Ruether (ed.), *Religion and Sexism*, New York, 1974.

69 See Elizabeth A. Clark, *Jerome, Chrysostom and Friends*, New York and Toronto, 1979.

70 The point is made by A. Momigliano, 'The Life of St. Macrina by Gregory of Nyssa', in J. Ober and J. W. Eadie (eds), *The Craft of the Ancient Historian*, Lanham, Maryland, 1985, 443–58.

71 See especially the collection of articles by Elizabeth A. Clark, *Ascetic Piety and Women's Faith*, Lewiston, NY, 1986; Franca Ela Consolino, 'Modelli di comportamento e modi di santificazione per l'aristocrazia femminile dell'occidente', in Giardina (ed.), I, 273–306.

72 See Averil Cameron, *Christianity and the Rhetoric of Empire*, 165ff. The complex of ideas and associations surrounding the concept of Mary in relation to women: E. Pagels, *Adam, Eve and the Serpent*, London, 1988.

73 Averil Cameron, 'Virginity as metaphor', in Averil Cameron (ed.), *History as Text*, London, 1989, 184–205; A. Rousselle, *Porneia*, Eng. trans., Oxford, 1989.

74 See Ward, *Harlots of the Desert*.

75 See the very detailed and interesting treatment by J. Beaucamp, *Le statut de la femme à Byzance (4e–7e siècle) I. Le droit impérial*, Paris, 1990, *II. Les pratiques sociales*, Paris, 1992. See also A. Arjava, 'Women and law in late antiquity', Diss. Helsinki. For a western comparison see Wendy Davies, 'Celtic women in the early Middle Ages', in Averil Cameron and Amélie Kuhrt (eds), *Images of Women in Antiquity*, London, 1983, rev. 1993, 145–66.

76 Authoritarianism: Averil Cameron, *Christianity and the Rhetoric of*

Empire, esp. ch. 6; Brown, *Power and Persuasion in Late Antiquity*, ch. 4.

7 URBAN CHANGE AND THE END OF ANTIQUITY

1 For discontinuity: C. Mango, *Byzantium. The Empire of New Rome*, London, 1980, ch. 3, 'The disappearance and revival of cities', with bibliography at 310–11. Discussion: J. Haldon, *Byzantium in the Seventh Century*, Cambridge, 1990, 99–124; Alan Harvey, *Economic Expansion in the Byzantine Empire 900–1200*, Cambridge, 1989, 22–31.

2 The basis of the figures is extremely problematic: brief introduction for Rome in Hodges and Whitehouse, 48–52. Constantinople: see Mango, *Byzantium. The Empire of New Rome*, 75–8 (sharp decline in the seventh and eighth centuries). In general, J. Durliat, *De la ville antique à la ville byzantine*, Paris, 1990, is important (see p.174 below).

3 Fourth-century Antioch is one of the few cases where we have the evidence to see this relation in action: see the study by J. H. W. G. Liebeschuetz, *Antioch. City and Imperial Administration in the Later Roman Empire*, Oxford, 1972. For Antioch in later periods see G. Downey, *A History of Antioch in Syria*, Princeton, NJ, 1961; and the excellent survey by J. H. W. G. Liebeschuetz and H. Kennedy, 'Antioch and the villages of northern Syria in the fifth and sixth centuries AD: trends and problems', *Nottingham Medieval Studies* 23 (1988), 65–90 (reprinted in J. H. W. G. Liebeschuetz, *From Diocletian to the Arab Conquest*, London, 1990, XVI).

4 For a good introduction, with discussion of specific examples, see K. Greene, *The Archaeology of the Roman Economy*, London, 1986, ch. 5.

5 T. Potter, *The Changing Landscape of South Etruria*, London, 1979. For other Italian surveys, such as those of the Molise, the *ager Cosanus*, the Liri valley: Greene, *Archaeology of the Roman Economy*, 103–9.

6 Greene, *Archaeology of the Roman Economy*, 114–22.

7 P. Leveau, *Caesarea de Maurétanie: une ville romaine et ses campagnes*, Rome, 1984. Libyan valleys survey; see Greene, *Archaeology of the Roman Economy*, 127–32. In general see also D. R. Keller and D. W. Rupp (eds), *Archaeological Survey in the Mediterranean Area*, Oxford, BAR, 1983.

8 Annual reports on archaeological work in Greece are published together with the *Journal of Hellenic Studies* as *Archaeological Reports*.

9 G. Tchalenko, *Villages antiques de la Syrie du nord*, I–III, Paris, 1953–8. Tchalenko's arguments have only recently begun to be revised, in particular by the work of G. Tate and his colleagues (see, e.g., G. Tate, 'Les campagnes de la Syrie du nord à l'époque proto-byzantine', in C. Morrisson and J. Lefort (eds), *Hommes et richesses dans l'empire byzantin I, IVe–VIIe siècle*, Paris, 1989, 61–77 and cf. Liebeschuetz and Kennedy, 'Antioch and the villages of northern Syria', 70–2).

10 J. -M. Dentzer (ed.), *Le Hauran I–II*, Paris, 1985; see the review article by H. Kennedy, 'Recent French archaeological work on Syria and

Jordan', *Byzantine and Modern Greek Studies* 11 (1987), 245–52; and his article, 'The last century of Byzantine Syria', *Byz. Forsch.* 10 (1985), 141–3.

11 Greene, *Archaeology of the Roman economy*, 140; and further, Chapter 8.

12 See for instance J. -G. Gorges, *Les villas hispano-romaines: inventaire et problématique archéologiques*, Paris, 1979, who shows that the Guadalcuivir valley is not in fact typical of Spain as a whole.

13 For example, Edith Wightman, *Roman Trier and the Treveri*, London, 1970; Liebeschuetz, *Antioch*.

14 C. Mango, *Le développement urbain de Constantinople (IVe–VIIe siècle)*, Paris, 1985, shows, largely from textual evidence, how gradually the city actually took shape; for St Polyeuktos see above, p. 60.

15 For the earlier inscriptions, from the Triumviral period to the third century, see Joyce Reynolds, *Aphrodisias and Rome*, London, 1982; Diocletian onwards: C. M. Roueché, *Aphrodisias in Late Antiquity*, London, 1989, *Performers and Partisans at Aphrodisias*, London, 1993; R. Cormack, 'Byzantine Aphrodisias: changing the symbolic map of a city', *PCPhS* 36 (1990), 26–41, argues against the conceptual framework of 'decline'.

16 R. R. R. Smith, 'Late Roman philosopher portraits from Aphrodisias', *JRS* 80 (1990), 127–55. In general on Aphrodisias see K. Erim, *Aphrodisias. City of Venus Aphrodite*, London, 1982 (illustrated).

17 See Roueché, *Aphrodisias and Rome*, esp. 60–84; I. Sevčenko, 'A late antique epigram and the so-called elder magistrate from Aphrodisias', *Synthronon* 2 (1968), 29–41.

18 Roueché, *Aphrodisias and Rome*, 153–4; Cormack, 'Byzantine Aphrodisias'.

19 See R. R. R. Smith, 'The imperial reliefs from the Sebasteion at Aphrodisias', *JRS* 77 (1987), 88–138.

20 Ephesus: see Clive Foss, *Ephesus after Antiquity. A Late Antique, Byzantine and Turkish City*, Cambridge, 1979; Apamea: see J.-Ch. and J. Balty, *Actes du Colloque Apamée de Syrie*, I–III, Brussels, 1969–80; J. -Ch. Balty, *Guide d'Apamée*, Brussels, 1981; id., 'Apamée au VIe siècle', in Morrisson and Lefort (eds), *Hommes et richesses* I, 79–96.

21 Above, Chapter 5; and see Frank E. Wozniak, 'The Justinianic fortification of Interior Illyricum', in R. L. Hohlfelder (ed.), *City, Town and Countryside in the Early Byzantine Era*, New York, 1982, 199–209, also pointing out the actual inadequacy of Justinian's defensive works in the face of the Avar and Slav invasions of the late sixth and early seventh centuries. See also B. Isaac, *The Limits of Empire*, Oxford, 1990, 366–8, on the value of Procopius' evidence.

22 See generally K. W. Russell, 'The earthquake chronology of Palestine and northwest Arabia from the 2nd through the mid-8th century AD', *Bull. American Schools of Oriental Research* 260 (1985), 37–60.

23 Ideological, because a strong view of urban decline ('collapse', in Mango's terms) also implies rejection of the idea of continuity between Byzantium and its classical past, which has for different reasons been dear to many in the past.

24 Two recent articles provide very useful introductions, with extensive

bibliography: S. Barnish, 'The transformation of classical cities and the Pirenne debate', *Journal of Roman Archaeology* 2 (1989), 385–400; M. Whittow, 'Ruling the late Roman and early Byzantine city: a continuous history', *Past and Present* 129 (1990), 3–29 (mainly on the Near East). Many other relevant papers are to be found in J. W. Rich (ed.), *The City in Late Antiquity*, London, 1992 (see especially W. Liebeschuetz, 'The end of the ancient city', at 1–49); and J. Drinkwater and H. Elton (eds), *Fifth-Century Gaul: a Crisis of Identity?*, Cambridge, 1992.

25 The great period fell in the mid-second to early third century, though it came somewhat later in North Africa, where the remains of such cities as Dougga, Bulla Regia, Maktar and El Djem are particularly impressive.

26 For the process seen on a grand scale, see G. M. Rogers, *The Sacred Identity of Ephesos*, London, 1991.

27 See Isaac, *The Limits of Empire*, 368–9. For the typical buildings of such cities, see D. Claude, *Die byzantinische Stadt im 6. Jahrhundert*, Munich, 1969, 69–106.

28 See Mango, *Byzantium. The Empire of New Rome*, 69–71 for a very strong statement.

29 See the paper by A. Poulter, 'The use and abuse of urbanism in the Danubian provinces of the later Roman empire', in Rich (ed.), *The City in Late Antiquity*, 99–135.

30 See T. E. Gregory, 'Fortification and urban design in early Byzantine Greece', in Hohlfelder (ed.), *City, Town and Countryside*, 54–5. Others may have retreated to the islands: Sinclair Hood, 'Isles of refuge in the early Byzantine period', *Annals of the British School at Athens* 65 (1970), 37–45.

31 See C. Bouras, 'City and village; urban design and architecture', *16th Int. Byz. Congress*, 12, Vienna, 1981, 255–78; G. L. Huxley, 'The second dark age of the Peloponnese', *Lakonikai Spoudai* 3 (1977), 84–110; P. Charanis, 'The Chronicle of Monemvasia and the question of Slavonic settlements in Greece', *Dumbarton Oaks Papers* 5 (1950), 139–66.

32 See the survey of evidence in Hodges and Whitehouse, 56–61 and generally (though on this book see, e.g., Barnish, 'The transformation of classical cities').

33 Alison Frantz, *The Athenian Agora XIV. Late Antiquity AD 267–700*, Princeton, NJ, 1988, 93–4, 117–22. Coin evidence: see D. Metcalf, 'The Slavonic threat to Greece', *Hesperia* 31 (1962), 134–57; id., 'Avar and Slav invasions into the Balkan peninsula (c. 575–625): the nature of the numismatic evidence', *Journal of Roman Archaeology* 4 (1991), 140–8.

34 See Liebeschuetz and Kennedy, 'Antioch and the villages of northern Syria', 66–7, and Chapter 8.

35 Anemurium: J. Russell, 'Byzantine *instrumenta domestica* from Anemurium: the significance of context', in Hohlfelder (ed.), *City, Town and Countryside*, 133–4.

36 See Clive Foss, *Byzantine and Turkish Sardis*, Cambridge, Mass., 1976, 53ff.; id., *Ephesus after Antiquity*, 103ff.; and especially his articles,

'The Persians in Asia Minor and the end of antiquity', *English Historical Review* 90 (1975), 721–47 (on which see F. R. Trombley, 'The decline of the seventh-century town: the exception of Euchaita', in Sp. Vryonis Jr, *Byzantine Studies in Honor of M. V. Anastos, Byzantina and Metabyzantina* 4 (1985), Appendix III); and 'Archaeology and the "Twenty Cities" of Byzantine Asia', *AJA* 81 (1977), 469–86 (both reprinted in his *History and Archaeology of Byzantine Asia Minor*, London, 1990). W. Brandes, *Die Städte Kleinasiens im 7. und 8. Jahrhundert*, Berlin, 1989, is a detailed discussion of the evidence for the cities of Asia Minor generally and especially the question of 'relative continuity' for individual sites.

37 See the excellent discussion by Hugh Kennedy, 'From Polis to Madina: urban change in late antique and early Islamic Syria', *Past and Present* 106 (1985), 3–27; 'encroachment' upon the colonnaded main street at Antioch: Liebeschuetz and Kennedy, 'Antioch and the villages of northern Syria', 65–6. See also H. Kennedy, 'Antioch: from Byzantium to Islam and back again', in Rich (ed.), *The City in Late Antiquity*, 181–98.

38 Caesarea: Robert L. Vann, 'Byzantine street construction at Caesarea Maritima', in Hohlfelder (ed.), *City, Town and Countryside*, 167–70. An imperial inscription guarantees the identification of the very impressive remains of the Nea church at Jerusalem: N. Avigad, 'A building inscription of the Emperor Justinian and the Nea in Jerusalem', *Israel Exploration Journal* 27 (1977), 145–51.

39 See Whittow, 'Ruling the late Roman and early Byzantine city', 13–15. For the mosaics, see G. W. Bowersock, *Hellenism in Late Antiquity*, Cambridge, 1990, ch. 6; M. Piccirillo, *Chiese e mosaici di Madaba*, Jerusalem, 1989; id., 'The Umayyad churches of Jordan', *Ann. Dept of Antiquities of Jordan* 28 (1984), 333–41.

40 Whittow, 'Ruling the late Roman and early Byzantine city', 17 (part of a general argument from the silver treasures of Syrian churches, for which see Chapter 3).

41 See T. J. W. Wilkinson, *Town and Country in S. E. Anatolia. Settlement and Land Use at Kurban Höyük*, Chicago, Ill., 1990, 117f., 131–2. Among possible reasons for the earlier growth are the construction of roads following Osrhoene's incorporation as a province (end of second century), the military build-up and consequent military needs prior to the Persian wars of the sixth century; as Wilkinson points out (and see Chapter 8), this expansion was common to other parts of the east, from northern Syria to southern Palestine. The 'precipitous decline' in settlement seems to have resulted from the Persian and Islamic invasions; it is also argued that by the eighth century there was a flight from villages in the region round Edessa, Harran and Amida (Diyarbekir).

42 Whittow, 'Ruling the late Roman and early Byzantine city', 16, with bibliography.

43 Ed. with French trans., A. J. Festugière, Paris, 1974.

44 R. Cormack, *Writing in Gold*, London, 1985, ch. 2; text, ed. P. Lemerle, *Les plus anciens recueils des miracles de Saint Démétrius*, 2 vols, Paris, 1979–81.

45 See the discussion in F. R. Trombley, 'The decline of the seventh-century town', 65–90. The *Lives* of Theodore of Sykeon and John the Almsgiver are translated in E. Dawes and N. Baynes, *Three Byzantine Saints*, Oxford, 1948, repr. 1977.

46 Mango, *Byzantium. The Empire of New Rome*, 68–9, lays great emphasis on the presumed demographic effects; contra, Whittow, 'Ruling the late Roman and early Byzantine city', 13, and for a reasoned argument against over-reliance on the literary evidence see J. Durliat, 'La peste du VIe siècle', in Morrisson and Lefort (eds), *Hommes et richesses I*, 107–19. Cemeteries in the west do however seem to show such traces.

47 Y. Hirschfeld, *The Judaean Desert Monasteries in the Byzantine Period*, New Haven, Conn., 1992, 228. The source is the *Life* of the saint by Cyril of Scythopolis.

48 See Whittow, 'Ruling the late Roman and early Byzantine city', 15, on Anemurium, with bibliography. Antioch: Liebeschuetz and Kennedy, 'Antioch and the villages of northern Syria'. The excavators believe that the large city of Scythopolis (Bet Shean) in northern Galilee, then still flourishing, was badly hit by the earthquake recorded for the mid-eighth century.

49 See S. Thomas Parker, *Romans and Saracens. A History of the Arabian Frontier*, Winona Lake, 1986.

50 See I. Sevčenko and N. P. Sevčenko, *The Life of St. Nicholas of Sion*, Brookline, Mass., 1984, paras 52–5. Slaughtering and offering up oxen, which then provide feasts, seems to have been one of Nicholas' specialities – see paras 87–91. He was also good at financing church restoration and ensuring good crops (paras 91–5).

51 See further on this G. Dagron, 'Le christianisme dans la ville byzantine', *Dumbarton Oaks Papers* 31 (1977), 3–25 (repr. in his *La romanité chrétienne*, London, 1984).

52 For a good discussion see J. M. Spieser, 'L'évolution de la ville byzantine de l'époque paléo-chrétienne à l'iconoclasme', in Morrisson and Lefort (eds), *Hommes et richesses I*, 97–106, esp. 102–6.

53 For the steady increase in central demands on cities since the Principate see F. G. B. Millar, 'Empire and city, Augustus to Julian: obligations, excuses, status', *JRS* 73 (1983), 76–96, and above, Chapter 4. The 'flight of the curiales' is discussed by Whittow, 'Ruling the late Roman and early Byzantine city', 4–12.

54 For these developments see Jones, *LRE*, II, 757–63. For the *pater tes poleos* see C. M. Roueché, 'A new inscription from Aphrodisias and the title "Pater tes poleos"', *Greek, Roman and Byzantine Studies* 20 (1979), 173–85.

55 *LRE*, II, 762.

56 See E. Patlagean, *Pauvreté économique et pauvreté sociale à Byzance, IVe–VIIe siècles*, Paris, 1977.

57 Spieser, 'L'évolution de la ville byzantine', 102.

58 The new governing class: F. Winkelmann, *Byzantinische Rang- und Amterstruktur im 8. und 9. Jahrhundert. Faktoren und Tendenzen ihrer Entwicklung*, Berlin, 1985; id., *Quellenstudien zur herrschenden Klasse von Byzanz im 8. und 9. Jarhundert*, Berlin, 1987; see also M. Angold,

'The shaping of the medieval Byzantine "City"', *Byzantinische Forschungen* 10 (1985), 1–37.

59 See M. C. Mundell Mango, *Silver from Early Byzantium*, Baltimore, Maryland, 1986, 3–6, 11–15; and see Whittow, 'Ruling the late Roman and early Byzantine city', 16–18, who rightly draws attention to the phenomenon, but wrongly concludes that it is a sign of general prosperity. The general point is well made by Spieser, 'L'évolution de la ville byzantine', 103–6.

60 See Whittow, 'Ruling the late Roman and early Byzantine city', 21–8; Thessaloniki offers an unusual combination of visual and textual evidence: see Cormack, 'Byzantine Aphrodisias'; and the *Life* of Theodore is also extremely important for its indications of the visual environment (ibid., 17–49). Further on the *Life* of Theodore of Sykeon, F. R. Trombley, 'Monastic foundations in sixth-century Anatolia and their role in the social and economic life of the countryside', *Greek Orthodox Theological Review* 30 (1985), 65–90, an article which is valuable for its discussion of the interactions of monasteries, villages (like Sykeon itself) and towns.

61 Hodges and Whitehouse, 30 (in terms of 'the west').

62 See Chapter 3, with G. Fowden, 'Bishops and temples in the eastern Roman empire 320–435', *JThS* n.s. 29 (1978), 53–78.

63 For a good discussion of urban violence and its social and economic causes in the general context of late antique urbanism see Patlagean, *Pauvreté économique et pauvreté sociale*, 203–31.

64 See ibid., 216–17.

65 See C. M. Roueché, *Performers and Partisans at Aphrodisias*, London, 1993, with a wealth of epigraphic and other evidence.

66 Alan Cameron, *Circus Factions*, Oxford, 1976, 237ff., citing Liebeschuetz, *Antioch*, 210f.

67 Alan Cameron, *Porphyrius the Charioteer*, Oxford, 1972 discusses all the evidence and provides an ingenious reconstruction of the monuments; for factional violence see 232–3.

68 Alan Cameron, *Porphyrius*, 214–22.

69 R. Cormack, 'The wall-painting of St. Michael in the theatre', *Aphrodisias Papers* 2, Ann Arbor, Michigan, 1991, 109–22.

70 Alan Cameron, *Porphyrius*, 257.

71 Patlagean, *Pauvreté économique et pauvreté sociale*, 215. Acclamations: C. M. Roueché, 'Acclamations in the later Roman empire: new evidence from Aphrodisias', *JRS* 74 (1984), 181–99.

72 Durliat, *De la ville antique à la ville byzantine*, 585ff.

8 THE EASTERN MEDITERRANEAN – SETTLEMENT AND CHANGE

1 But see further below.

2 See Y. Tsafrir *et al.*, *Excavations at Rehovot-in-the-Negev*, I, Qedem 25, Jerusalem, 1988.

3 Balance: Y. Tsafrir and G. Foerster, *Excavations and Surveys in Israel* 9 (1989–90), 126; Bet Shean was rebuilt after the earthquake, but on a

reduced scale. Hammat Gader inscription: Y. Hirschfeld and G. Solar, 'The Roman thermae at Hammat Gader: preliminary report of three seasons of excavation', *Israel Exploration Journal* 31 (1981), 203–5.

4 For striking illustrations of the latter, see D. Kennedy and D. Riley, *Rome's Desert Frontier from the Air*, London, 1990, 70–6.

5 B. Isaac, *The Limits of Empire*, Oxford, 1990, 247–8. For similar dealings with Arab tribes under Justinian, see Procopius, *BP* I.19.8–13 (Abukarib); for all this see M. Sartre, *Trois études sur l'Arabie romaine et byzantine*, Coll. Latomus 178, Brussels, 1982.

6 The kingdom of Himyar is known from several important but difficult sources; see the detailed discussion by Z. Rubin, 'Byzantium and southern Arabia – the policy of Anastasius', in D. H. French and C. S. Lightfoot (eds), *The Eastern Frontier of the Roman Empire*, II, Oxford, BAR, 1989, 383–420, especially 386ff.; I. Shahid, *The Martyrs of Najran*, Brussels, 1971; id., 'Byzantium in south Arabia', *Dumbarton Oaks Papers* 33 (1979), 23–94. Arabia: see also D. T. Potts, *The Arabian Gulf in Antiquity*, II, Oxford, 1990 (discussion arranged diachronically by region).

7 See Z. Rubin, 'Diplomacy and war in the relations between Byzantium and the Sassanids in the fifth century AD', in P. Freeman and D. Kennedy (eds), *The Defence of the Roman and Byzantine East*, Oxford, BAR, 1986, 677–97; against the traditional idea of Mecca as a centre of long-distance trade: P. Crone, *Meccan Trade and the Rise of Islam*, Princeton, NJ, 1987.

8 See the useful introduction in S. P. Brock and S. Ashbrook Harvey, *Holy Women of the Syrian Orient*, Berkeley and Los Angeles, Calif., 1987; G. W. Bowersock, *Hellenism in Late Antiquity*, Cambridge, 1990, ch. 3.

9 Importance of Ephrem: R. Murray, *Symbols of Church and Kingdom: a Study in Early Christian Tradition*, Cambridge, 1975; Greek influence: S. Griffith, 'Ephraem, the deacon of Edessa and the church of the empire', in T. Halton and J. P. Williams (eds), *Diakonia. Studies in Honor of Robert T. Meyer*, Washington DC, 1986, 22–52. The only history of Edessa in English is J. B. Segal, *Edessa. The Blessed City*, Oxford, 1970, but a recent book in Spanish concentrates on Edessa and Greek culture, and is a useful corrective to the over-romantic view of Ephrem: J. Teixidor, *La Filosofía Traducida*, Barcelona, 1991.

10 The notion of 'Hellenism' has received some attention recently: see Fergus Millar, 'Empire, community and culture in the Roman Near East: Syrians, Jews and Arabs', *Journal of Jewish Studies*, 38 (1987), 143–64; and (for the Hellenistic period) Amélie Kuhrt and Susan Sherwin-White (eds), *Hellenism in the East*, London, 1987; Bowersock, *Hellenism in Late Antiquity*.

11 See Averil Cameron, 'The eastern provinces in the seventh century AD. Hellenism and the emergence of Islam', in S. Said (ed.), Ἑλληνισμός. *Quelques jalons pour une histoire de l'identité grecque*, Actes du Colloque de Strasbourg, 25–7 October 1989, Leiden, 1991, 289–313.

12 Emphasized by I. Shahid, *Rome and the Arabs*, Washington DC, 1984; id., *Byzantium and the Arabs in the Fourth Century*, Washington DC,

1984; id., *Byzantium and the Arabs in the Fifth Century*, Washington DC, 1990. The emphasis is justified, though the problem of definition remains.

13 Potts, *Arabian Gulf*, II, 221, 227, 241ff. Christian and Jewish communities continued to exist in the area after the coming of Islam (221, n. 105).

14 ibid., 339.

15 ibid., 244–5.

16 Stylites: see Chapter 3; debates in Constantinople: S. P. Brock, *Syriac Perspectives on Late Antiquity*, London, 1984, no. XI; Christianization of Syria: J. H. W. G. Liebeschuetz, *From Diocletian to the Arab Conquest*, London, 1990, nos VIII and IX.

17 We are well informed about these campaigns from the *Histories* of Theophylact Simocatta, written in the reign of Heraclius (AD 610–41); the history written by Menander Protector, which continued that of Agathias, is preserved only in fragments, but thanks to the interest of later Byzantine compilers in diplomacy, we have substantial sections relating to Byzantine/Persian relations under Justin II and Tiberius. See Select critical bibliography p. 242.

18 The chronology of some of these events, of which only an outline can be given here, is very difficult to establish because of the nature of the sources (in particular the Byzantine chronicles of Theophanes and the *Chronicon Paschale*, and the history in Armenian attributed to Sébéos, trans. F. Macler, Paris, 1904); for Asia Minor see Clive Foss, 'The Persians in Asia Minor and the end of antiquity', *EHR* 90 (1975), 721–47 (but see Chapter 7); general outline: J. Herrin, *The Formation of Christendom*, Oxford, 1987, 186–200, 203–4.

19 See J. Frendo, 'The poetic achievement of George of Pisidia', in A. Moffatt (ed.), *Maistor: Classical, Byzantine and Renaissance Studies for R. Browning*, Canberra, 1985, 159–88.

20 The events of the conquests are equally hard to date, and indeed to establish, but this is not the place to go into more detail; see further H. Kennedy, *The Prophet and the Age of the Caliphates*, London, 1986, ch. 3; detailed discussion, based mainly on the Arabic sources: F. M. Donner, *The Early Islamic Conquests*, Princeton, NJ, 1981, 128–55; and see W. E. Kaegi Jr, *Byzantium and the Early Islamic Conquests*, Cambridge, 1992. Students should be warned that the chronology of apparently straightforward narratives in modern works on the conquests may be seriously misleading.

21 See Herrin, *Formation of Christendom*, 197–200.

22 Brief narrative, Jones, *LRE*, I, 315f.; faction rioting in eastern cities: see pp. 172f. above.

23 Discussion: P. Mayerson, 'The first Muslim attacks on southern Palestine', *TAPA* 95 (1964), 155–99.

24 See A. Sharf, *Byzantine Jewry from Justinian to the First Crusade*, London, 1971; S. Leder, 'The attitude of the population, especially the Jews, towards the Arab-Islamic conquest of Bilad al-Sham and the question of their role therein', *Die Welt des Orients* 17 (1986), 64–71. Several important articles dealing with Jews in this connection, including a French edition, translation of, and commentary on the *Doctrina*

Jacobi (see n. 26) can be found in the journal *Travaux et mémoires* 11 (1991).

25 An introduction to these complicated matters can be found in J. Meyendorff, *Imperial Unity and Christian Divisions: the Church 450–680 AD*, Crestwood, NY, 1989. For Byzantine reactions to the Arab invasions see W. E. Kaegi Jr, 'Initial Byzantine reactions to the Arab conquests', *Church History* 38 (1969), 139–49.

26 Ed. with French translation and commentary by V. Déroche, with G. Dagron, *Travaux et mémoires* 11 (1991), 47–273.

27 See F. G. B. Millar, 'Emperors, frontiers and foreign relations, 31 B.C. to 378 A.D.', *Britannia* 13 (1982), 1–23; J. C. Mann, 'Power, force and the frontiers of the empire' (review discussion of Luttwak's book), *JRS* 69 (1979), 175–83; Isaac, *The Limits of Empire*; in general see also Freeman and Kennedy (eds), *The Defence of the Roman and Byzantine East*; S. Thomas Parker, *Romans and Saracens. A History of the Arabian Frontier*, Winona Lake, 1986; useful historical survey, maps and splendid pictures in Kennedy and Riley, *Rome's Desert Frontier from the Air*.

28 Fergus Millar, 'Empire, community and culture', 143–64 at 145ff.

29 On the 'Saracen threat' to Rome see the important paper by D. Graf, 'The Saracens and the defence of the Arabian frontier', *Bull. Am. Schools of Oriental Research* 229 (1978), 1–26; with id., 'Rome and the Saracens: reassessing the nomadic menace', in T. Fahd (ed.), *L'Arabie préislamique et son environnement historique et culturel*, Colloque Strasbourg, June 1987, Leiden, 1989, 341–400.

30 For these arguments see in particular Isaac, *The Limits of Empire*, ch. 4, 161–218; with Kennedy and Riley, *Rome's Desert Frontier from the Air*, 32–7, 237–8; Isaac has also argued that the term *limes* does not actually mean 'frontier', as it is usually understood to mean, but rather simply 'border zone'. The main source for Julian's campaigns, and the loss of Nisibis is Ammianus Marcellinus; see John Matthews, *The Roman Empire of Ammianus*, London, 1989, with M. H. Dodgeon and S. N. C. Lieu, *The Roman Eastern Frontier and the Persian Wars AD 226–363*, London, 1991 (sources).

31 Above, Chapter 2. Legions and legionary numbers: Kennedy and Riley, *Rome's Desert Frontier from the Air*, 43–5; *limitanei*: B. Isaac, 'The meaning of "limes" and "limitanei" in ancient sources', *JRS* 78 (1988), 125–77. This is not to deny that such soldiers sometimes farmed land; witness the fifth-century tax edict from Beersheba (see Parker, *Romans and Saracens*, 146).

32 See R. N. Frye, 'The political history of Iran under the Sasanians', *Cambridge History of Iran* III.1 (1983), 116–80.

33 Michael Whitby, *The Emperor Maurice and his Historian*, Oxford, 1988, 292–304. Theophylact's narrative of the restoration of Chosroes II is found at *Hist.* V.1–3.

34 For discussion see R. Schick, *The Christian Communities of Palestine from Byzantine to Islamic Rule: a Historical and Archaeological Assessment*, Princeton, NJ, 1993.

35 Isaac, *The Limits of Empire*, 239–40; Millar, 'Empire, community and culture', 154.

36 This is al-Harith b. Jabala, not to be confused with al-Harith b. 'Amr,

killed by the Lakhmid pro-Persian phylarch al-Mundhir in AD 528 (Malalas, *Chronicle*, trans. Jeffreys, 252); al-Harith b. 'Amr had a Christian daughter, Hind: see Martindale, *PLRE*, II, 139–40.

37 For all of this see Isaac, *The Limits of Empire*, 238–49; Sartre, *Trois études*, 153–203; Parker, *Romans and Saracens*, 149–54; Kennedy and Riley, *Rome's Desert Frontier from the Air*, 36–9; Parker, *Romans and Saracens*, 153; further, J. H. W. G. Liebeschuetz, 'The defences of Syria in the sixth century', in his *From Diocletian to the Arab Conquest*, no. XX.

38 See further Bowersock, *Hellenism in Late Antiquity*, ch. 6, 'Hellenism and Islam'; and G. Fowden, *Empire to Commonwealth. The Consequences of Monotheism in Late Antiquity*, Princeton, NJ, 1993.

CONCLUSION

1 Jones, *LRE*, I, 304–7.

2 See Theophylact's excursus on the subject, VII.7.6.ff.; cf. M. Whitby, *The Emperor Maurice and his Historian*, Oxford, 1988, 315–17. In general, see D. Obolensky, *The Byzantine Commonwealth. Eastern Europe AD 500–1453*, London, 1971.

3 See J. Tainter, *The Collapse of Complex Societies*, Cambridge, 1988; Greg Woolf, 'World-systems analysis and the Roman empire', *Journal of Roman Archaeology* 3 (1990), 44–58.

4 So K. Randsborg, *The First Millennium AD in Europe and the Mediterranean. An Archaeological Essay*, Cambridge, 1991. See also Z. Rubin, 'The Mediterranean and the dilemma of the Roman Empire in late antiquity', *Mediterranean Historical Review* (1986), 32–47.

5 For the former, see, e.g., J. Le Goff, *Medieval Civilization*, Eng. trans., London, 1988; A. Kazhdan and A. Wharton Epstein, *Change in Byzantine Culture in the Eleventh and Twelfth Centuries*, Berkeley and Los Angeles, Calif., 1985, ch. 1; Alan Harvey, *Economic Expansion in the Byzantine Empire 900–1200*, Cambridge, 1989, ch. 1. For the latter, A. Hourani, *A History of the Arab Peoples*, London, 1991.

6 Benedict Anderson, *Imagined Communities. Reflections on the Origin and Spread of Nationalism*, London, 1983; cf. E. Gellner, *Thought and Change*, London, 1964, 150ff., 174ff.

Select critical bibliography

INTRODUCTION

Averil Cameron, *The Later Roman Empire*, Fontana History of the Ancient World, London, 1993, covers the period up to AD 395, but not far beyond; readers are referred to that for the relevant period and for further bibliography. Though there are many introductory books dealing with east and west separately from AD 395, few cover the entire area; one that does is R. Collins, *Early Medieval Europe 300–1000*, London, 1991, which gives a good chronological account. Jones, *LRE*, provides a narrative in chs 6–10, with source references; see also Bury, *LRE* (though of course old, still the most detailed treatment in English). Volumes XIII and XIV of the revised edition of the *Cambridge Ancient History* will cover the period AD 337–c. 600. Martindale, *PLRE I–III* are works of reference in the form of a biographical dictionary of all secular office-holders in the period AD 395–641, giving source references for their lives and careers. A. Demandt, *Die Spätantike*, Mullers Handbuch der Altertumswissenschaft, Munich, 1990 (in German), is an immensely detailed work of reference with very full bibliography up to AD 565. Students will find many relevant entries in *The Oxford Dictionary of Byzantium*, New York, 1991. Much more than an atlas, and with many excellent illustrations, is Tim Cornell and John Matthews, *Atlas of the Roman World*, Oxford, 1982.

Sources in translation: A. H. M. Jones, *A History of Rome through the Fifth Century II: The Empire*, London, 1970; N. Lewis and M. Reinhold, *Roman Civilization. Sourcebook II: The Empire*, New York, 1955, rev. edn 1966. Sources relating to the church in the fifth century: Stevenson, *Creeds*.

For the 'Pirenne thesis', and for the archaeology of the period, see Hodges and Whitehouse; and K. Randsborg, *The First Millennium AD in Europe and the Mediterranean. An Archaeological Essay*, Cambridge, 1991; see ch. 4. Although there are a number of abridged versions available, Edward Gibbon's great work, the multi-volume *Decline and Fall of the Roman Empire*, is best read in the edition edited by J. B. Bury, 4th edn, London, 1906. M. I. Rostovtzeff's negative views on the later Roman empire can be found in his *SEHRE*. The title of MacMullen's *Corruption* speaks for itself; a negative view also (for different reasons) in de Ste Croix,

Class Struggle; and Alföldy, *Social History*, ch. 7. For critique of the nationalistic view of the Germanic invaders, common in German scholarship, see H. Wolfram, *History of the Goths*, Berkeley and Los Angeles, Calif., 1988; and W. Goffart, *Barbarians and Romans*, Princeton, NJ, 1980, ch. 1. For M. I. Finley and his influence see his classic book *The Ancient Economy*, Berkeley and Los Angeles, Calif., 1973, rev. edn London, 1985, with the late Roman essays in Peter Garnsey, Keith Hopkins and C. R. Whittaker (eds), *Trade in the Ancient Economy*, London, 1983. Relevant books by Peter Brown include *The Cult of the Saints*, London, 1981, and *Society and the Holy in Late Antiquity*, collected essays, Berkeley and Los Angeles, Calif., 1982. For late Roman pottery the classic work is John Hayes, *Late Roman Pottery*, London, 1972. Current Italian scholarship on the period is represented in the essays in the four-volume collection edited by Giardina, on vol. III of which see C. Wickham, 'Marx, Sherlock Holmes and the late Roman economy', *JRS* 78 (1988), 183–93; see also the essay by Carandini in Garnsey, Hopkins and Whittaker (eds), *Trade in the Ancient Economy*, and various articles on economy and society in the French collection edited by C. Morrisson and J. Lefort, *Hommes et richesses dans l'empire byzantin I, IVe–VIIe siècle*, Paris, 1989. For the debate about when Byzantium began, see A. Kazhdan and A. Cutler, 'Continuity and discontinuity in Byzantine history', *Byzantion* 52 (1982), 429–78; considerable diversity of terminology is used of the period – Kazhdan here favours 'proto-Byzantine', while N. H. Baynes called it 'the east Roman empire', A. H. M. Jones 'the later Roman empire' and others simply refer to it as 'Byzantium'. *The Oxford Dictionary of Byzantium* reverts to 'late Roman' or 'late antique', both used in this book. However, in order to deal with the period, students of ancient history will need to get used to consulting books which prima facie seem to be about Byzantium.

For Augustine see Peter Brown, *Augustine of Hippo*, London, 1967. W. Goffart, *The Narrators of Barbarian History (AD 550–800)*, Princeton, NJ, 1988, deals with Jordanes and Gregory of Tours; for Cassiodorus see J. J. O'Donnell, *Cassiodorus*, Berkeley and Los Angeles, Calif., 1979; and for Cassiodorus' *Variae*, the translation with notes by S. Barnish, Translated Texts for Historians 12, Liverpool, 1992. Gregory the Great: Carole Straw, *Gregory the Great. Perfection in Imperfection*, Berkeley and Los Angeles, Calif., 1988. There is a Penguin translation of Gregory of Tours, *History of the Franks*, trans. L. Thorpe, Harmondsworth, 1974, and his hagiographical works are translated with notes in the Translated Texts for Historians Series (*Glory of the Confessors* and *Glory of the Martyrs*, trans. R. Van Dam, Liverpool, 1988; *Life of the Fathers*, trans. E. James, Liverpool, 1985). For Venantius Fortunatus see George, *Venantius Fortunatus*. The Greek secular historians of the fifth and sixth centuries are edited by Blockley. For Procopius see Cameron, *Procopius*; Malalas' chronicle is now available in English translation by Jeffreys *et al*; and see Elizabeth Jeffreys, with Brian Croke and Roger Scott (eds), *Studies in John Malalas*, Sydney, 1990. On saints' lives and related religious literature see, e. g., C. Stancliffe, *St. Martin of Tours and his Biographer Sulpicius Severus*, Oxford, 1983; Alison Goddard Elliott, *Roads to Paradise. Reading the Lives of the Early Saints*, Hanover and London, 1987; S. Hackel (ed.), *The Byzantine Saint*, London,

1981. Church councils: Judith Herrin, *The Formation of Christendom*, Oxford, 1987; the *Codex Theodosianus* (= *CTh*) is available in the English translation by Clyde Pharr, *The Theodosian Code*, Princeton, NJ, 1952; on the *Notitia Dignitatum* see Jones, *LRE*, app. II and see above, Chapter 2. Greek inscriptions: see C. M. Roueché, *Aphrodisias in Late Antiquity*, London, 1989.

1 CONSTANTINOPLE AND THE EASTERN EMPIRE IN THE FIFTH CENTURY

Basic narratives: Jones, *LRE*; Bury, *LRE*, I; see also E. Demougeot, *De l'unité à la division de l'empire romain: 395–410*, Paris, 1951. J. H. W. G. Liebeschuetz, *Barbarians and Bishops. Army, Church and State in the Age of Arcadius and Chrysostom*, Oxford, 1990, includes an interesting chapter on the preaching of John Chrysostom; and Synesius has attracted several recent studies including J. Bregman, *Synesius of Cyrene. Philosopher-Bishop*, Berkeley and Los Angeles, Calif., 1980; for his relation to the landowning aristocracy of Cyrenaica see D. Roques, *Synésios de Cyréne et la Cyrénaïque du Bas-Empire*, Paris, 1987. The emergence of Alaric and the Visigoths has recently been well served, especially by Peter Heather, *Goths and Romans 332–489*, Oxford, 1991, based on a new interpretation of the central source on Gothic history, the sixth-century *Gothic History* of Jordanes. For ecclesiastical politics and councils see the source-book by J. Stevenson, *Creeds, Councils and Controversies*, London, 1966, with S. G. Hall, *Doctrine and Practice in the Early Church*, London, 1991; for the personalities and their writings see also F. M. Young, *From Nicaea to Chalcedon*, London, 1983. The acts of the councils are translated in *Nicene and Post-Nicene Fathers*, XIV, repr. Grand Rapids, Michigan, 1977; and the church histories of Socrates and Sozomen can be found in ibid., vol. II, repr. Grand Rapids, Michigan, 1976; see also G. Chesnut, *Three Christian Histories*, Paris, 1977. The Greek fifth-century historians including Olympiodorus of Thebes, Priscus and Malchus are edited and translated, with discussion, by Blockley, 1981, 1983; and see the brief critical description in Heather, *Goths and Romans*, 71–83.

2 THE EMPIRE, THE BARBARIANS AND THE LATE ROMAN ARMY

The association of AD 476 with the transmission of power to the Germanic peoples has been built into theories of the 'decline and fall' and, neglecting continuity of government, administration and institutions in the east, to many interpretations of the end of the ancient world, especially but by no means only in Marxist scholarship (see, e.g., Perry Anderson, *Passages from Antiquity to Feudalism*, London, 1974; however, de Ste Croix, *Class Struggle*, takes c. 600 as the turning point, following Jones, *LRE*). AD 476 is also a convenient closing date for books on ancient history; see, e.g., C. G. Starr, *The Roman Empire, 27 BC to AD 476*, Oxford, 1982; and cf.

239

Alföldy, *Social History*, 189. The importance of the date has much to do with each author's own ideology and orientation in relation to the medieval west and Byzantium; see A. Momigliano, 'La caduta senza rumore di un impero nel 476 D.C.', *Annali Scuola Normale di Pisa* ser. 3, 3.2 (1973), 397–418; B. Croke, 'AD 476: the manufacture of a turning point', *Chiron* 13 (1983), 81–119; E. A. Thompson, *Romans and Barbarians. The Decline of the Western Empire*, Madison, Wisconsin, 1982, 61–76. K. Randsborg, *The First Millennium AD in Europe and the Mediterranean*, Cambridge, 1991, shows the continuity of the archaeological evidence. In general on Gaul in the fifth century, see J. Drinkwater and H. Elton (eds), *Fifth-Century Gaul: a Crisis of Identity?*, Cambridge, 1992. Two collections with relevant chapters on east and west in this period are J. Shepard and S. Franklin (eds), *Byzantine Diplomacy*, Aldershot, 1992 and E. K. Chrysos and A. Schwarcz (eds), *Das Reich und die Barbaren*, Vienna and Cologne, 1989.

The contemporary sources for military affairs and invasions are often difficult to use, because they are one-sided and tendentious or because they survive only in part or because of the nature of chronicles evidence. Among the most important which do survive are the pagan *New History* of Zosimus (Greek, Constantinople, late fifth- or early sixth-century), trans. Ridley, drawing on the important earlier history of Olympiodorus; the ecclesiastical histories of Socrates and Sozomen (see p. 239). Jordanes' *Getica* (Latin, sixth-century), trans. C. C. Mierow, Princeton, NJ, 1915, is a fundamental source for the history of the Goths, but needs careful handling: see, e.g., Peter Heather, *Goths and Romans 332–489*, Oxford, 1991, ch. 2. The western chroniclers Prosper and Hydatius, and the Latin Chronicle of AD 452 are important but difficult sources for the events in the west in this period; the Latin texts are in T. Mommsen (ed.), *MGH* (*Monumenta Germaniae Historica*), Auct. Ant. IX, *Chronica Minora*, I–II, Berlin, 1982, 1894; and see S. Muhlberger, *Fifth-Century Chronicles*, Liverpool, 1990. For the several fifth- and sixth-century historians who wrote in Greek about this period, including Priscus and Olympiodorus, but whose works survive only indirectly in quotations see Chapter 1, with C. D. Gordon, *The Age of Attila. Fifth-Century Byzantium and the Barbarians*, Ann Arbor, Michigan, 1960 (translated extracts). The *Notitia Dignitatum* has still to be read in the Latin edition by O. Seeck, Berlin, 1876; for the *De Rebus Bellicis* see the translation and discussion in R. Ireland, M. W. C. Hassall and R. I. Ireland, *De Rebus Bellicis*, London, 1979.

3 CHURCH AND SOCIETY

Further aspects of Christianization and religious life in the period are discussed in Chapter 6, 'Culture and mentality'. There is a host of books on relevant topics, but among recent contributions the following may be singled out. Peter Brown's works are basic, including especially *The Cult of the Saints*, London, 1981 (mainly on the west); *Society and the Holy in Late Antiquity*, Berkeley and Los Angeles, Calif., 1982 (an important collection of articles); *The Body and Society. Men, Women and Sexual Renunciation in Early Christianity*, New York, 1988; *Power and Persuasion in Late Antiquity*, Madison, Wisc., 1992. R. A. Markus, *The End of Ancient Christianity*, Cambridge, 1990, is a recent and innovative book, again with a western focus. See also J. Richards, *The Popes and the Papacy in the Early Middle Ages, AD 476–750*, London, 1979; F. M. Young, *From Nicaea to Chalcedon*, London, 1983 (an excellent introduction to doctrinal controversies and to the contemporary Christian literature, mainly Greek); S. G. Hall, *Doctrine and Practice in the Early Church*, London, 1991 (also to AD 451); P. Chuvin, *A Chronicle of the Last Pagans*, Cambridge, Mass., 1990, Eng. trans. of larger French edition. On monasticism: O. Chadwick, *John Cassian*, Cambridge, 1968; D. J. Chitty, *The Desert a City*, Oxford, 1966; P. Rousseau, *Ascetics, Authority and the Church*, Oxford, 1979; id., *Pachomius*, Berkeley and Los Angeles, Calif., 1985.

Imperial legislation concerning the church is found in the *Codex Theodosianus*, bk XVI; translated sources: Stevenson, *Creeds* (up to AD 451); Mango, *Art* (a very useful collection); V. Wimbush (ed.), *Ascetic Behavior in Greco-Roman Antiquity. A Sourcebook*, Minneapolis, Minnesota, 1990.

Christian art and architecture: R. Krautheimer, *Early Christian and Byzantine Architecture*, Harmondsworth, 1965, rev. 1975; C. Mango, *Byzantine Architecture*, New York, 1986; A. Grabar, *Byzantium. From the Death of Theodosius to the Rise of Islam*, London, 1966, 5–100, with splendid plates; K. Weitzmann (ed.), *The Age of Spirituality*, New York, 1979; R. Milburn, *Early Christian Art and Architecture*, Berkeley and Los Angeles, Calif., 1988.

4 LATE ROMAN SOCIAL STRUCTURES AND THE LATE ROMAN ECONOMY

Much of the secondary literature presents the later Roman empire as a crumbling, top-heavy economy with too few producers, too many consumers (the army, the church, the bureaucracy) and a too heavy or otherwise inadequate system of taxation: so, e.g., Jones, *LRE*, and see the essays by Jones in P. Brunt (ed.), *The Roman Economy*, Oxford, 1974; Alföldy, *Social History*, ch. 7. This view is increasingly being revised: see the items mentioned above in the Introduction. For settlement patterns, trade and archaeological evidence in general see also K. Greene, *The Archaeology of the Roman Economy*, London, 1986. Earlier discussion of the economic aspects of the transition from the ancient to the medieval world has been distorted by excessive emphasis on the so-called 'Pirenne thesis' (see Introduction); for discussion see Hodges and Whitehouse. A similarly dominant issue has been that of the relation between ancient slavery and medieval feudalism; see C. Wickham, 'The other transition: from the ancient world to feudalism', *Past and Present* 103 (1984), 3–36; and further, Chapter 6 above. M. Hendy, *Studies in the Byzantine Monetary Economy c. AD 300–1450*, Cambridge, 1985, contains a great deal of important material about the fiscal and economic working of the late Roman and early

Byantine state; since the book is largely arranged thematically the student needs to be warned to make energetic use of the index. The main thrust in recent work has been in the direction of archaeological investigation aimed at uncovering local economic conditions and settlement patterns rather than individual buildings; some of the more accessible literature is cited in the notes to this chapter and to Chapters 2, 7 and 8, and an overview is provided by K. Randsborg, *The First Millennium AD in Europe and the Mediterranean. An Archaeological Essay*, Cambridge, 1991.

5 JUSTINIAN AND RECONQUEST

A detailed treatment of the reign of Justinian is badly needed: in general see R. Browning, *Justinian and Theodora*, London, 1971, rev. 1987; J. Barker, *Justinian and the Later Roman Empire*, Madison, Wisconsin, 1966; on the evidence of Procopius (the main source) see Cameron, *Procopius*. E. Stein, *Histoire du Bas-Empire*, II, rev. J.-R.Palanque, Paris, 1949, repr. Amsterdam 1968, remains the fullest guide. See also Tony Honoré, *Tribonian*, London, 1978, ch. 1.

All Procopius' works (*Wars*, comprising two books on the Persian wars (*BP = Bellum Persicum, Persian War*), two books on the Vandal wars (*BV = Bellum Vandalicum, Vandal War*) and four books of Gothic wars (*BG = Bellum Gothicum, Gothic War*), the *Buildings* (*De Aedificiis*) and the *Secret History* (*Anecdota*) are available in English translation in the Loeb edition; the *Secret History* is also available both in Penguin Classics and trans. A. E. R. Boak, Ann Arbor, Michigan, 1961. For John the Lydian see A. C. Bandy, *John Lydus, On Powers or the Magistracies of the Roman State*, Philadelphia, Pennsylvania, 1983; Maas, *John Lydus*; Cameron, *Procopius*, ch. 14. The *Histories* of Agathias Scholasticus, who continued Procopius' narrative of the wars up to AD 559, are translated by J. D. Frendo, Berlin, 1975; and see Averil Cameron, *Agathias*, Oxford, 1970; the *History* of Menander Protector (only surviving in part), which picked up the story where Agathias left off, is edited with trans. and notes by Blockley, *Menander the Guardsman*. The *Chronicle* of John Malalas also belongs to the reign of Justinian (trans. Jeffreys); see Elizabeth Jeffreys, with Brian Croke and Roger Scott (eds), *Studies in John Malalas*, Sydney, 1990.

6 CULTURE AND MENTALITY
7 URBAN CHANGE AND THE END OF ANTIQUITY

For these chapters, which rely on a wide range of detailed evidence, the reader is referred to works cited in the notes. Source-books for Chapter 6 include Elizabeth A. Clark (ed.), *Women in the Early Church*, Wilmington, Delaware, 1983; V. Wimbush (ed.), *Ascetic Behavior in Greco-Roman Antiquity. A Sourcebook*, Minneapolis, Minnesota, 1990; and R. S. Kraemer (ed.), *Maenads, Martyrs, Matrons, Monastics*, Philadelphia, Pennsylvania, 1988.

8 THE EASTERN MEDITERRANEAN – SETTLEMENT AND CHANGE

A useful introduction with good bibliographies for those who can read French is A. Ducellier, M. Kaplan and B. Martin, *Le Proche-Orient médiéval*, Paris, 1978 (with maps). See also P.-L. Gatier, B. Helly and J.-P. Rey-Coquais, *Géographie historique au Proche-Orient (Syrie, Phénicie, Arabie grecques, romaines, byzantines)*, Paris, 1988.

We have substantial sections relating to Byzantine/Persian relations under Justin II and Tiberius from the history by Menander Protector (see above, Chapter 5). Part 3 of the Syriac *Ecclesiastical History* of John of Ephesus (text and Latin trans. by E. W. Brooks, CSCO Scriptores Syri 55, Louvain, 1935–6, repr. 1952; the English translation by R. Payne Smith, Oxford, 1860, is not reliable), and the *Chronicle* of Michael the Syrian (text and French trans. by J.-B. Chabot, 2 vols, Paris, 1899–1901), the latter much later, but using early material, are essential, but there is still no modern study of either text. For the Greek *Ecclesiastical History* of Evagrius see P. Allen, *Evagrius Scholasticus the Church Historian*, Louvain, 1981. For the reign of Maurice (AD 582–602) see the excellent annotated translation of Theophylact Simocatta's history by Michael Whitby and Mary Whitby, *The History of Theophylact Simocatta*, Oxford, 1986; with Michael Whitby, *The Emperor Maurice and his Historian*, Oxford, 1988, 250–394. For the *Chronicon Paschale* (ends AD 628) see the English translation by Whitby and Whitby, Liverpool, 1989.

The *Chronicle* of Theophanes (died AD 814), is translated (for the years AD 602–813 only) by Turtledove, *Chronicle*. For John of Nikiu's *Chronicle*, see the trans. by R. H. Charles, London, 1916. The *Doctrina Jacobi nuper baptizati* is edited with French trans. and discussion by V. Déroche and G. Dagron, *Travaux et Mémoires*, 11 (1991), 47–273.

The best introduction to Syriac culture is provided by the various articles by Sebastian Brock, conveniently collected in his *Syriac Perspectives on Late Antiquity*, London, 1984, esp. II and III, on translation, and V, 'From antagonism to assimilation: Syriac attitudes to Greek learning'; and id., *Studies in Syriac Christianity*, London, 1992; see also the useful introduction in Sebastian P. Brock and Susan Ashbrook Harvey, *Holy Women of the Syrian Orient*, Berkeley and Los Angeles, Calif., 1987; and G. W. Bowersock, *Hellenism in Late Antiquity*, Cambridge, 1990, ch. 3.

Index